Mastering the Art of Equity Trading through Simulation

Founded in 1807, John Wiley & Sons is the oldest independent publishing company in the United States. With offices in North America, Europe, Australia and Asia, Wiley is globally committed to developing and marketing print and electronic products and services for our customers' professional and personal knowledge and understanding.

The Wiley Trading series features books by traders who have survived the market's ever changing temperament and have prospered—some by reinventing systems, others by getting back to basics. Whether a novice trader, professional, or somewhere in-between, these books will provide the advice and strategies needed to prosper today and well into the future.

For a list of available titles, visit our Web site at www.WileyFinance.com.

Mastering the Art of Equity Trading through Simulation

The TraderEx Course

ROBERT A. SCHWARTZ
GREGORY M. SIPRESS
BRUCE W. WEBER

WILEY

John Wiley & Sons, Inc.

Published by John Wiley & Sons, Inc., Hoboken, New Jersey.
Published simultaneously in Canada.

For general information on our other products and services or for technical support, please contact our Customer Care Department within the United States at (800) 762-2974, outside the United States at (317) 572-3993 or fax (317) 572-4002.

Wiley also publishes its books in a variety of electronic formats. Some content that appears in print may not be available in electronic books. For more information about Wiley products, visit our web site at www.wiley.com.

Library of Congress Cataloging-in-Publication Data:

Schwartz, Robert A. (Robert Alan), 1937–
  Mastering the art of equity trading through simulation : the traderEx course / Robert A. Schwartz, Gregory M. Sipress, Bruce W. Weber.
      p. cm. – (Wiley trading series)
  Includes index.
  ISBN 978-0-470-46485-4 (paper/website)
  1. Stock exchanges–Computer simulation.   2. Speculation–Computer simulation.   3. Stocks.
4. Securities.   I. Sipress, Gregory M.   II. Weber, Bruce W., 1961–   III. Title.
  HG4551.S3933 2010
  332.63′2280113–dc22

                                                                                    2010003140

Printed in the United States of America

10   9   8   7   6   5   4   3   2   1

Contents

Foreword

This book is about trading, and it is for traders and those who want to gain a hands-on understanding of trading. But trading affects many professions in the financial area, and I highly recommend this book to asset managers, regulators, and also exchange operators. Bob Schwartz, Greg Sipress, and Bruce Weber have written this book to further the development of state-of-the-art trading. In this time of global financial crisis it is a sign of professional bravery to write such a book. And if we are serious in our desire to improve trading in the equity markets, then such a book is absolutely necessary.

When I first met Bob Schwartz, many years ago, I immediately knew that this encounter would not be without consequences. Never before had I met someone who was so dedicated to analyzing and understanding the world of global trading. And I have yet to meet anyone who is as interested in improving trading and educating traders through professional advice. Now that Bob has become a friend and a trusted expert in discussing questions of how to further improve trading, it is a great honor for me to write a few lines as a Foreword to this book.

For all three authors, their great achievement is that their writing is instructive. This book is not about abstract models of trading, or theoretical "ifs," or purely academic analysis. It puts you right in the middle of simulated markets and successfully shows you how financial markets operate, how to handle your strategic decisions, how to react to market conditions, how to be honest, and on top of all of that, how to trade with a long-run perspective. Beyond this, the simulation lets you operate in an environment where the characteristics of the stock you are trading and the structure of the market that you are trading in can be changed. Altering parameters and structural features is a key learning feature of the simulation: You can see, feel, and better understand how the realities of a marketplace impact your strategic trading decisions.

The simulation is realistic. The key generic forms of market structure that today's exchanges offer can be experienced, and a spectrum of trading challenges encountered. Results can be assessed, mistakes in decision making identified, and understanding delivered. A newcomer can be turned loose both with and without position constraints or other trading restrictions that would otherwise have to be imposed on a novice. If losses are incurred because of either bad luck or a lack of skill, it does not matter. TraderEx is only an educational simulation.

Providing good, liquid markets for mid-cap and small-cap stocks is one of the problems our markets are facing today. For all stocks, handling the large orders of institutional investors is another big challenge. You come face-to-face with these market realities in this book. You will finish its exercises with a better understanding of the trading skills that illiquid markets and large orders call for, and you will better appreciate the difficulties of designing trading systems that cater to the needs of a broad and diverse group of participants who are trading a wide spectrum of stocks.

In today's fast-moving electronic environment, traders, and increasingly asset managers, appreciate the importance of the complexity of trading, and trading has acquired professional status. But something is missing. To be established fully as a profession, a formal educational program is required. Moreover, formal education is needed not just for traders, but also for the broader set of people who are part of and who interact with the profession.

A formal education in this field is simply not currently available. Rather, today a trader's "education" consists largely of sitting at a trading desk, watching experts, and finally being allowed to handle simple orders. It takes a year or more for an apprentice trader to cease being a novice. This book helps professionalize the approach to "education."

The book is pragmatic, the simulation is realistic, and the target is clear and good: To improve the quality of trading and the quality of traders. That is a precondition to running successful markets and to creating successful traders. What more could we wish for?

Dr. Reto Francioni
CEO Deutsche Boerse

Preface

Trading has been transformed by information technology. In today's markets, not only are orders being sent electronically to exchanges where they are turned into trades by a computer, but a substantial percentage of the very orders themselves are being computer generated. Two relatively new terms capture this development: algorithmic trading and high-frequency trading.

The world of trading is far too intricate, too subtle, and too dynamic to be negotiated with static computer-driven responses. It may be important to appreciate the high-frequency trading and computer-driven algorithms that are such a prominent part of today's markets, but computers will never be able to do it all. TraderEx itself is based on computer-driven, *algo* models. Much of our discussion of how you might operate in the TraderEx marketplace involves decision rules that could potentially be programmed as algorithms. On an ongoing basis, human judgment will always be called for. That is why the title of this book refers to the *art* of equity trading.

Whatever your background, TraderEx will let you experience the real thing. Can you make split-second market judgments and implement crucial trading decisions? With practice, this is possible. Can you beat a trading benchmark consistently? In the real world, this would earn you big bonuses. Can you contribute several percentage points of return to an investment fund, and sense the appreciation of your money manager? In the real world, this could put your fund in the top decile of returns for its category. Would you like to find out what it is like to open a trading day with no position in a stock, build up a scary risk position as a market maker, and then unwind it profitably? In the real world, you would go home happy with a large gain and no overnight risk.

But trading, for sure, is not all milk and honey. With TraderEx, you will at times see a market slam through your orders and turn your unrealized profit into a realized loss. You can incur a big opportunity cost by delaying the submission of a buy order and missing a golden chance to get your shares at the low price of the day. You might have a substantial short position when, suddenly and much to your dismay, a positive earnings surprise or a takeover rumor drives up the price of the stock you want by twenty percent and leaves your P&L deep in the red. And you can experience what it is like to be a dealer when the bid-ask spread has narrowed by 50 percent and turned your previously profitable trading into a break-even proposition, at best. Our goal is to let you experience all of this, to operate in different market environments, under different market structures, and in the capacity of different market professionals. As you do, you will learn more about what the professionals do, better appreciate what they feel and, whatever your own professional intentions might be, understand more deeply what trading involves.

Most books on financial markets treat a market as a mechanical abstraction that simply produces prices, and individual participants are left with little scope for understanding market structure and for making good trading decisions. We treat the situation differently. You sit at your computer, call up the TraderEx screen, roll up your sleeves, and trade. It is you and a market operated by the computer. It is you against a flow of orders that the software generates. It is you fighting it out in a marketplace where knowledge of market structure and good trading decisions are rewarded, and where poor trading decisions are, let us say, costly.

HOW TRADEREX WORKS

TraderEx is designed to be a learning tool. With it, you can learn about trading, and you can find out whether or not you are cut out to be a trader. You can also gain much insight into the dynamic behavior of a marketplace that is noted for its complexity, its intrigue, and its enormous importance to the broad economy: the marketplace where already issued equity shares are traded. And there is something else. You can have fun, for TraderEx is, all said and done, a game.

At the end of a simulation run you find out how well you have done. If you were given an order to work, did you get the job done? Did you buy at low prices and sell at high prices? Did you follow a prudent course or did you take excessive risk? What was your profit or loss? After finding out how well you have done, you sit back, smile, and then go back and trade some more. There is nothing to worry about, your bank account will not be affected by how much you have won or lost. You are only playing with simulated dollars.

TraderEx has played a major role in various courses that we teach in business school programs. The simulation has also been put to good use in seminars and training programs that we have conducted for industry participants including trading managers, regulatory officials, and stock exchange executives. We have run simulations in labs and classrooms with college undergraduates, with MBAs with PhDs, with new industry recruits, and with seasoned industry professionals. After a short introduction, we get them started. One step at a time, the greenhorns learn how to read the TraderEx screen, they find out how to enter orders and, before they know it, they are in the middle of a market trading. We show them the close correspondence between the TraderEx simulation and the real stock markets. The software is easy to use, but the beginners soon realize that successful outcomes are not a given, and that acquiring trading skills requires thought and effort. Seasoned professionals already know this.

A simulation run typically takes twenty minutes. In our training sessions, we introduce a simulation, talk about its parameters and market structure, and then turn the class loose. After a run, we discuss the results and then move on and launch another one. The participants learn by repetition. They generally begin the program quietly, focusing intently on their screens. With practice, they ease into it, they get more excited, and some of them start making noise. Exclamations of victory can be heard along with the cries of defeat. The words, "Hit me, hit me" are shouted out, along with "Come on, dude, where are you!" That is what we want. A simulation session is not just learning by talk and by lecture, it is learning by doing, and doing calls for engagement.

WHO THIS BOOK IS FOR

Investing is a traditional topic in financial economics. Trading, the implementation of an investment decision, is now receiving serious attention in academia. Trading is a solid topic for two business school subjects in addition to finance: computer information systems and economics. Students in computer information systems gain valuable experience with market concepts and the role of information technology in operating a market, providing a trading interface, and offering software functionality to trading participants.

Trading is particularly germane to economics. Microeconomics considers how economic agents interact in the marketplace to determine the pricing and distribution of goods, services, and assets. Equity shares are financial assets and the equity markets, as we have noted, are enormously important and exciting markets in which to study supply, demand, and pricing. Microeconomics strictly focuses on markets. And that is what TraderEx is—it is a market. TraderEx's structure, the principles upon which it is based, and the insights that it provides are grounded in microeconomic theory, and its integral relationship to a microeconomics course naturally follows.

We do not treat markets in the abstract. We operate in the context of specific market structures and specific sets of trading rules. You will certainly find out that a market's structure matters. TraderEx is built around four generic types of markets: a continuous order book market (participants post prices and trade against the posted prices), a call auction (orders are cumulated for simultaneous execution at a common clearing price), a dealer market (market makers post the prices that public participants can trade at), and a block trading facility (where large orders meet and transact against each other). Each of these markets represents a different economic environment, and each presents different decisions to make. You may not fully appreciate this in an economics theory course, but you will in the TraderEx Course: market structure matters.

OVERVIEW OF THE BOOK

The book is broken into two parts. The first part establishes a background on trading and markets from an economics perspective, and provides an overview of the simulation model and the TraderEx software. The second part gives you a sequences of exercises in which you will trade in different market environments created by the TraderEx software and its settings.

Here is a more detailed overview of Part One:

Chapter 1, Equity Market Trading: This chapter provides a broad overview of the equity markets, paying particular attention to trading costs and liquidity, two intimately related concepts. The four generic market structures that we have already noted are presented: the continuous order driven market, the call auction, the quote driven dealer market, and the negotiated block market. A crossing network, a facility that in a number of respects resembles the call auction, is also introduced. The concept of informational efficiency (or the lack thereof) is addressed, and the Efficient Markets Hypothesis (EMH) and random walk theory are included in the discussion.

We then turn to investor expectations. Expectations link the fundamental information that investors possess to security prices that are set in the marketplace. In discussing this link, we distinguish between the standard academic assumption that informed investors have homogeneous expectations, and the marketplace reality that informed investors have divergent expectations (very importantly, TraderEx allows for such divergency).

The chapter also sets forth the key players in the marketplace. Buy-side investors are distinguished from sell-side broker/dealer intermediaries. In turn, the buy-side participants are categorized as information traders, liquidity traders, and technical traders.

Chapter 2, Simulation as a Learning Tool: Chapter 2 explains what a simulation model requires to be an effective learning tool, and establishes the underlying economic structure of the TraderEx simulator. We distinguish between simulations based on historic (canned) data, and those run using computer-generated data. Canned data come from real markets and thus reflect reality, but constrain the exercises to what happened without regard to any impacts that your own orders can have. Our TraderEx computer generated simulation offers flexibility and control that would otherwise be unobtainable. To deliver its promise and to be engaging, the computer-driven trading model must have four properties that are next discussed: it must capture the pricing dynamics of a real-world marketplace, it must give you some basis for anticipating future price movements, it must let you replay a simulation with some parameter and/or market structure feature changed, and it must provide meaningful benchmarks against which your performance can be assessed.

TraderEx's order flow is based on draws from various distributions, but underlying the statistical events are economic stories that pertain to the three types of traders that we introduce in Chapter 1: informed traders, liquidity traders, and technical traders. The chapter explains the economic models that support our statistical procedures.

Chapter 3, How to Use TraderEx: This chapter provides details about the TraderEx simulation software. After giving an overview of the simulation environment and specifying the requirements for running TraderEx, further detail is presented concerning the specific market structures that you will be trading in: the continuous order driven (order book) market, the quote driven dealer market, the order driven periodic call auction, a block trading facility, and a crossing network.

Chapter 4, Introduction to Trading Exercises: This chapter provides further information about markets and market participants so that you might have a good conceptual framework when undertaking the simulation exercises. Particular attention is paid, in turn, to the perspectives of buy-side participants and of sell-side market intermediaries. The TraderEx performance measures are then set forth and explained.

The material in Part One is also discussed in two related books: *Equity Markets in Action* (by Robert A. Schwartz and Reto Francioni) and *The Equity Trader Course* (by Robert A. Schwartz, Reto Francioni, and Bruce W. Weber). Both of these books provide further information on equity market structure, on the role and operations of exchanges, and on a spectrum of other topics including trading costs, public policy, and government regulatory intervention. If you are familiar with this material, you might wish to skim Chapters 1 and 2. Chapters 3 and 4 show you how to use the TraderEx software and introduce you to the trading exercises.

Part Two presents exercises along with additional discussion of the software and trading mechanisms that you will be operating within. The following is an overview of the five chapters containing hands-on trading exercises:

Chapter 5, Microeconomics Goes to Market: This chapter is the first of five that contain exercises that give you specific instructions for using the simulator. The eight exercises in this chapter are based on end-of-chapter material presented in the Wiley book, *Micro Markets: A Market Structure Presentation of Microeconomic Theory* (by Robert Schwartz). The first exercise gets you started with the simulator, and the seven that follow pertain to basic microeconomic formulations. They are:

1. Let's Look at a Market
2. What Are Your Attitudes Toward Risk?
3. Call Market Trading
4. Trading Costs in Action
5. Dealer Costs and Inventory Control
6. Inter-Market Competition for a Stock Exchange
7. Finding an Equilibrium Value
8. Economic Effects of an Order Protection Rule

Chapter 6, The Order Book Market Structure: This chapter and the three that follow present exercises that target specific market structures. The exercises in this chapter first get you entering orders in a simple order book system that characterizes trading in an order driven market. After becoming familiar with the sizing and pricing of your orders, you will encounter the challenge of handling a really big order, of trading in an illiquid market, and of coping with heightened volatility. In the later simulation exercises you will, among other things, be given news releases, and you will be introduced to trading in a crossing network.

Chapter 7, The Call Auction Market Structure: The chapter first presents further information about call auction trading that includes an explanation of how your own orders can affect the clearing price that is set in a call. The exercises that follow first enable you to get comfortable interacting with the call auction, and then challenge you with working a large order when call and continuous trading are both available. You will also play the role of a proprietary trader who is presented with news releases. The last of these exercises is structured to emphasize different dimensions of your trading performance, and you will be able to assess and analyze your performance score.

Chapter 8, Dealer Markets—What Do The Trading Intermediaries Do? The chapter begins by giving you further information about the operations of a dealer market. The exercises then challenge you to manage your inventory position and risk by appropriate quote setting. You will also be exposed to the effect that preferencing has on your quote setting and inventory management. You will experience the challenge of market making in volatile markets, and in low liquidity markets. From the perspective of a market maker, you will also discover the value of having an alternative trading system available for use.

Chapter 9, Dark Pools—How Undisclosed Liquidity Works: The final set of simulation exercises places you in a hybrid environment that includes both the standard, transparent order book facility and a dark pool, block trading facility. After introducing you to the mechanics of the TraderEx dark pool, we face you with the challenge of working a large order in the hybrid marketplace. Additionally, we will periodically present you with news releases. Once again, we will call attention to the different dimensions of your trading performance, and you will be able to assess and analyze your performance score.

DOWNLOADING THE TRADEREX SOFTWARE

The TraderEx software can be downloaded at: www.wiley.com/go/traderex.

HOW TRADEREX WORKS WITH MICRO MARKETS

As noted, this TraderEx book has a companion, Robert A. Schwartz, *Micro Markets: A Market Structure Presentation of Microeconomic Theory* (John Wiley & Sons, 2010). *Micro Markets* is about how these markets operate from a microeconomics perspective, and it devotes particular attention to the equity markets. The end-of-chapter material in each of the eight chapters of *Micro Markets* includes a computer simulation exercise (these are the ones listed above) that can be undertaken with the software and additional instructions that we provide in the current book. These exercises, with some further detail added, are presented in Chapter 5 of this book.

Robert A. Schwartz
New York, NY

Gregory M. Sipress
New York, NY

Bruce W. Weber
London, England
April, 2010

Acknowledgments

We are most grateful for the constant support and encouragement that we have received throughout the production process from our friend and TraderEx partner, Bill Abrams. We also thank Pamela van Giessen and Emilie Herman, our editors at John Wiley & Sons, for their counsel, support, and advice. Gregory Sipress would like to thank his parents, Mannie and Carol, and his wife, Lisa, for their unwavering love and support. Finally, our wonderful children Emily, Lindsay, John, and Hayden kept us happy and smiling through the project.

Mastering the Art of Equity Trading through Simulation

PART ONE

An Overview of Equity Market Trading

CHAPTER 1

Equity Market Trading

Dealing rooms are no longer loud, boisterous places where intuition and personal contacts determine how traders buy and sell securities. Trading floors today are hushed, studious spaces, with individual traders scanning dozens of screens to monitor markets and track trading positions. As the decibel level has fallen, the complexity of trading decisions has increased.

Today, financial markets offer traders more functionality, features, and tools than ever before. Navigating the choices requires a thorough understanding of alternative market structures and a sharper insight into the drivers of trading performance. Gaining knowledge and understanding of the more sophisticated opportunities and difficult decisions is not easy.

This book and the simulation software that comes with it will do two things. First, it will sharpen your understanding of what equity trading is all about. Trading involves the conversion of an investment decision into a desired portfolio position. It is the last part of the asset management process, and it is a treacherous part where all of your best efforts in selecting an investment can be squandered due to excessive trading costs or delays. Investors want their trading to be completed at the least possible cost and in a timely fashion. Trading is also about finding pricing discrepancies in the market, and entering the appropriate buy and sell orders to realize profits from a market imperfection.

The book's second objective is to detail how a micro market operates, for this knowledge can better your trading decision-making. A micro market is a market for a specific good, service, factor of production, or asset (in contrast to the *macro market*, which is all of a country's micro markets in aggregate). In this book, we deal with one specific micro market: the secondary market where already issued equity shares are traded. This micro market specifies the institutions, rules, transparency level, and matching algorithms that determine how traders act and which orders trade.

Micro markets are at the heart of microeconomic theory. Microeconomics is about how households, firms, industries and asset managers interact in the marketplace to determine the pricing, production, and distribution of a society's scarce resources and assets. But is microeconomic theory *real-world*? Much microeconomics, as traditionally presented, makes one big simplifying (and for us unacceptable) assumption: that a marketplace is a frictionless environment. The equity markets are far from frictionless, and we treat them as such. The interaction of orders, the setting of prices, and the determination of trading volumes are very much affected by various costs, blockages, uncertainties, and other impediments. This calls for analysis. Only when these marketplace realities are properly understood will a portfolio decision be properly formulated and implemented. In addition, as the trading world's adoption of algorithmic trading increases, the technologists designing the software need to take account of market imperfections when structuring their systems.

Equities are a critically important financial asset for scores of investors and corporations, and they are essential to the vibrancy and growth of the macro economy. Corporate equities represent shares of ownership in public companies and, as such, equity financing is an essential source of the financial capital that firms must have to undertake their operations. According to the World Federation of Exchanges, the total market capitalization of all publicly traded companies in the world was $40 trillion in the fourth quarter 2008. On a national level, equities comprise a major part of the portfolios of both individual and institutional investors such as mutual funds and pension funds. And, in light of its dynamic properties, an equity market is a particularly intriguing micro market to study.

Trading is not investing, and traders are a very different breed of people than portfolio managers. Portfolio managers (PMs) focus on stock selection. They take careful account of the risk and return characteristics of different stocks and, with increasing attention, their liquidity. Traders implement the PMs' decisions. Traders bring the orders they are given to the market, interact with other traders and, in the process, they focus out of necessity on liquidity (or the lack thereof).

A trader's environment is very different from that of the PM. Once a decision has been made and passed on to the trading desk, time acquires a different meaning. The clock suddenly accelerates. Prices in the marketplace can move sharply in brief intervals of time. As they do, trading opportunities pop up and quickly vanish. Your own order handling can cause a price to move away from you. Poor order placement and imperfect order timing are costly. A hefty portion of the gains that an asset manager might otherwise have realized from a good investment decision can be eroded by a poor trading decision.

In *Blink* (Little Brown and Company, 2005), a fascinating book about how we can think quickly and intuitively without literally figuring out our answers, Malcolm Gladwell analyzes decision making from a perspective that is very germane for a trader. Perhaps you are at the trading desk of a mutual fund, a hedge fund, or a pension fund. You are an active, short-term trader, and you have orders to work. You see the numbers flicker on your screen. You follow the market as it becomes fast moving and then, sensing the situation, act on your snap judgment. Without having the luxury of time to figure it all out, you (or the trading algorithm that you have designed), buy the shares, sell the shares, or hold back. A trading day is replete with these blink experiences. Moreover, feedback and performance measures are presented almost immediately and your decisions and the outcomes are assessed. How well have you done (or not)? Obviously you cannot win them all, but with training, your blink experiences will work a whole lot better for you.

As a trader, you may take liquidity or supply it. Traders who are successful often choose to wait a bit before becoming aggressive. Al Berkeley of Pipeline has characterized the strong incentive *not* to display your trading intentions until the other side has revealed itself. *"Pipeline's order matching algorithm . . . price improves the first order that has been placed. It removes the perverse incentive to be passive and wait, and it solves the Prisoner's Dilemma problem."* [*] Successful traders often refer to the importance of consistency and not altering their decision-making approach when losses arise, and they remain steady on the plow. Quality decisions must be made under a spectrum of conditions, including when the market is under stress, as when stabilizing buy orders are cancelled, a rush of sell orders arrives, and the market turns one-sided. Daily openings and closings are also stressful times when volume is high, volatility accentuated, and the clock is ticking.

It takes much experience to think and to act instinctively. Professional traders become good traders only after gaining experience and learning what works. Think of the basketball player who, after having spent hundreds of hours shooting baskets for practice, makes a clutch shot on instinct just before the buzzer at the end of a championship game. And so it is with the equity trader. Only after many months of training will the good trader trade well on instinct. On this score, simulated trading can help. Our TraderEx software is designed to accelerate your learning process.

THE COSTS OF TRADING

Trading is costly because the marketplace is not a frictionless environment. Costs fall into two broad categories: *explicit costs* and *execution costs* (which, by their

---

[*]Schwartz, Francioni, and Weber, *The Equity Trader Course*, John Wiley & Sons, 2006, p. 200.

nature, are implicit). Explicit costs are visible and easily measured; they include, most prominently, commissions and taxes. Execution costs are not easily measured; they exist because, given the relative sparseness of counterpart orders on the market, a buy order may execute at a relatively high price, or a sell order may execute at a relatively low price. Along with reducing your returns, trading costs also cause investors to adjust their portfolios less frequently and, accordingly, to hold portfolios that they would not deem to be optimal in a perfectly liquid, frictionless environment.

To understand trading costs, one needs to know exactly how orders are handled and turned into transactions and transaction prices. We facilitate our discussion of order handling by defining the following:

- *Quotation:* A displayed price at which someone is willing to buy or to sell shares. A quote can be either *firm* or *indicative.* If firm, the participant setting the quote is obliged to honor it if a counterparty arrives. If indicative, the quoting participant is not obliged to.
- *Bid Quotation:* The price at which someone is willing to buy shares. The highest posted bid on the market is the "best bid" or the "inside bid."
- *Ask Quotation (offer price):* The price at which someone is willing to sell shares. The lowest posted ask on the market is the best or "inside ask."
- *Limit Order:* An individual participant's priced order to buy or to sell a specific number of shares of a stock. The limit price on a buy limit order specifies the highest (maximum) price a buyer is willing to pay, and the limit price on a sell limit order specifies the lowest (minimum) price a seller is willing to receive. The trader placing a limit order is a price *maker*, and limit orders that are posted on a market are *pre-positioned.* The pre-positioned orders to buy and to sell that are the most aggressive establish the best market quotes and thus the market's bid-ask spread.
- *Market Bid-Ask Spread:* The best (lowest) market ask minus the best (highest) market bid. The bids and offers can be market maker quotes and/or the prices that individual participants put on their pre-positioned limit orders. The market spread is sometimes referred to as the *inside spread* or as the *BBO* (best bid and offer).
- *Market Order:* An individual participant's un-priced order to buy or to sell a specific number of shares of a stock. A market order can execute against a dealer quote or against a pre-positioned limit order. Market orders to buy are typically executed at the best (lowest) quoted ask, and market orders to sell are typically executed at the best (highest) quoted bid. When placing a market order, you are a *price taker*.
- *Short Selling:* A participant who does not own shares of a company but believes that the shares are overpriced can act on his or her opinion by *selling short.*

A short sale involves selling borrowed shares. If the price does fall, the short seller will buy the shares back in the market and return them to the lender. Short selling enables a participant to have a negative holding. Negative holdings are called *short positions*, and positive holdings are called *long positions*. A short sale that is executed without the shares having been previously borrowed is a *naked short*.

- *Arbitrage trading: Arb* opportunities exist in two forms. In the rare risk-free form, a mispricing of related securities gives "free" money to someone. If a convertible bond can be bought for $9 and converted into a share worth $10, you arb the price difference until it has been whittled down to the cost of establishing the position. When one stock is seemingly overpriced relative to another stock, you may seek to profit from that discrepancy, but your trades will entail risk. Short selling enables arbitrage trading. An arbitrageur will exploit a pricing discrepancy by buying the underpriced asset (acquiring a long position in it) and shorting the overpriced asset (acquiring a short position in it). The arbitrageur then profits as the prices of the two stocks regain their proper alignment. We refer to arb operations in the next section of this chapter, where we focus on liquidity. As you will see, in the perfectly efficient, frictionless world of the Capital Asset Pricing Model, arbitrageurs are the ultimate source of the liquidity that characterizes that model.

It is helpful to distinguish between two types of traders: active and passive. During normal trading hours, an execution is realized whenever two counterpart orders cross. This happens if one of the following three events occurs:

1. A public trader first posts a limit order, and then another public trader submits a market order that executes against the limit order.

2. A market maker (dealer) sets the quote, and then a public market order executes against the quote.

3. Two or more public traders negotiate a trade. The negotiation may take place on the floor of an exchange; in a brokerage firm in the so called "upstairs market"; in a privately owned, alternative trading system; or via direct contact between the two trading partners.

For each trade, one party to it may be viewed as the active trader who is the instigator or liquidity taker, and the other party may be viewed as the passive trader who is the liquidity provider or price maker. The one who initiates is seeking to trade without delay and is the active trader. Active traders are the public market order traders (cases 1 and 2 above) and the trader who initiates the negotiation process (case 3). Passive traders include the limit order trader (case 1), the market maker (case 2), and the trader who does not initiate the negotiation process (case 3). If you are an active trader, you will generally incur execution costs; these payments are positive returns for passive traders. On the other hand, if you are a passive trader, you run the risk of a delayed execution or of not executing at all.

With these definitions, we can identify the implicit execution costs of trading. The major execution costs for a smaller, retail customer are the bid-ask spread and opportunity costs. A large institutional customer may also incur market impact costs.

- **The Bid-Ask Spread:** Because matched or crossed orders trigger transactions that eliminate the orders from the market, market bid-ask spreads are always positive and, with discrete prices, must be at least as large as the smallest allowable price variation (currently one cent in the United States for most traded stocks). An active trader typically buys at the offer and sells at the bid, and the bid-ask spread is the cost of taking a round trip (buying and then selling, or selling short and then buying). Conventionally, half of the spread is taken to be the execution cost of either a purchase or a sale (a one-way trip).
- **Opportunity Cost:** This cost refers to the cost that may be incurred if the execution of an order is delayed (commonly in an attempt to achieve an execution at a better price), or if a trade is missed. A buyer incurs an opportunity cost if a stock's price rises during the delay, and a seller incurs an opportunity cost if a stock's price falls during the delay.
- **Market Impact:** Market impact refers to the additional cost (over and above the spread) that a trader may incur to have a large order executed quickly. It is the higher price that must be paid for a large purchase, or the reduction in price that must be accepted for a large sale.

LIQUIDITY

Liquidity is a nebulous term that nobody can define with precision, but which many would accept is the ability to buy or to sell a reasonable number of shares, in a reasonably short amount of time, at a reasonable price. But what is reasonable? The inability to answer this question with precision suggests why formal liquidity models and empirical liquidity studies have not been forthcoming to anywhere near the extent that they have been for risk, the other major determinant of a stock's price.

Illiquidity is the inevitable product of market frictions. We do not operate in a frictionless environment (and never will). No matter how efficient our trading mechanisms may be, there are limits to the liquidity that participants can expect to receive. Of course there are trading costs, both explicit and implicit and, as a manifestation of trading costs, intra-day price volatility is elevated (especially at market openings and closings). Of course strategic decisions have to be made concerning how best to supply liquidity or whether to access the liquidity that others have provided.

Implicit trading costs such as spreads and market impact are manifestations of illiquidity, but they address only part of the story. To probe deeper, we focus on two major functions of an equity market: *price discovery* and *quantity discovery*. Price discovery is the process of finding a value that best reflects the broad market's desire to hold shares of a stock. The process is complex and it is protracted. In large part this is because of friction in the production, dissemination, assessment and implementation of information. Information sets are huge, information bits are generally imprecise and incomplete, and our tools for assessing information are relatively crude. Consequently, different individuals who are in possession of the same publicly available information may form different expectations about the risk and expected return parameters for any given stock or portfolio. Moreover, when participants have different expectations, they can also change their individual valuations at any time, particularly when they learn the valuations of others. A divergence of expectations and the attending interdependencies between different people's valuations profoundly impact the process of price formation.

Quantity discovery is also difficult. Large institutional participants, because of their size and the size of their orders, typically approach the market wrapped in a veil of secrecy, and secrecy is the root cause of the problem: how do the large participants find each other and trade if they are all trying to stay hidden? Quantity discovery may be viewed as liquidity discovery, and the incompleteness of quantity discovery is akin to latent liquidity (i.e., it is there if only it can be found). Large traders either "hold their orders in their pockets" until they are motivated to step forward and trade; or they send their orders to upstairs trading desks or to other non-transparent trading facilities; or they slice and dice their orders, feeding the pieces into the market over an extended period of time. One or more large buyers may be doing any or all of this at the same time that one or more large sellers are doing the same thing. Consequently, the contras may not meet, they may not be providing available liquidity to each other, and some trades that would be doable do not get made.

A number of our TraderEx exercises are designed to sharpen your understanding of the complexities of both quantity and price discovery.

MARKET STRUCTURE

How orders are translated into trades and transaction prices depends on the rules of order handling and trading that define the architecture of a marketplace. Much development has occurred on the market structure front in recent years. Nevertheless, despite striking technological advances, the emergence of new trading facilities, and a sharp intensification of inter-market competition, major problems persist, and equity market design remains a work in process. Two problems are paramount: (1) providing reasonable liquidity for mid-cap and small-cap stocks, and (2) amassing sufficient liquidity for large, institutional-sized orders for all stocks. The simulation exercises in this book will bring you face-to-face with these problems in the context of specific market structures.

Comprehensively viewed, trading facilities are classified into the four generic structures. Our exercises will enable you to trade in each of them and in pairwise hybrid combinations. We describe these structures in further detail in the context of the exercises but, in brief, here they are:

- **Continuous Order Driven Market.** For a trade to be made, a price first has to be established. In an order driven market, prices are set by the limit orders that have been posted by some of the participants. The limit orders to sell establish the prices at which market order traders can buy, and the limit orders to buy establish the prices at which market order traders can sell. In continuous trading, the limit orders are posted on a limit order book and a trade is made whenever a buy order matches or crosses a sell order at any time during normal trading hours.
- **Call Auction.** A call auction is a periodic rather than a continuous order driven market. With a call auction, participant orders are batched together for a simultaneous execution at a single clearing price at a pre-announced point in time. When the market is called, all buy orders equal to and greater than the clearing price are executable, as are all sell orders equal to or less than the clearing price.[*]
- **Quote Driven, Dealer Market.** In a dealer market, dealers state the prices at which public customers can trade. A dealer posts *two-sided quotes*: a bid quote at which the dealer will buy shares from you if you are looking to sell, and an ask quote at which the dealer will sell shares to you if you are looking to buy. A dealer market is commonly referred to as a *quote driven market* because the dealer quotes "prime the market."
- **Negotiated, Block Market.** Trades are made by two parties meeting and negotiating a trade. This market structure is used to handle the large block orders of big institutional investors, where a block is generally defined as an order

---

[*]When the executable number of shares to buy does not equal the executable number of shares to sell exactly, some of these shares remain unexecuted. When this occurs, a time priority rule is generally applied to determine the orders that do execute, with those that were placed first being filled first.

for 10,000 shares or more. A negotiation can be between two floor traders, or between an institutional customer and an upstairs block positioner, or it can be affected by two large traders meeting each other directly. A negotiation can be person-to-person (either face-to-face or via telephone), or it can take place via an electronic interface. Today's dark liquidity pools are the network-era equivalent of the deliberately discreet activities of block trading desks.

INFORMATIONAL EFFICIENCY (OR THE LACK THEREOF)

Smart trading is all about coping effectively with trading costs along with price trending and the accentuated price swings that characterize illiquid markets. You will encounter all of these as you use the TraderEx software. The trading costs, trending, and accentuated price swings are all attributes of a market that is not perfectly efficient. As we have already discussed, trading costs exist because trading is not a frictionless process. TraderEx will present you with feedback information on how well you are managing to trade in the presence of the inefficiencies.

In this section, we consider market efficiency on a more fundamental level by assessing the accuracy with which information is reflected in share prices. Strong inferences about the quality of market prices can be drawn by assessing how stock prices evolve over time. Let's start at the beginning.

The term *informational efficiency* refers to the accuracy with which prices that are set in a marketplace reflect the underlying information that the prices are based on. In an informationally efficient securities market, all existing information is reflected in share values perfectly, and no trader has an informational advantage that would allow him or her to realize excess risk-adjusted returns. The null hypothesis, which is referred to as the *Efficient Market Hypothesis* (EMH), is formalized as follows.

Excess returns cannot be realized from information that is contained in

- **Past prices**—this is referred to as weak form efficiency.
- **Any public information** (including past prices)—this is referred to as semi-strong form efficiency
- **All information**—this is referred to as strong form efficiency.

Our discussion focuses on the first bullet, weak form efficiency. The weak form tests address one concept in particular: whether or not stock prices follow *random walks*. Random walk is a cool concept. In a nutshell, it means that where you take your next step is totally independent of all other steps that you have previously taken. If you are taking a random walk, anyone following your path would have no ability whatsoever to predict where you might next be heading. Your friend who is trying to guess your destination will find that the path you have traced out thus far contains absolutely no useful information. It is as if your footprints did not exist.

The random walk concept applies to the stock market. Those of us with an interest in the equity markets like to follow prices. We try to predict where they might be going next. Is a stock heading up? Is it drifting down? Has it gone up too far (or down too low)? Is it about to reverse direction and revert back to an earlier value? Or perhaps, is price only following a random walk? Unless you have taken a finance course that deals with the subject, you might think that stock prices following a random walk is a preposterous idea.

It is not. Many financial economists are of the opinion that stock price movements are essentially free of any correlation pattern. For the most part they believe that, aside from transaction prices bouncing between bid and offer quotes, it is not possible to predict where a stock's price might next be heading. Our colleagues would be correct if markets were fully efficient, totally frictionless, and perfectly liquid. Why is that?

Here is the answer. Information is the input that drives investment decisions and trading, and security prices are based upon the information set. Informational efficiency means that security prices fully incorporate the entire information set. If this were not the case, some clever participant could grab hold of the information set and churn out some profitable trades. If someone could do this at some moment in time, then the price of a stock, at that moment, could not be reflecting the information set correctly. If this were the case, the EMH would not hold. But if there were to be a pricing error in the totally frictionless, perfectly liquid environment, the error would be immediately exploited by an arbitrage action, for this is what mispricing leads to.

There is a story about an economist and friend who were walking down a city street when the economist spotted a twenty-dollar bill on the sidewalk. He pointed the bill out to his friend but walked right by it. "Why didn't you pick it up?" asked the friend. "Because it isn't real," was the answer. "How do you know that?" was the follow-up question. "Because if it was, somebody else would have picked it up already," was the economist's explanation.

So let's presume that a stock's price, at any moment in time, does properly reflect the full information set. What then would cause the stock's price to change? With the current information fully adjusted to, no future price change can be attributed to the current information set. If it were, then the stock's price could not have been an appropriate reflection of the current information in the first place. For the EMH to hold, a stock's price can change only because of the advent of *new* information (news). The news would have to be totally unanticipated because any anticipation is part of the current information set. Now for the punch line: If the news must be totally unanticipated, its effect on the stock's price cannot be predicted. Therefore, neither can any future price change be predicted. Will the news be bullish or bearish? Who knows? Nobody knows. The stock's price must, therefore, be following a random walk.

But what if it doesn't? If share prices do not follow random walks, then their path into the future offers some predictability, which means that profitable decision rules based on recent price movements could possibly be formulated. Using recent price behavior to predict future price movements is called *technical analysis* (the older term that is not heard as much these days is *charting*). A more recent tool called *algorithmic trading* is often put to much the same purpose. While any decision rule can be called an algorithm, algorithmic trading refers specifically to computer driven trading rules. When an *algo* that is resident in a computer program is activated by, for instance, an intra-day price pattern, a trading decision is formulated and the order is shot into the market, all in tiny fractions of a second (milliseconds). Both technical analysis and algorithmic trading are widely used by stock market professionals although neither would have a payoff if share prices were taking random walks.

What do the data say about this? Going way back, to before the 1970s, random walk tests have been among the most important tests of the EMH. For years, the weak form of the EMH generally passed these tests, and the results were certainly sobering for any young buck poised to predict future price movements based on patterns that he or she seemingly saw in historical data. To this day, the EMH should keep us all acceptably humble. But this does not mean that prices actually follow random walks, or that correlation patterns do not exist, or that technical analysis and algorithmic trading do not have valid roles to play.

With the advent of powerful computers and high frequency data (complete, moment-to-moment records of all transaction prices, quotes, and transaction volume), financial economists are increasingly finding that stock returns are not entirely free of the correlation patterns that random walk theory says should not be there. And yet the EMH remains compelling. What is the missing element? Missing is full recognition of an important reality: markets are not fully efficient, they are not frictionless, and they are not perfectly liquid.

Of course we do not live and operate in a frictionless environment. Quite to the contrary, many markets are not perfectly competitive, the economic environment is far from static, a spectrum of costs and blockages exist that would not be there to perturb us in a frictionless marketplace, and there are various sources of market failure. The environment is also imperfect in another way: we have only a limited ability to deal with information sets that are so enormous, so complex, so incomplete, and so imprecise. Nevertheless, the efficient market hypothesis remains elegant, compelling, extraordinarily difficult to refute, and humbling. The EMH stands as a warning to all aspiring young masters of the universe who, armed with what they might think are magic formulas, believe that they will earn millions.

That said, cracks in the façade of the EMH and random walk theory have profound implications for an equity trader. Market timing gains importance, trading requires strategic decision making, technical analysis and algorithmic trading have a raison d'être, and trading acquires professional importance.

EXPECTATIONS

Expectations, being formulated on the basis of current information, link the information to the market value of shares. Investors form expectations about a company's future returns, and they trade shares based on these expectations. Expectations are a major, but not the only force that drives trading. Participants also trade because of their own liquidity needs, and technical traders are on the scene as well (as we will shortly discuss).

Do all of the informed investors form identical expectations? If so, they have *homogeneous expectations*. If not, investors have *divergent expectations*. Think about what you read in the papers and hear on TV. Think of the discussions that you and your friends enter into at cocktail parties and other social events. Consider why some people are buying shares of Pfizer or Cisco at the same time that others are selling. It is quite obvious, is it not, that investors disagree with each other's evaluations; that they have divergent expectations?

This simple observation that investors have divergent expectations (which, with some irony, we point out just about every industry practitioner agrees with) is of major importance. It is important for your investment decisions and your trading decisions. It is important because it has implications for the dynamic formation of quotes and transaction prices in the marketplace. It is important because when expectations are divergent, stocks cannot have intrinsic values, and no stock analyst can determine what a share of stock is worth. Prices can be found only in the marketplace. It is as simple as that.

This reality aside, much formal analysis in financial economics assumes that different investors have the same expectations concerning security returns. Even though we may agree that the assumption of homogeneous expectations is unrealistic, models based upon it (such as the standard capital asset pricing model) give much insight into how a market determines prices for various assets according to their risk and return characteristics.

But some academicians cite a further reason for assuming homogeneous expectations—one that goes well beyond the need for model simplicity. To some, rational decision making implies the homogeneity of expectations. This is because decision making considers what a rational person would conclude given "the facts." Presumably, what one rational person would conclude, all rational people *should* conclude (and, in any event, anyone not arriving at that conclusion would, in a

Darwinian sense, "die out"). However, having considered the elements that comprise the information set, we may better understand why the homogeneous expectations assumption is unrealistic. It is plausible for a group of investors to have homogeneous expectations only if they share the same information and if (and this is a big if) they process it in an identical way. Do they?

Think again about the realities of the world that we live in. Think again about information sets that are vast, complex, imprecise, incomplete, and a challenge to understand. Different individuals possess only part of the information that is publicly available, and they analyze the parts in different ways. To some extent we all resemble six blind men who, upon touching different parts of an elephant, reach different conclusions about what they are in contact with. "A spear," says one (whose hand is on a tusk). "A rope," says another (who is holding the elephant's tail). "A fan," declares a third (whose hand is on the huge animal's ear). And so on, as shown in Figure 1.1. Not one of the six blind men can put it all together. Not one knows that they are all touching an elephant.

Some of our TraderEx exercises include information stories. Some of the information stories are relatively straightforward and easy to translate into share values. You will also be given information stories that are more complex. When information is difficult to interpret, participants are more apt to have different opinions about it, their expectations will be more divergent, and reasonably accurate price discovery is not easily achieved. Our intention is for you to experience this as you play TraderEx.

FIGURE 1.1 Six blind men and an elephant.

THE PLAYERS

The different types of players who interact in the equity markets can be classified in a couple of different ways. By one classification, the entire industry is separated into two groups: buy-side participants and sell-side participants. By a second classification, buy-side participants fit into three groups: informed traders, liquidity traders, and technical traders. This trichotomy of buy-side traders is standard in the academic literature, it forms the basis for TraderEx's computer generated order flow, and we discuss each of these types of agents in the context of our simulation model.

Buy-Side versus Sell-Side Participants

Buy-side players include those participants who are looking to trade for their own portfolio reasons. The group includes retail customers and institutional customers such as pension funds, mutual funds, and hedge funds. These players are on the buy-side because they are buying trading services.

The sell-side of the market (the sellers of trading services) includes broker-dealer intermediaries who (for the most part) are employed by banks and brokerage houses. *Intermediation* means the participation of a third party in trading. Intermediaries fit into the value chain between the investor as the final owner of the securities, and the stock market as the price discoverer and exchange operator. Intermediaries include brokers, dealers, market makers, and specialists. One can also view the term *intermediary* more broadly to include the computerized intermediation functions of the market centers themselves, of electronic brokers, and of electronic order routing systems. For the most part, however, when we refer to *intermediaries* we have in mind two types of human agents: brokers and market makers.

A *broker* handles customer orders as an agent, routing an order into the order book of an exchange or to a designated dealer intermediary. The broker may be bound by fiduciary obligations to ensure that customers receive favorable treatment in the market and that they obtain fair prices. In markets with *dealer* intermediaries, the dealers create value by committing capital to trade beyond the sizes that are available in the order book. Exchanges often place special obligations on dealer intermediaries to make fair and orderly markets by buying for, and selling from, their own inventories, by trading in a stabilizing manner against public orders, and by taking the corresponding position risk. Dealers in the equity markets are widely referred to as *market makers*. We use the terms *dealer* and *market maker* interchangeably.

Informed Traders

Informational change about the value of a stock is the most important reason for a security's valuation to change. Informed traders are those who trade knowing that the current price level diverges from the value that would be observed in the market if all participants were fully informed. In TraderEx, the equilibrium price is called P^*. When the P^* valuation is greater or less than the stock's market price, informed orders are motivated.

In a hypothetical world with costless trading and complete, instantaneous information dissemination, price adjustments are instantaneous, one-shot events. In real-world markets, informationally motivated orders arrive at the market sequentially, and price adjustments are noisy and non-instantaneous. As we discuss further in Chapter 2, price changes that reflect new information take place sequentially in TraderEx.

Informed participants are informed in TraderEx simply because they know the value of P^*, and they act upon this knowledge in the market by buying or selling. The informed trader will send a buy order to market if P^* is above the value at which shares can be bought (i.e., if it is above the market offer). Similarly, an informed trader will send a sell order to market if P^* is below the value at which shares can be sold (i.e., if it is below the market bid)[*]. P^* itself changes over time according to a statistical jump process with the times between jumps determined by random draws from a statistical distribution. We discuss this further in Chapter 2.

Liquidity Traders

Liquidity traders play a different role than information traders in actual markets and in TraderEx. They come to the market because of their own idiosyncratic desires to trade. Orders from liquidity traders are two-sided, they can be either market orders or limit orders, and they arrive randomly. That is, these orders are uncorrelated with each other.

The term "liquidity trading" is in the tradition of good old Keynesian economics. A key building block in the Keynesian model is the *liquidity preference function*, which describes the aggregate demand of people to hold cash. This demand, when matched with the money supply, establishes the interest rate. Cash is the ultimate, perfectly liquid asset because it is the generally accepted medium of exchange. Keynes recognized two reasons for holding cash—a *transaction motive* (you need cash to buy goods and services, and you are paid in cash when you sell a good or service), and a *speculative motive* (you hold more cash if you think that interest rates will rise and thus that bond prices will fall, and you hold less cash if you think that interest rates will fall and bond prices will rise).

Keynes's transaction motive leads to liquidity trading. To illustrate, consider a liquidity trader who suddenly becomes cash rich and buys some shares. Perhaps his Uncle has just passed away and our liquidity trader has been remembered in

---

[*]Operationally, when P^* is above the offer or below the bid, the arrival rate of market orders to buy or to sell is increased from 50 percent to about 70 percent of TraderEx's total order flow.

his Uncle's will. Across town, another liquidity trader has a bill to pay for her son's college tuition, and she sells some shares. These cash flows are unique to each individual. The two liquidity orders are completely independent of each other, and neither is correlated with market information.

Technical Trading

Technical traders are prevalent in the market, and you might be one yourself. You could be a market technician using charting techniques, or an *algo* trader relying on software to react to tick-level change in the market, or an arbitrageur, or a day trader who is wearing one of these hats. In the TraderEx software, our machine resident technical traders use one simple rule, that of a momentum player—buy if price starts to rise, and sell if price starts to fall[*]. This simple rule is all that is necessary to include this third type of real-world player, and for the dynamics of our simulated market to be complete. We provide further details about this in Chapter 2.

SUMMARY

Trading is a complex activity and equity markets are intricate environments. Three major tools exist for studying the markets: institutional description, theoretical modeling, and simulation analysis. The third, simulation, lets you actually participate in trading, and you can do so without losing (or winning) real money. To be valid, however, the simulation must capture the pricing dynamics of real-world markets. That is what the TraderEx software does. We explain how this objective is accomplished in the next chapter.

---

[*]Specifically, the machine-resident momentum players operate according to the following algorithm: if a sequence of four or more buy-triggered (or sell-triggered) trades and/or upticks (down ticks) in the midquote occurs, the conditional probability is increased that the next machine-generated order will be a market order to buy (or a market order to sell).

CHAPTER 2

Simulation as a Learning Tool

Talking about trading is one thing; experiencing it is another. But the experience can be way too costly if it involves putting actual money into an actual market. In TraderEx's simulated trading environment, you need not worry that your real cash position will wind up in the tank. You can experiment with different trading strategies simply to see how they work out. You can evaluate the effects of different trading rules and of alternative market structures on your trading decisions and on the quality of market outcomes. You will be able to compare and understand alternative market structures, and you can participate in an economic process that translates news about the stock you will be trading into the price of its equity shares. You can do all of this, you should have fun, and the only thing that you will lose (or gain) will be simulated dollars.

In this chapter we explain what is required for a simulation model to be an effective learning tool. In so doing, we show you the underlying economic structure of the TraderEx simulation.

CANNED VERSUS COMPUTER GENERATED PRICES AND QUOTES

A computer driven financial market simulation can be based on either (1) replays of historic (canned) data or (2) computer generated data. With the canned data approach, quotes, orders, prices, and trades are taken from an historic transaction record, and a live participant trades against the historic values. The historic data approach has been used to back-test investment or trading strategies, where you hypothetically follow a rule using market prices for a prior period of time.

Many strategies, when implemented, fail to live up to the expectations established by back testing. A major reason is that when back testing a hypothetical trading strategy with the data replay approach, your own orders cannot affect the record of past prices—the prices are what they were. And so, with a canned data simulation, you can trade any quantity that you want without affecting the prices at which you trade. How realistic is that? In the real world, your larger orders can have a big impact on market prices and quotes. Your buys will push prices up and away from you, and your sells will push prices down and away from you. Canned data have one clear advantage, however. You know that the stream of quotes and transaction prices that you are trading against reflects reality because they were produced by real-world dynamics.

The transaction record used, however, is the product of the specific date, stock, and market that produced it. Perhaps the transaction record is for Wal-Mart (WMT) on April 21, 2009, a day that the stock opened at $49.66, traded in a range from $48.93 to $50.00 (a $1.07 or 2.2 percent high-low range), and closed at $49.83, which was 56 cents higher than its previous close, on a volume of 15.6 million shares. WMT trades on the New York Stock Exchange, and on that date the stock experienced a particular level of volatility, a particular pattern of bid-ask spreads, a particular price trend, and so forth. You could not replay the WMT record with a higher level of volatility, or a lower volume, or with any other parameter or market structure feature altered. Canned data are linked exclusively to the environment that generated them.

This is not so with computer-generated data. TraderEx generates its own market data to address the deficiencies of canned data. With TraderEx, you can affect market prices. You can rerun the TraderEx simulations to assess the impact of a parameter change, or of a strategy change, or of a market structure change, while experimenting with just one thing at a time. This selective change of the environment is classic economic methodology—we are able to analyze one thing at a time while "holding all else constant," or *ceteris paribus* for those who speak Latin. Consequently, machine generated data can have a decided advantage over canned data, but something major is required for this advantage to be realized: the machine generated order flow must capture the pricing dynamics of a real-world marketplace. This chapter explains how TraderEx does this.

What a Trading Simulation Requires

To deliver its promise and to be truly engaging, a trading simulation must have four critical properties:

1. The machine generated order flow must capture the pricing dynamics of a real-world marketplace.

2. The simulated market must give you some basis for anticipating future price movements.

3. The software must enable you to replay a simulation run so that you can see the effect of a change of your strategy, or of market structure, or of a market parameter.

4. The simulation must provide you with meaningful performance benchmarks against which to assess how well you are doing during a run, and at the end. Performance measures allow you to compare your results against others, and to know whether you are improving with experience.

Each of these is next discussed in greater detail.

The Pricing Dynamics of a Real-World Marketplace Must Be Captured

At the heart of the TraderEx simulation is a set of statistical distributions (e.g., a normal distribution) that are randomly drawn from. But while the draws are random, the resulting quotes and transaction prices are not. Capturing the pricing dynamics of a real marketplace requires that quotes and transaction prices in the simulated environment do not follow random walks. Indeed, the returns traced out as the simulation progresses reflect an intricate correlation pattern that is attributable to the way in which the orders are handled in our simulated market (e.g., entered into a limit order book) and turned into trades (e.g., the arrival of a market order triggers the execution of a limit order). We discussed random walk in Chapter 1, and we provide more information about returns correlations in the appendix to this chapter.

With regard to market prices, if you enter an order that betters the best bid or offer quote in the market, you may trigger a trade that would not otherwise have happened. Moreover, if you enter a large buy order, you can push price up. Or, if you enter a large sell order, you can push price down. These things happen all the time in the real world, as they do in TraderEx.

Price Changes Can Be Anticipated So that you might be able to anticipate future price movements, we give you other signals to go on other than guesswork. As we have just noted, prices and quotes in TraderEx do not simply move randomly (and neither do they in real equity markets). Trading strategies and order placement skills can be developed and used to good advantage with TraderEx that would not be possible if the simulation's prices and quotes followed random walks. Patterns of runs and reversals co-exist in real-world markets, and they do so in TraderEx as well. Consequently, you should not determine when to act in our simulation simply by throwing darts at a time clock. Your orders should be timed, priced and sized in relation to your assessment of current conditions and your anticipation of future market changes. After you have completed several simulation runs, you might better understand that good trading decisions are not just a matter of guessing.

Simulation Runs Can Be Replayed   You can replay the TraderEx simulation runs and observe the effect of a change of your strategy or parameter settings. If you have traded impatiently and have suffered the consequences, you are able to go back and see what would have happened if you had followed a more patient strategy. You can repeat a run and see what would have happened if you had been less aggressive, or if you had been operating under a different market environment.

Each TraderEx run is based on a random number seed that is called a *scenario number.* There are 100 scenario numbers for you to pick from. Keeping the scenario number the same means that, all else equal, the random outcomes in the run will be repeated if you yourself do nothing differently. However, by making changes in your decisions, you are able to see exactly how your actions can change history. That is, you will see how outcomes change because you have done something different, or because you have changed one particular parameter setting, or because you have changed the market structure in some specific way, with everything else remaining as before (the *ceteris paribus* condition).

Performance Can Be Assessed   The fourth and last requirement is that you have meaningful performance benchmarks that let you know how you are doing, and how you are improving with experience. You can also use the benchmarks to assess the relative success of different trading strategies that you might want to experiment with. For instance, how does trading patiently by using limit orders compare with trading aggressively by using market orders?

TraderEx has four targeted performance measures. These measures are set forth in further detail in the context of our simulation exercises. In brief, they are:

1. **P&L:** The net profit or loss that you have generated over the course of a simulation run. As on real trading desks, TraderEx profit is divided into realized profit and unrealized profit. Realized profit is money you can put in the bank. You bought shares and opened a position, and then closed part or all of it by selling shares at higher prices than you paid. Or you have sold shares short and then closed part or all of the position by buying shares back at lower prices than you had sold at. Unrealized profits are determined by the position that you have, and by the amount of cash that you would be left with if you were to close the position at the current bid quote if you have a long position, or at the current ask quote if you have a short position (in other words, your inventory positions are marked to market). Notice that due to price movements, there is no certainty that the unrealized profits of a position can be realized. The higher your profits are, the higher is your score.

2. **VWAP:** VWAP, the volume weighted average price, is computed throughout a TraderEx simulation as:

$$\text{VWAP} = \text{Total value traded} \div \text{Total volume traded in shares}$$

The measure shows the average price a share has changed hands at up to that point in the trading day. Traders monitor the difference between VWAP and their average buying price (or average selling price) over the simulation run. The better you have done vis-à-vis the VWAP benchmark (the lower your average buying price, or the higher your average selling price), the higher is your score.

3. **Risk:** Holding a large order that you have been asked to fill or carrying a large inventory that you have been asked to liquidate is risky. If you trade too slowly, the price might move away from you. It is also risky if you trade too quickly since you might miss out on an opportunity to transact later at better prices. Our risk measure reflects how the instruction to buy or to sell a number of shares is completed over the course of a simulation run vis-à-vis a benchmark that reflects a relatively prudent execution pattern. The lower your risk measure, the higher is your score.

4. **Job Completion:** If you are instructed to buy or to sell a certain number of shares by the end of a simulation run, what percentage of your order have you filled as of the market's close? The closer the percentage filled is to 100 percent, the higher is your score.

After each simulation run, you will receive a single composite performance score that is a weighted average combination of your four targeted scores. The weight for each of the four measures reflects the measure's relative importance in any given simulation exercise. For instance, the P&L score will be given a heavy weight if you are playing the role of a proprietary trader (i.e., a market maker or a day trader). The VWAP score will get the heavy weight if you are playing the role of an order entry firm seeking to obtain "good" prices for your customers. The risk score will receive a heavy weight if you are playing the role of a relatively new trainee who is being held to strict position limits. The job completion measure will receive a heavy weight if you are working for a portfolio manager who has emphatically stated, "I want you to get the job done!"

The Forces that Drive Trading

TraderEx's machine generated order flow is based on draws from various statistical distributions. Underlying the statistical events are economic stories that pertain to the three classes of traders that we have discussed in Chapter 1:

1. **Informed traders:** they are motivated by the arrival of news.
2. **Liquidity traders:** they are motivated by the individual cash flow needs of the different participants.
3. **Technical traders:** they are motivated by their beliefs that they have observed exploitable patterns in the stock's price movements.

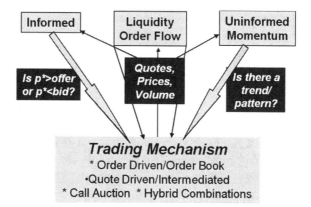

FIGURE 2.1 Types of trades and market mechanisms in TraderEx.

These three types of order flow are shown in Figure 2.1. Each motive for trading generates order flow. For any given order in TraderEx, you will not know what its motive is. Order flow brings liquidity to the market and, consequently, trades can be made.

We first look at a simple model in which orders to buy and to sell have arrival rates that vary with current market prices and with an equilibrium value of the security that we describe in more detail later in this chapter. As in Chapter 1, we call the equilibrium value P^*.

Now consider Figure 2.2. In this diagram, we show orders being generated at the average (expected) rates that are indicated by the downward-sloping buy curve, and sell orders being generated at the average (expected) rates that are given by the upward-sloping sell curve. For this particular setting, with the market bid and ask quotes centered on $P^* = \$48$, the buy and sell orders are both expected to arrive at the rate of seven orders per hour.

If the quotes in Figure 2.2 were centered on a price above \$48, the arrival of sell orders would, on expectation, exceed the arrival of buy orders. Or, if the quotes were centered on a price below \$48, the arrival of buy orders would, on expectation, exceed the arrival of sell orders. Absent changes in P^*, the market quotes will tend to self-correct and remain centered on P^*. That is, at higher quotes, selling pressure will move the market back down toward \$48, and at lower quotes buying pressure will move the market back up to \$48.

Suppose that P^* shifts up from \$48 to \$48.50. The graph would then center on \$48.50. If the quotes did not immediately move up with P^*, buy order arrivals would (on expectation) be greater than sell order arrivals, and the buying pressure would push the quotes up until they did center on the new value of P^*. The opposite would occur if P^* were to shift down from \$48 to, say, \$47.50.

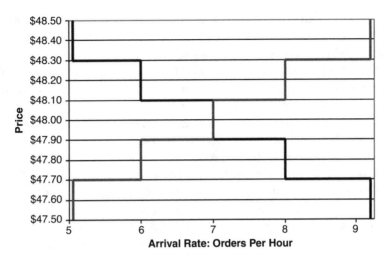

FIGURE 2.2 Buy and sell order arrival rates.

We have identified the three trader types: information traders, liquidity traders, and technical traders. The information traders and the liquidity traders respond to external events—the former to the advent of new information, and the latter to whatever impulses drive their own individual desires to trade. The technical traders respond to the price and quote behavior that they observe in the marketplace. Shortly, we will focus in greater detail on each of these three trader types. First, however, we explain how arrival rates for orders and events can be modeled as a statistical process.

Poisson Arrival Rates   The arrival of information driven and liquidity driven orders is modeled with the use of a stochastic process known as the *Poisson Arrival Process*. The Poisson process has the interesting property of being memoryless. *Memoryless* means that, no matter how much time has passed since the last event, the probability that P* will jump again in the next segment of time (e.g., the next minute) remains constant. Consequently, it is not possible to predict when P* will next change based on the amount of time that has passed since it last changed.

To illustrate, imagine that you are waiting to catch a number 3 city transit bus. While the timetable says that a number 3 bus should arrive every 20 minutes, you do not believe bus timetables and have observed that in fact, buses arrive, on expectation, every 20 minutes according to a Poisson process. You get to the bus stop. Q: What is your expected wait for the number 3? A: 20 minutes. Q: After waiting 5 minutes, what is your expected wait? A: Again, 20 minutes.

Think about this more closely. Knowing that, when on schedule, a number 3 bus arrives every 20 minutes, you would figure that the probability that one will arrive in the next minute should increase with each passing minute. But what if you are not sure that you are standing in the correct stop for the number 3? In this case, as the minutes go by, the probability of a number 3 appearing could start to fall off. Now, if in one case the probability of the next event occurring increases with the passage of time, and if in another case the probability falls, you might conceive of a third case, a neutral one—one where the probability of a new arrival neither increases nor decreases with the passage of time. This is the Poisson.

The Poisson has several nice properties. First, it has the efficient markets property that it is not possible to predict when information change will next occur (or, for that matter, if the news will be good or bad). Second, the Poisson is simple. The order arrival rate, λ, is its one and only parameter. This parameter describes both the mean and the variance of the distribution. An active stock will have a high λ value; an inactive stock will have a low λ value. By changing λ, we can change the rate at which orders arrive and information events occur in a TraderEx simulation run.

P* Changes   The magnitude of information change, when it occurs, is reflected in the size of the jump in P*. Jump size is also determined by a random draw. Each change in P* is an investment return to holders of the stock. P* jumping up (a positive return) means that the stock has become more valued, while P* jumping down (a negative return) means bad news (if you are long the stock). In our TraderEx simulation, the P* returns are lognormally distributed with a mean of zero. Each new value of P* is obtained by multiplying its previous value by one plus the return given by the draw from a lognormal distribution.

Over any simulation run, P* may drift up or it may drift down but, with a mean return of zero, there is no systematic tendency for it to move in one direction or the other over any simulation run. We can change the magnitude of the information events, and thus the underlying level of market volatility, by changing the variance parameter of the lognormal returns distribution. Because the P* returns are obtained by random draw, successive changes in P* are not serially correlated. P* moves randomly through time. In other words, our equilibrium price follows a random walk.

New values of P*, however, need not be determined by draws from the lognormal distribution. For some of the exercises, we have pre-configured P*. We do this when an information story is provided for the simulation run. Thus, P* will rise appropriately following an unexpectedly bullish news release, or fall appropriately following an unexpectedly bearish news release. Accordingly, the news release itself should give you an expectation about P* and, if you respond accurately and quickly, you may get your trades done before the new information is fully incorporated in share price.

Informed Traders

Informational change about the value of a stock is the most important reason for a security's valuation to change. Informed traders are those who trade knowing that the current price level diverges from the true, equilibrium value that you would observe in the market if all participants were fully-informed, and if there were no trading costs or frictions. In TraderEx, when the P* valuation is greater than or less than the stock's market price, informed orders will be triggered.

An important area in financial economics deals with the speed with which markets adjust to new information. In a hypothetical world with costless trading and complete, immediate information dissemination, price adjustments are instantaneous, one-shot events. In real-world markets, informationally motivated orders arrive at the market sequentially, and price adjustments are noisy and non-instantaneous. Price changes that reflect new information take place sequentially in TraderEx. This is shown in Figure 2.3 for a three-day simulation that we have run.

Informed participants are informed in TraderEx simply because they know the value of P*, and they act upon this knowledge by buying or by selling. The informed trader will send a buy order to market if P* is above the value at which shares can be bought (i.e., if it is above the market offer). Similarly, an informed trader will send a sell order to market if P* is below the value at which shares can be sold (i.e., if it is below the market bid). The informed orders are small enough that a number of them is generally required to move prices into alignment with a P* value. This treatment reflects the reality that better informed participants, by trading in

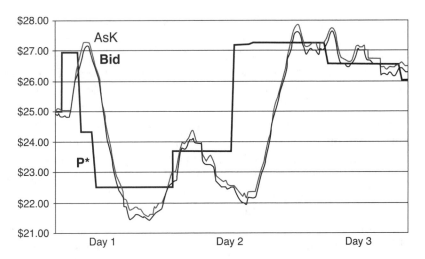

FIGURE 2.3 A graph of P* and market quotes showing lagged information assimilation in one run of a TraderEx simulation.

relatively small quantities, can more delicately exploit their information advantage rather than banging in too precipitously with one big order. This thinking conforms to the pricing dynamics described with reference to Figure 2.2.

Figure 2.3 shows that, at the start of day 1, P^* is $25 and is between the quotes. Soon it jumps to $27 and, after a lag, the quotes respond. When the quotes do react, they overshoot, rising above $27. Meanwhile, as the quotes are heading toward new highs, P^* has jumped down in two steps to a low of $22.50. In response, the quotes are pulled down and again they overshoot, reaching a low of $21.50. P^* recovers on day 2, but twice falls a bit on day 3. With this by way of background, note the following:

- Throughout the three day period, P^* is rarely between the quotes.
- After each of the big P^* changes on days 1 and 2, the quotes have over-adjusted.
- By inspection, it is easy to tell that the quotes are more volatile than P^*, and this is because of the overshooting of quotes (they reach higher highs than P^* and drop to lower lows than P^*).
- We know that P^* is following a random walk jump process. The quotes, quite clearly, are not. After each big P^* jump, the quotes trend toward the new equilibrium price, which implies a first order returns autocorrelation that is positive. But the quotes overshoot the new value and then revert back to it, which implies higher orders of returns autocorrelation that are negative (see the appendix for further explanation).
- The negative higher order returns autocorrelation is consistent with the quotes being more volatile than P^*.

Operationally, when P^* is above the offer (or below the bid), the arrival rate of market orders to buy (or to sell) is increased from 50 percent to 70 percent of TraderEx's total order flow. When P^* is below the bid, there will be 7/3, or 2.33 sell orders for every buy order, on average. Similarly, when P^* is above the offer, there will be 7/3, or 2.33 buy orders for every sell order on average. When P^* is between the bid and the offer, no informed orders are generated and market orders to buy and to sell arrive with equal probability. The imbalance between buy and sell market orders that occurs when P^* is outside of the quotes pulls the market in the direction of P^*. This is a key dynamic to be sensitive to. As you play TraderEx, keep asking yourself, "Where is P^*?" If truth be known, P^* typically is not between the bid and the offer (look again at Figure 2.3). Like the children's book character, Waldo, P^* is very hard to find.

Informed orders are perfectly directionally correlated with each other. If one informationally motivated order to buy arrives at the market, another will also arrive, and then a third, and a fourth, and so on until the market ask is pushed above P^*. Of course, due to the random arrival of other orders, some sell orders will be intermingled with the informed buys. Similarly, if one informationally motivated sell order arrives, other similarly motivated sell orders will also come in (most likely laced with some buys) until the market bid is pushed below P*. This is in contrast with our second type of machine generated orders—the liquidity motivated orders. The liquidity orders are uncorrelated with each other. In the next section, you will see how the liquidity motivated orders are generated by TraderEx.

In TraderEx, P* periodically jumps from one value to another. Recall that the time span from one jump to the next is determined by a random draw from a Poisson distribution. We have already noted the following about the Poisson arrival process:

- It is *memoryless* (the probability of a new value arriving in the next moment of time remains constant as time passes).
- It is a simple process to work with—it has just one parameter, λ, that describes both its mean and variance.
- The rate at which information events can, on expectation, occur in a simulation run can be controlled by changing λ.

Moreover, the magnitude of the information events, and thus the stock's price volatility, can be controlled by changing the variance parameter of the lognormal returns distribution.

As we have said, P* is an equilibrium value, and informed orders are activated whenever P* is above the posted offer or below the posted bid. This does not imply, however, that our machine-resident informed traders have homogeneous expectations. On the contrary, our statistical procedure is consistent with an economic environment where expectations are divergent among the group of informed traders. The reason for this is that P* represents a common expectation among the better informed of what the equilibrium is, but P* is not necessarily any one individual's personal assessment of share value, and the personal assessments need not be the same for all.

Liquidity Trading

The liquidity orders in TraderEx are equally likely to be buy orders or sell orders, and the assignment for each newly-generated liquidity order is done randomly and independently. Whatever motivates them, the important thing for us is that these orders are uncorrelated with each other. Recognizing this, the liquidity motive that we discussed in Chapter 1 can be expanded to include all reasons that are unique to an individual. Most importantly, let's include a trader's own, individual reassessment of share value. Each investor, having his or her own opinion about a security's value, is free to change that opinion for a reason that only he or she knows.

Accordingly, a better term for *liquidity motive* may be *idiosyncratic motive.* But we will stick with the former. *Liquidity motive* is widely used (and also it is easier to say).

In the TraderEx simulation, liquidity orders may be either limit orders or market orders, whereas with our standard treatment of P*, informed orders are always market orders. Informed traders are impatient because they know that the market will soon adjust and erode their profit opportunities. The informed traders arrive only when P* is not within the market quotes, but liquidity traders can arrive at any time. For each liquidity order, its time of arrival, size, type (limit or market), and price are determined by random draws from the relevant distributions.

The price attached to each machine-generated liquidity order is set with the use of a distribution that we call *the double triangular.* The distribution is double triangular because it has two modes, one that is located with reference to the current market bid, and the other that is located with reference to the current market ask. One double triangular distribution is used for the liquidity driven buy orders and another, a mirror image of the first, is used for the liquidity driven sell orders. The double triangular distribution for liquidity driven sell orders is shown in Figure 2.4.

In Figure 2.4, price is on the vertical axis, and the probability of a price being selected for an incoming liquidity order is on the horizontal axis. The top triangle has a maximum probability of 24 percent at $44.70 at the market offer, and the lower triangle has a maximum probability of 18 percent at the market bid of $44.40. If the price that is picked by the random draw is above the $44.40 bid, the order is placed on the book as a priced order to sell. For a sell order, the price is a *price*

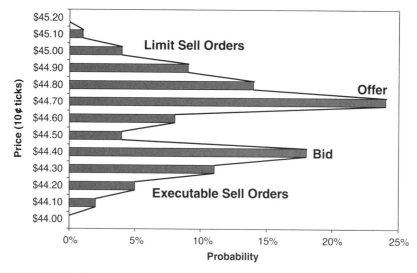

FIGURE 2.4 Double triangular distribution used for generation of liquidity motivated sell orders.

limit below which the order is not to be executed. For a buy order, the price is a *price limit* above which the order is not to be executed. These priced orders are *limit orders*.

If the price that is picked is at the $44.40 bid or below, the order is executable (at least partially) up to the amount available at the bid quote. If the limit sell price produced by the TraderEx software is below the bid, the order will execute down to that price as a market order. Any remaining units to sell are entered as a limit sell (an offer) at the limit price picked from the double triangular distribution.

The liquidity orders are picked from a distribution that is double triangular because liquidity traders enter limit orders on the book, and the double triangular preserves a meaningful market bid-ask spread. In Figure 2.4, the tick size is 10¢, the bid is $44.40, the offer is $44.70, and we have a 30¢ (or a three-tick) spread. A new limit sell at $44.60 or at $44.50 would narrow the spread appreciably, but the probabilities for either of these two events occurring are 8 percent and 4 percent, respectively. On the other hand, the probability of a new sell limit coming in at $44.70 (at the offer) is 24 percent. Consequently, wide spreads (e.g., three ticks or more) have a good chance of being narrowed, but the spread will nevertheless in all probability remain substantial (e.g., greater than one tick)[*] .

Because the market bid and offer quotes are location parameters for the double triangular distribution, the distribution shifts with the bid and the offer. The distribution itself has a neutral effect on prices. If informed orders pull the quotes up (or down), the double triangular rises (or falls). Whatever the price level may be, the liquidity motivated orders will not cause it to revert back to a previous level. Neither will they reinforce a trend to a new level.

The distribution, because of the relative size of the two triangles, maintains about a 70/30-percent split in TraderEx between limit orders and market orders among the liquidity traders. This is roughly consistent with many real-world, order book markets. In TraderEx's quote driven market structure without a limit order book, all orders are market orders, so liquidity motivated orders are drawn only from the "executable" part of the double triangular.

In TraderEx, any drift that, by chance, is caused by liquidity trading is constrained by the information-motivated order flow. If a buy-sell imbalance from liquidity orders (without any P* change) causes the quotes to move up, informed sell orders kick in once the bid quote rises above P*. Similarly, informed buy orders kick in whenever an order imbalance causes the offer to fall below P*. Accordingly, the informed orders keep the quotes loosely aligned with the fundamental determinant of share value, our informed order driver, P*. Alternatively stated, the informed

---

[*]The existence of a meaningful bid-ask spread is discussed further in Robert A. Schwartz, *Micro Markets: A Market Structure Presentation of Microeconomic Theory*, John Wiley and Sons, 2010.

orders cause price to *mean revert* to a previous value whenever a preponderance of liquidity motivated buy (or sell) orders has caused the quotes to move above (or below) P*. *Mean* refers to an average, and *mean reversion* signifies that the price reverts back to an equilibrium value (which has the properties of an average) if liquidity orders and/or technical trading have pushed the price away.

Technical Trading

TraderEx incorporates just one kind of technical trader, a momentum player. Momentum trading is an essential component of TraderEx. Without uninformed momentum traders, it would be too easy for you to detect P* shifts from the evolution of trade prices. This is because any jump in P* that puts it above the offer (or below the bid), triggers a preponderance of machine generated market orders to buy (or market orders to sell), and these market orders cause prices to run up (or to run down) toward the new value of P*. This pattern must be obscured in some way, or you could profit too easily by buying or selling whenever price appears to be trending up or down. We do not want you to be a monopolist with respect to this strategy, and momentum trading is the answer. Momentum trading can compete with you if you try to jump on a trend by buying when the quotes rise, or selling when they fall.

Trends can also mislead you. The momentum driven machine orders make your life more complicated, partly by jumping onto a run faster than you might be able to do. They can also cause very realistic uncertainty for you by reinforcing false momentum moves. Do you see price trending up? Perhaps several liquidity motivated buy orders happened to have arrived simply by chance. The machine generated momentum orders to buy will then kick in and reinforce the trend, possibly tricking you into thinking that P* has jumped up when it has not. If you are not careful, your own orders can activate the machine generated momentum orders. Or, perhaps several liquidity motivated sell orders (and/or your own orders) have led to machine generated momentum selling, which could trick you into thinking that P* has just dropped when it hasn't. But you never know. Perhaps P* has changed. Even then, the machine generated momentum orders can trick you by causing an otherwise justified price run to overshoot its mark, the new value of P*.

Both "false" runs and overshooting commonly cause price to rise too high or to fall too low. Either way, price will then reverse course and revert back to P*. Consequently, by including machine generated momentum orders, we have built patterns of reversals as well as runs into TraderEx. This makes it considerably more difficult for you to exploit any price move. You can never be sure if a run is real, or when and how it will end. The co-existence of positive and negative serial correlation in real-world markets (as well as in TraderEx) masks the existence of each, and can prevent each from being arbitraged away.

There is another reason for including momentum trading in the simulation model, one that has to do with liquidity trading. As we have said, our liquidity traders (but not our informed traders) submit limit orders in the TraderEx order driven environment (as they do in real-world order driven markets). For this to happen, however, there must be compensation for the participant who submits a limit order and thereby accepts the risk that it will not execute. The compensation is from the higher return that is realized if the limit order does execute. But where does this higher return come from? It is attributable to price being pulled back to a previous level (a higher level for a buy limit order and a lower level for a sell limit order) after the limit order has executed.

The term that we have used to describe the "pulling back" is *mean reversion*, and it occurs whenever momentum buy orders drive prices above P* and whenever momentum sell orders drive prices below P*. Look again at Figure 2.3 and you will see this. If you have placed a limit buy order at a lower price and it executes because momentum orders have driven price below P*, you profit when informed order flow brings the prices back up to the P* level. Similarly, if you have sold short by a limit sell order placed at a higher price and which has executed because momentum orders have driven price above P*, you profit when informed order flow brings prices back down to the P* level.

The overshooting caused by momentum orders provides compensation that is necessary for limit orders to be submitted. A relatively wide bid-ask spread also provides further compensation. Accordingly, when you are formulating your trading strategy in the TraderEx order driven environment, pay attention to the price swings and to any relative sparseness of the book, for both can make limit order submission a profitable trading strategy for you to employ.

APPENDIX: INTER-TEMPORAL RETURNS CORRELATION

The term *inter-temporal* refers to events that occur in different time periods. For instance, if the price change for a stock in one period is correlated with the price change for that same stock in another period (e.g., one hour or one day later), the stock's returns are *inter-temporally correlated*. When the return is for the same stock, this inter-temporal correlation is referred to as *auto-correlation*, or as *serial correlation*.

Returns are positively auto-correlated when positive returns are more likely to be followed by other returns that are positive, and when negative returns are more likely to be followed by other returns that are negative. Therefore, if returns are *positively auto-correlated*, a series of price changes includes a larger number of price continuations (up-ticks followed by other up-ticks, or down-ticks followed by other down-ticks) than would be expected in a random sequence of price changes. If, on the other hand, returns are *negatively auto-correlated*, a series of price changes includes a larger number of price reversals (an up-tick followed by a down-tick, or a down-tick followed by an up-tick) than would be expected in a random sequence of price changes.

The inter-temporal correlation need not be between sequentially adjacent returns. For instance, the return in one period may be correlated with the return two or more periods later. The correlation between sequentially adjacent returns is *serial correlation*, or *first order auto-correlation*. The correlation between nonadjacent returns is called *higher order auto-correlation*. The term *auto-correlation* simply means that the returns for an issue are auto-correlated, although not necessarily of first order.

The return on one stock in one period of time may also be correlated with the return on another stock (or stock index) in another period of time. This is *serial cross-correlation*. Serial cross-correlation exists when different stocks do not adjust simultaneously to common information change.

Positive Inter-Temporal Correlation

Four factors can cause the returns for a security to be positively auto-correlated: (1) sequential information arrival, (2) the limit order book, (3) market maker intervention in trading, and (4) non-instantaneous price discovery after change in investor demand.

> *Sequential Information Arrival.* The sequential arrival of information (or, equivalently, the sequential adjustment of expectations) can cause a security's returns to be positively auto-correlated.
>
> *The Limit Order Book.* If orders on the book are not quickly revised after informational change, new orders based on the information transact at prices set by existing limit orders. As a series of such transactions eliminates the older orders sequentially from the book, a security's transaction price rises or falls in increments to a new equilibrium value.
>
> *Market Maker Intervention.* The affirmative obligation of stock exchange specialists leads these market makers to intervene in trading when transaction-to-transaction price changes would otherwise be unacceptably large. This can cause a security's price to adjust in increments to a new equilibrium value after the advent of news.
>
> *Inaccurate Price Discovery.* Price discovery is inaccurate when new equilibrium values are not instantaneously achieved. Price discovery is inaccurate because investors do not instantaneously transmit their orders to the

market, because orders left on the market are not continuously revised, and because, when they write their orders, investors do not know what the equilibrium prices are or will be. With inaccurate price determination, actual prices differ from equilibrium values. Some price changes are too small (they under-adjust to news), and other price changes are too large (they over-adjust to news). *Ceteris paribus*—if inaccurate price determination that involves partial adjustment (under-shooting) predominates, returns will be positively auto-correlated.

Negative Inter-Temporal Correlation

Three factors may cause negative inter-temporal correlation in security returns: (1) the bid-ask spread, (2) the temporary market impact exerted by large orders, and (3) non-instantaneous price discovery after change in investor demand propensities.

> *The Bid-Ask Spread.* With a spread, orders to sell at market execute against the bid, and orders to buy at market execute against the ask. In the process, transaction prices will bounce between the bid and the ask. The bid and ask quotes themselves change over time with the arrival of new orders and the elimination of old orders (that either execute or are withdrawn). Nevertheless, the bouncing of transaction prices between the quotes causes transaction-to-transaction price returns to be negatively auto-correlated. To see this, assume the quotes are fixed. Then, if at some moment in time the last transaction in a particular stock is at the bid, the next transaction that generates a nonzero return must be at the ask, and a positive return (price change) is recorded. If the quotes remain unchanged, the next nonzero return must be negative (when a market sell once again hits the bid). Thus price reversals occur as the transaction price moves back and forth between the bid and the ask. Even if the quotes change randomly over time, the price reversals attributed to the spread introduce negative inter-temporal correlation in transaction price returns.

> *Market Impact Effects.* The effective spread is generally greater for larger orders. Consider the arrival of a large sell order, for instance. If the book is relatively sparse, the transaction price will be depressed so that the order may be absorbed by the relatively thin market. In this case, the lower price itself attracts new buy orders to the market and price once again rises. Therefore, the initial price decrease is followed by a reversal (an increase). The reverse pattern would be caused by the arrival of a large buy order. Either way, the successive price changes are negatively auto-correlated.

Inaccurate Price Discovery. We have noted that, with inaccurate price discovery, actual prices wander about their equilibrium values. If inaccurate price determination that involves overreaction to news (overshooting) predominates, returns are negatively auto-correlated. Further, it can be shown that returns are negatively auto-correlated if an underlying equilibrium price changes randomly over time and transaction prices wander randomly about their equilibrium values. This can be understood intuitively with the aid of the following visualization. Picture a man walking his dog on a leash across a field, with the dog racing randomly about the man, but never straying too far because of the leash. If the man follows a random path, the leash causes reversals in the dog's path, and thus the animal's movements are negatively auto-correlated.

Serial Cross-Correlation

The returns on two (or more) different securities are generally correlated with each other. This inter-stock correlation is referred to as *cross-correlation*. The returns for two different securities are *serially* cross-correlated if the correlated price adjustments do not occur simultaneously (that is, if they are non-synchronous). The TraderEx simulation model is for one risky asset (not two or more) and cash, and thus serial cross-correlation is not in the software that you will be using. We include discussion of this dynamic property of real-world price behavior in this appendix for completeness only.

If all price adjustments were instantaneous for all securities (as would be the case in the perfectly liquid, frictionless market), the price adjustments across the different securities would be synchronous. However, the factors that we have discussed in relation to the auto-correlation of returns also cause price adjustment delays, which lead to non-synchronous adjustments across stock, and consequently to serial cross-correlation.

The prices of some securities tend to adjust faster than others to changing market conditions. Some large, intensely watched issues may lead the market, and other smaller issues may lag behind. This gives rise to a pattern of serial cross-correlation where the price adjustments for securities such as IBM and Exxon precede the price adjustments for thinner issues such as Liquidity Inc. and Podunk Mines.

Serial cross-correlation patterns are no doubt diffuse, complex, and not readily subject to exploitation by a clever trader. The reason is twofold: the time lags involved are not stable, and imperfect price discovery may entail both overshooting and undershooting. TraderEx does not explicitly incorporate other securities with correlated returns, but some price changes could be explained as a reaction to another stock.

SUMMARY

To be instructive, a computer simulation model of trading order flow must satisfy a number of conditions. First, your actions must be able to influence the market in which you are operating. This rules out using canned data from prior markets, since your actions would not impact what is in the past. Second, the simulation's machine generated order flow must reflect the dynamics of real markets, including information change, lagged adjustments, trend-following orders, and mean reversion in short-period returns. These dynamics give you, much like the real world, a basis for anticipating future price movements. Third, you should be able to replay a simulation run so that you can see the results of different trading tactics when all else is held constant. Fourth, the simulation must provide meaningful performance benchmarks to compare your results to others, and to know whether you are improving your trading decisions with experience. TraderEx satisfies these requirements and gives us a platform for analyzing and gaining experience with trading decision making. The chapters that follow will show you how to use the software and provide trading exercises to build your knowledge and skills.

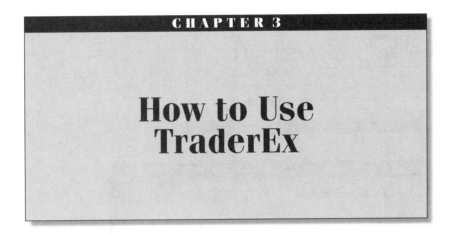

CHAPTER 3

How to Use TraderEx

This chapter explains how to use the TraderEx software. To log on, go to the Internet, www.eTraderEx.net for the TraderEx homepage, and then click on "Member Log-In" and follow the on screen instructions.

Followed by:

Once you enter your Log-In details, the simulation will begin downloading. This chapter will detail TraderEx's features, and how you can use the software to learn about trading decisions and trading performance in the key market structures available in equity exchanges.

AN OVERVIEW OF THE TRADEREX ENVIRONMENT

The TraderEx simulation provides a market for trading in a single security. Trading takes place in five trading mechanisms: an order book market, a dealer market, a call auction, a crossing network and a block trading facility. Unnecessary complexity is avoided in TraderEx. There are two order types in the simulation, market orders and limit orders. In TraderEx there are no explicit trading costs (e.g., commissions) or short selling constraints. You have two assets: a risky security and cash. You will generally begin each simulation run with a zero position in both the security and in cash.

New orders to buy and to sell in the simulation will be generated by the computer and by you. While the market background is computer-generated, your orders will influence both the orders that the computer generates and the evolution of quotes and prices as a simulation run progresses.

Short-term changes in TraderEx quotes and transaction prices do not follow random walks. They include realistic patterns of runs (trends) and reversals (reversion). Remember, your trading will impact the market. A large buy order can drive the market up, and a large sell order can drive it down.

Each simulation is run with a pre-set scenario number, which is a random number seed. A simulation can be rerun with the same random number seed if you wish to repeat a run. However, if your own trading changes, you will see some different market results. Or, you can rerun a simulation with the same parameter settings and a different random number seed and, again, you will see different results.

The computer:

- Generates a flow of machine-generated public orders.
- Establishes and maintains the limit order book in order driven market structures.
- Operates a number of rules-based market maker participants in the quote-driven market structure.
- Maintains a screen display, including trade history.
- Captures data for post game analysis.

A training version of TraderEx can be played at a pace that you choose. You can manually advance the simulation from event to event by hitting the "GO" button, or you can put the simulation run on a time clock. The simulation runs in a *continuous time mode* at a slow, medium, or fast pace as you choose. At a medium pace, a one-trading-day simulation will take about 15 to 25 minutes to run.

Requirements for Running TraderEx

You will need 1) the Java Development Kit (JDK) to download and run the simulation. This is a free download available at www.java.sun.com.

1. Go to our web site (www.eTraderEx.net) and log in.
2. A valid copy of the book to access the software download.

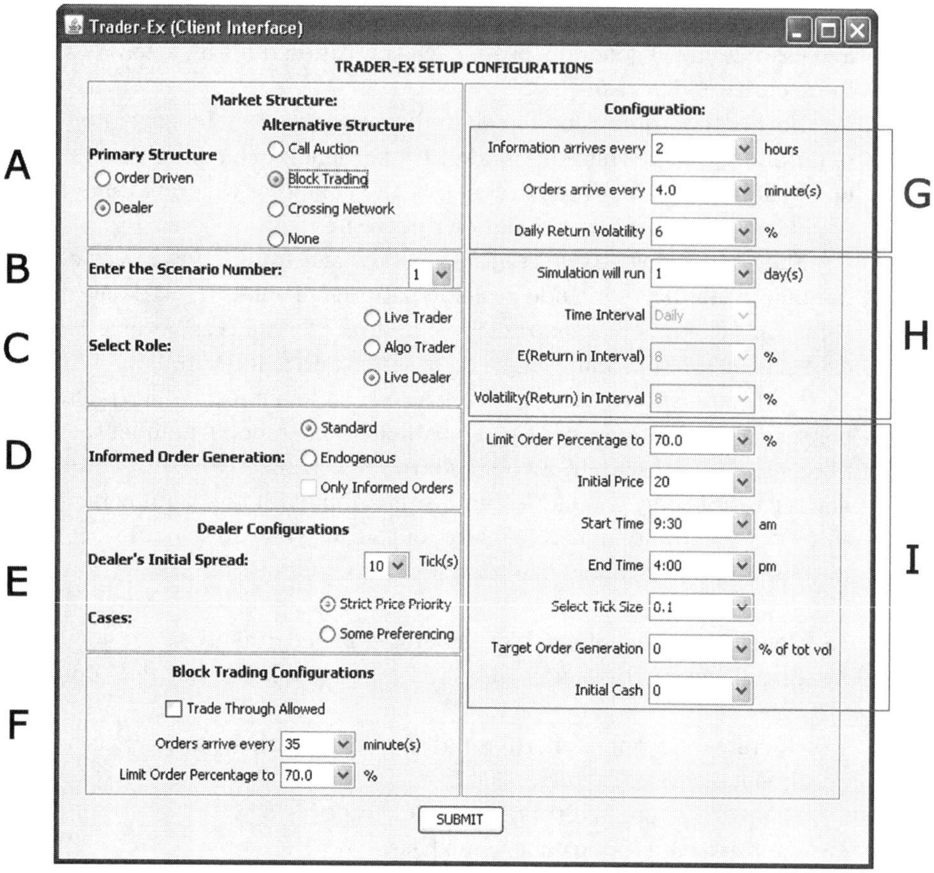

FIGURE 3.1 Initial configuration screen.

Setting Up a TraderEx Simulation

The configuration screen in Figure 3.1 allows you to customize the market conditions and the specific properties of the underlying equity. The remainder of this section explains how to do this.

There are four main settings for a simulation highlighted as A-D in Figure 3.1:

1. **Select Simulation Features (A):** There are two primary features shown here:
   - Order Driven market
   - Dealer market

Next to them are the alternative trading structures:
- Call Auction
- Block Trading/Dark Pool
- Crossing Network

2. **Enter the scenario number (B):** This is a random number seed that will allow you to replay a simulation holding everything constant except your own interaction with the system, or any other parameter or market structure feature that you might wish to change at the start of the next simulation run.

3. **Select Trader Role (C):** Select your role in the marketplace. You can be either an equity trader or a market maker (dealer).

4. **Select Informed Order Generation (D):** In the standard informed order generation mode, the computer will generate market orders whenever P* is below the bid (generating an informed sell market order) or whenever P* is above the offer (generating an informed buy market order). See Chapter 2 for a further discussion of P*. We also have an endogenous P* mode that is slightly more complex. With endogenous P*, the live trader's actions can influence the equilibrium price P*.

The alternative trading structures have configuration panels.
- Dealer Configurations (E): This configuration panel will only be visible if you select Dealer Market as your primary feature in Section A. More on these configuration settings in the Dealer Market section of this chapter.
- Block Board Configurations (F): This configuration panel will only be visible if you select Block Board as the alternative trading structure in Section A. More on these configurations in the Block Trading Facility section of this chapter.
- Call Auction Configurations (not shown). This configuration panel will only be visible if you select Call Auction as the alternative trading structure in Section A. More on these configurations in the Call Auction section of this chapter.
- Crossing Network Configurations (not shown). This configuration panel will only be visible if you select Crossing Network as the alternative trading structure in Section A. More on these configurations in the Crossing Network section of this chapter.

There are 14 additional configuration settings available on the right side of the screen. These are shown as G through I in Figure 3.1:

1. **Select Information Arrival (G):** This parameter sets the expected number of P* changes throughout the trading day. The default setting is for a change in P* to occur every two hours on expectation.

2. **Select Order Arrival (G):** This parameter sets the expected arrival rate of orders that are generated by the computer. For a relatively liquid, big cap stock, this setting might be one or two minutes. For a relatively illiquid, small cap stock, this setting can be 6 minutes or more.

3. **Select Volatility (G):** The volatility parameter is the variance of the (log normal) returns distribution used to get new values for the underlying equilibrium price, P^*. For a relatively low volatility stock, this setting can be 1 percent or 2 percent, while for a relatively high volatility stock it can be set closer to 10 percent (or more, if you wish). The information arrival setting and the volatility parameter work together to form the price pattern. For example, if you set the information arrival to 2 (the default setting), you will have a change in P^* every 2 hours (on average), which will produce (on average) three changes to P^* per trading day. By setting the intraday volatility (which is dimensioned as a standard deviation) to 6 percent, changes to P^* will be 2 percent (on average). Providing you with an average of three P^* changes, each of which on average is 2 percent, results in an intraday volatility of 6 percent.

4. **Select Days (H):** One-day and multiple-day simulations are available. If you choose a multiple-day simulation. To skip to the next day click the Fast Forward ("FF") button in the simulation control panel.

5. **Select Time Interval (H):** For multiple day simulations, this represents the amount of time between successive days. For example, if you wanted to simulate four trading days within a year, the time interval would be quarterly.

6. **Select Expected Return in Interval (H):** The expected return is set for the given time interval set above. So if the time interval selected above is quarterly, this is the three-month expected return of the stock.

7. **Select Volatility of Returns in Interval (H):** This is the volatility of the expected return for the given time interval.

8. **Select Limit Order Percentage (I):** Recall there are three sources of order flow in the TraderEx simulation: informed, liquidity, and momentum orders. Liquidity orders can be generated at any time. An incoming liquidity trade order can be a market or a limit order. The limit order parameter sets the percentage of liquidity orders that come into the system as limit orders. If you wish to work with a relatively liquid order book, this parameter should be relatively high. The lower the setting, the less liquidity will be in the order book. The default setting is 70 percent.

9. **Select Initial Price (I):** This is the opening price.

10. **Select Start Time (I):** Daily start time for the simulation. The default start time is 9:30 A.M.

11. **Select End Time (I):** Daily end time for the simulation. The default end time is 4:00 P.M.

12. **Select Tick Size (I):** You can choose the minimum price variation. The default setting is 10¢.

13. **Select Target Order Generation (I):** The computer can automatically generate a target position that the user must obtain. This simulates the role of an equity trader. The pace and risk will be based on the target generated. The target is based on a percentage of the total trading volume. The initial target (stated as a number of units) is delivered to the participant at the start of the simulation. Targets will be updated throughout the simulation, as well.

14. **Set Initial Cash (I):** The computer can start you with an initial amount of cash.

For the demonstration that follows, retain the default settings. Click "SUBMIT" on the bottom of the page. We will describe the operations of the different markets' structures.

THE CONTINUOUS ORDER BOOK MARKET

The TraderEx software maintains a limit order book that enforces strict price and time priorities when executing orders in an order driven setting. In other words, the limit orders to buy (sell) at the highest (lowest) prices trade first and, at the same price, the order that arrived earliest trades first. All orders sent to the order book are sized in terms of units where 1 unit is 100 shares. An order for 55 can be thought of as an order for 5,500 shares. This saves us from displaying numerous zeroes on the screen. With the order book, you can do the following:

- Buy shares immediately with a market order. You will execute against the sell limit orders (OFFER) that others have entered into the book. The lowest priced offers will execute first.
- Attempt to buy shares by placing your own limit buy orders (BID) and hoping that they execute against incoming sell orders.
- Sell shares immediately with a market order. You will execute against the buy limit orders (BID) that others have entered into the book. The highest priced bids will trade first.
- Attempt to sell shares by placing your own limit sell orders (OFFER) and hoping that they execute against incoming buy orders.

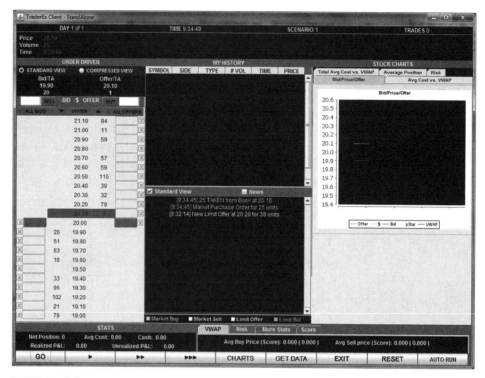

FIGURE 3.2 Order book screen at market open.

Figure 3.2 shows a representative screen in the order book market, and Figure 3.3 is the book soon after in the trading day.

As the simulation progresses, even if you enter no orders, the computer will generate both limit and market buy and sell orders, and market quotes, trades, and transaction prices will evolve. The machine orders are statistically generated to reflect the three motives for trading:

- **Information motives**—informed traders will buy when the market price is below an equilibrium price (P*), and sell at prices above P*.
- **Liquidity motives**—Liquidity traders buy to put cash to work and sell to raise cash for other purposes.
- **Momentum motive**—trend-following traders will buy if price is trending up and sell if it is trending down.

Each of these three motives for trading react to market conditions and to you as a trader. Remember, TraderEx prices may not evolve in a random walk pattern in the short term. Trends and reversals will occur during a trading day.

ORDER DRIVEN
VOLUME 391
HIGH 20.20
LOW 19.80
VWAP 20.059
STANDARD VIEW
COMPRESSED VIEW
Bid/TA 20.00 40
Offer/TA 20.10 53
SELL
BID $ OFFER
BUY
ALL BIDS
CENTER
ALL OFFERS
21.10 115
21.00
20.90 11
20.80 59
20.70
20.60 116
20.50 73
20.40 81
20.30 57
20.20 64
20.10 53
40 20.00
46 19.90
62 19.80
63 19.70
43 19.60
36 19.50
33 19.40
96 19.30

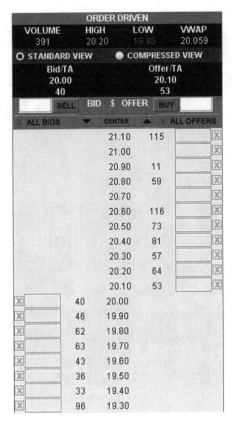

FIGURE 3.3 Order book display.

Order Book: The TraderEx Screen

Figure 3.4 shows the first 2 rows of the simulation screen. The top row provides the day and the time of day in the simulation; below that row is the ticker of recent trades.

The top lines on the screen are straightforward:

Day and time	Where we are in the simulated trading day
Scenario	Scenario number
Trades	Total number of trades

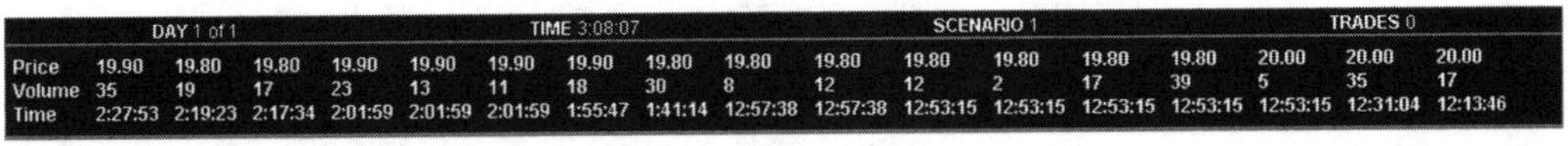

DAY 1 of 1
TIME 3:08:07
SCENARIO 1
TRADES 0
Price 19.90 19.80 19.80 19.90 19.90 19.90 19.90 19.80 19.80 19.80 19.80 19.80 19.80 19.80 20.00 20.00 20.00
Volume 35 19 17 23 13 11 18 30 8 12 12 2 17 39 5 35 17
Time 2:27:53 2:19:23 2:17:34 2:01:59 2:01:59 2:01:59 1:55:47 1:41:14 12:57:38 12:57:38 12:53:15 12:53:15 12:53:15 12:53:15 12:53:15 12:31:04 12:13:46

FIGURE 3.4 Ticker of trade prices, sizes, and time.

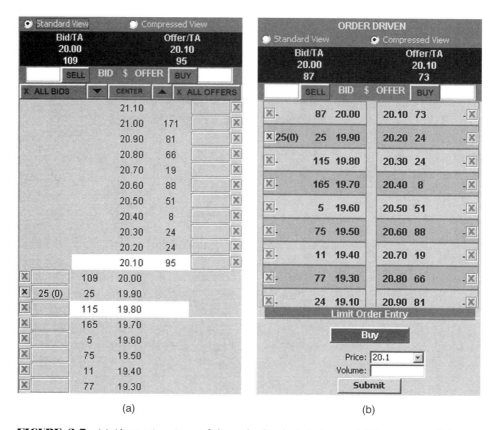

(a)   (b)

FIGURE 3.5   (a) Alternative views of the order book: Full view and (b) compressed view.

An alternative look for the order book is called "Compressed View." When selected, it places bids and offers side by side. See Figure 3.5.

As shown in Figure 3.6, your orders are time stamped and logged in the middle third of the screen. The list is scrollable, and columns can be rearranged by
dragging and dropping. The data are available in spreadsheet format for analysis.

In the TraderEx simulation software, the price levels in the order book that are
shaded in Figure 3.5 and highlighted in red and green on your PC's screen are the
low and the high prices of trades so far in the day.

MY HISTORY				
TIME	**SIDE**	**PRICE**	**TYPE**	**# VOL**
11:01:43	Sell	20.10	Limit	21
10:36:44	Sell	19.90	Market	31
10:36:44	Sell	20.00	Market	58
10:25:07	Sell	20.10	Limit	23

FIGURE 3.6   History of all user trades.

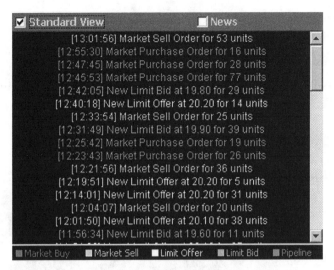

FIGURE 3.7 Stream of market events with the most recent on the top.

The Event Viewer displays the sequence of orders and trades. As illustrated in Figure 3.7, all limit orders will be displayed. Market Orders are color-coded—green for market purchases and yellow for market sells. Block Trades appear in orange.

At the bottom of the screen is the total number of shares in your net position and your average price. This is shown in Figure 3.8. We also see that the user is short 133 units of the stock.

From this data we see that to make a profit, he or she must buy the stock back at a price that is less than the average selling price for the current short position, which is $20.01. If the user is a day trader, he/she will want to be flat and have a zero Net Position by the end of the day. For this user that means that 133 shares will have to be purchased to return to a zero inventory position by the close of the market.

There are six in-game chart graphs available by clicking on the tabs, all shown in Figure 3.9. The charts can display the changes over time for the following measures:

a. Market Bid/Offer quotes

b. Average Cost vs. VWAP

STATS		
Net Position: -133	Avg Cost: 20.01	Cash: 2661.33
Realized P&L: 0.00	Unrealized P&L:	- 11.97

FIGURE 3.8 User's current price, P&L, and position data.

   c. Total Average Buying/Selling vs. VWAP

   d. Average Position

   e. Risk

   f. Supply vs. Demand (This is only available in the Call Auction Alternative Market Structure).

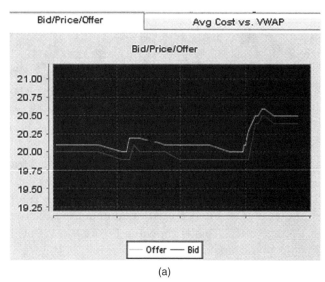

(a)

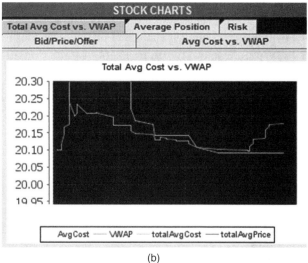

(b)

FIGURE 3.9 The six in-game charts.

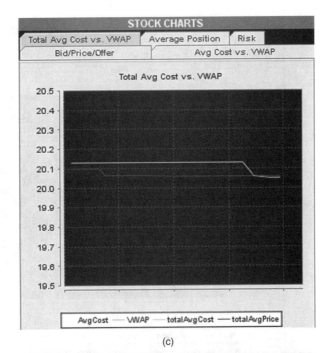

(c)

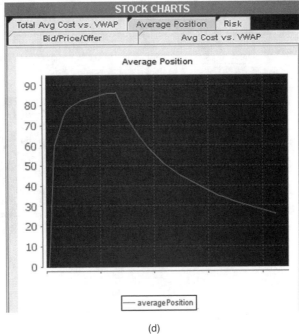

(d)

FIGURE 3.9 (*Continued*)

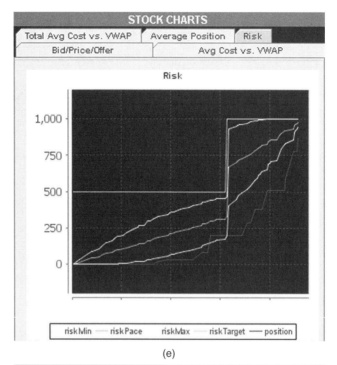

(e)

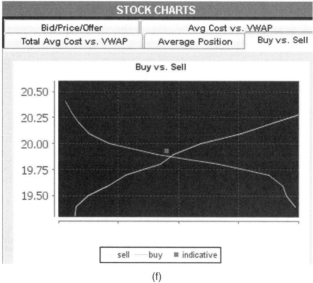

(f)

FIGURE 3.9 *(Continued)*

STATS		
Net Position: 361	Avg Cost: 20.14	Cash: -7209.50
Realized P&L: 0.00		Unrealized P&L: -13.40

FIGURE 3.10 Display of general statistics.

By following how the bid and the ask quotes evolve, you can better gauge the color of the market. By watching the spread between the quotes, you can roughly gauge the liquidity of the market. The second chart includes VWAP (Volume Weighted Average Price), and the last sale price. You can toggle between the charts.

Performance Measures and Statistics

The performance measures in TraderEx consist of your trading record statistics, which are gathered and calculated throughout the trading day. These raw values are then translated into a score that is an evaluation of your trading performance. The software will provide you with a number of measures of performance during a simulation run.

The General Statistics, shown in Figure 3.10, include:

- Net Position: Current net position in units.
- Avg. Cost: This is the cost of your current position.
- Cash.
- Realized P & L is the profit (loss) that you have captured thus far in the day from shares that were bought and then sold (or sold and then bought back).
- Unrealized P&L is the current inventory of shares marked to market. We use standard accounting principles and mark long positions to the bid quote and short positions to the ask quote.

Under the VWAP Tab, shown in Figure 3.11, the following measures are shown:

- Avg. Buy Price (Score): This is the Average Buying Price—the average price paid for all shares purchased.
- Avg. Sell Price (Score): This is the Average Selling Price—the average price received for all shares sold.

VWAP	Risk	More Stats	Score
Avg Buy Price (Score): 20.137 (-3.461)		Avg Sell price (Score): 0.000 (0.000)	

FIGURE 3.11 VWAP information.

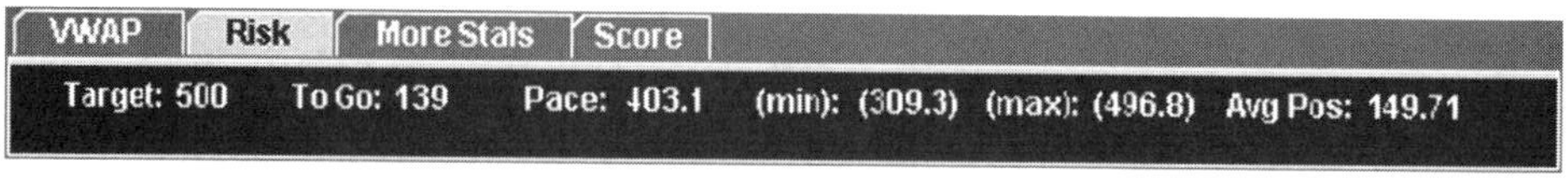

FIGURE 3.12 Risk information.

Under the RISK Tab, shown in Figure 3.12, two measures are shown:

- Target, To Go, Pace, (min), (max): The Target position is what you are expected to have at the end of the simulation. The default is zero. You can edit the target amount by clicking on the word ⟨⟨Target⟩⟩ and entering the desired target. To Go is the number of shares to reach your target. The Pace amount is the position you would have if you executed the order at a constant rate. (min) and (max) which pertain to our risk measure will be explained in Chapter 4.
- Avg Pos: This is the average position the trader had throughout the trading day.

The next tab is the More Stats Tab, shown in Figure 3.13:

- My Vol (% Market Share): This is your total volume and your volume relative to the market's total volume. The market's total volume is the number of shares traded.
- Mkt Order Vol: Volume of stock you have acquired through market orders.
- Lmt Order Vol: Volume of stock you have acquired through limit orders.
- Total Vol: The total number of shares you have traded. If you buy 10 units and then sell 10 units, your net position is zero and your total volume is 20 units.
- Trades: Total number of trades you were involved in.

In TraderEx, the user's score is based on four measures: Risk, P&L, VWAP, and job completion. The Total Score displayed during a simulation is a weighted sum of the performance measures listed here.

- VWAP Score: The sum of your volume weighted Buys vs. VWAP Score and your volume weighted Sells vs. VWAP Score.
- P&L Score: Sum of your realized and unrealized P&L.

FIGURE 3.13 Additional information during simulation run.

VWAP	Risk	More Stats	**Score**					
VWAP:	22.446	P & L :	54.00	RISK:	843700.75	% DONE:	75.00	TOTAL: 76.447
Weight:	100	Weight:	100	Weight:	0%	Weight:	0	

FIGURE 3.14 Components of total trading score.

- Risk Score: This is based on our risk measure within TraderEx, which is detailed in Chapter 4's section on Performance Measures.
- Job completion is only calculated at the end of a run, and is discussed in further detail in Chapter 4.

In assigning weights to these four factors, you might put all of the weight on VWAP. To do this, click on the "VWAP" label (shown in Figure 3.14), change the VWAP weight to 100, and click "Submit Changes." If you are running a dealer simulation, you might want to increase the weights on Risk and on P&L. See the section Performance Measures and their weights for more details about the measures and their weights. Chapter 6 provides exercises on VWAP trading and Chapter 8's exercises consider risk and return in dealer market trading.

To set the weights, click on a performance measure, type the desired weight into the text box and hit "Enter." The weights will be normalized to sum to 100 percent. If you put weights of 10, 10, and 30, they would be scaled to 20 percent, 20 percent, and 60 percent in the software. The software will also adjust for the mean and standard deviation of the VWAP, P&L, and Risk scores. Our adjustment ensures that the three components influence your score depending on their relative distance above or below their respective expected values.

Several of the market structures have measures that are unique to their market:

1. Block Trading. (See Figure 3.15.)
   - My Block Vol (% Of All Block Volume): Your volume traded in the dark pool, i.e., the ratio of your volume to the total volume traded in the dark pool.
   - Total Block Volume (% of Total Volume): Total volume traded in the dark pool, i.e., the ratio of the total block volume to the total volume traded.

VWAP	Risk	More Stats	Block Stats	Score
My Block Volume (% Market Share): 00 (0%)		Block Volume (% Total Volume): 00 (0%)		

FIGURE 3.15 Adjusting the weight on VWAP to be 50 percent of the total score.

2. Call Auction.
   - My Call Volume (% of all Call Volume): Your volume traded in the call auction, i.e., the ratio of your volume to the total volume traded in the call auction.
   - Total Call Volume (% of Total Volume): Total volume traded in the call auction, i.e., the ratio of the total call auction volume to the total volume traded.
3. Crossing Network.
   - My Crossing Volume (% of all Call Volume).
   - Crossing Volume (% of Total Volume).

Advancing Time in TraderEx

In all of the TraderEx market structures, the clock for the market day in TraderEx can be advanced by the user with time effectively stopped between market events. Alternatively, time can progress continuously under the control of the computer at a slow, medium, or fast rate. There are three arrow buttons and one "GO" button to adjust the advance of time (see Figure 3.16).

- **GO Button:** This is used to advance the simulation manually, one event at a time, at a pace of your choosing. In this mode you do not face time pressure, as the clock only progresses when you click on "GO".
- **Arrow buttons for continuous time:** When these are used, the time clock advances the simulation. Hit the one-arrow button for a relatively slow pace, the two-arrow button for a medium pace, and the three-arrow button for a relatively fast pace. With an automatic time advance, you are under time pressure to make decisions and to place or cancel orders.

The opening screen of the central limit order book (CLOB) is shown in Figure 3.17. It operates as a standard price–time priority market. The quotes are $19.90 bid and $20.10 offer. The book shows that 20 units are at the $19.90 bid, and that 26 units are at the $20.10 offer. Other limit buy orders are shown below the best bid, and other limit sell orders are shown above the best offer. The total number of units posted at each price level is shown next to each price. Focus on the middle of the order book, for this is where you will find the best bid and offer.

FIGURE 3.16 Options for advancing time in simulations.

FIGURE 3.17 Opening TraderEx screen.

Now advance the simulation by clicking the "GO" button. You will see that a limit sell order for 38 units arrives at the market at $20.20. This price level will flash for a few moments, indicating that a change is coming, and then the volume next to the $20.20 price will increase from 41 units to 79 units.

Now advance the simulation by again clicking the "GO" button. The next event is the arrival of a market buy order for 25 units. It appears in the Blotter and updates the order book. In addition, the trade is shown in the ticker at the top of the screen.

Entering a Market Order

To submit a market order, type in the quantity you wish to buy or to sell in one of the boxes at the top of the book. As we have noted, quantity is measured in units, where a unit is 100 shares. Let us enter a 20-unit order (2,000 shares) to buy at market. We do this by entering 20 in the white box to the right of the label "BUY" (just above the limit order book) and hitting "Enter" or by clicking the "BUY" button. This will result in your buying 20 units at the lowest posted offer on the book (see Figure 3.18).

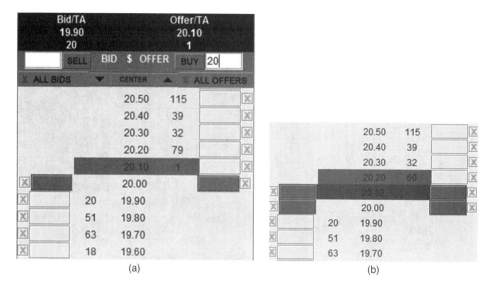

FIGURE 3.18 The effect of a market purchase order on the continuous order book and the event feed.

If your market order is for a number of units equal to or less than the volume at the posted quote, your order will execute completely at that price level. Market orders that are larger than the quantity at the best bid and ask quotes will "walk the book" to the next price level(s). That is, if your order is for a larger number of units, it will execute at successively inferior prices until it is completely filled. For instance, Figures 3.18 and 3.19 show that a market order to buy 90 units will purchase 79 at $20.10 and the next 11 at $20.20 for an average purchase price of $20.112.

Entering a Limit Order

You can enter a limit order into the order book by clicking on the box next to the price limit that you want your order placed at. Once you have entered an order, it will be visible in the book. In Figure 3.20(a), you will see the buy limit order placed in the book at $20.00. The size of your order is 30 units. In Figure 3.20(b), which applies after you have entered your order. As indicated in parentheses, 0 units to

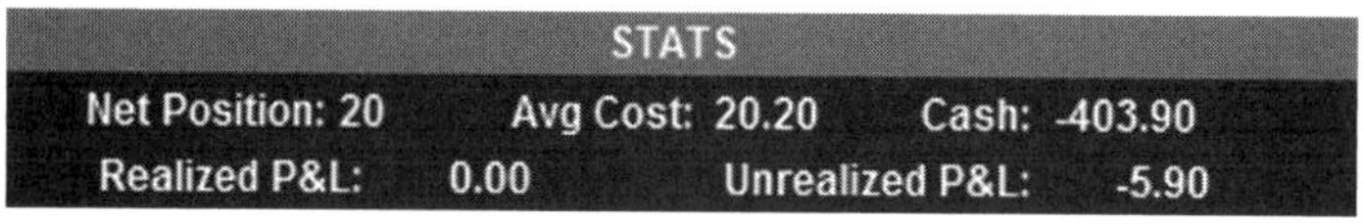

STATS		
Net Position: 20	Avg Cost: 20.20	Cash: -403.90
Realized P&L: 0.00	Unrealized P&L: -5.90	

FIGURE 3.19 The effect of a market purchase order on the user's statistics.

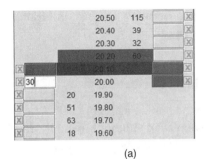

(a)

[9:43:51] New Limit Bid at 20.00 for 30 units
[9:38:38] 19 TAKEN from Book at 20.20
[9:38:38] 1 TAKEN from Book at 20.10
[9:38:38] Market Purchase Order for 20 units
[9:34:34] 25 TAKEN from Book at 20.10
[9:34:34] Market Purchase Order for 25 units
[9:32:15] New Limit Offer at 20.20 for 38 units

(b)

FIGURE 3.20   The effect of a new limit buy order in the book.

buy from other traders have time priority over you, and thus your order will be the first to execute if a market order to sell arrives. Because there are no other orders at the price, the total bid quantity at $20.00 is 30.

Limit orders can be made larger by clicking on the existing order and adding a new amount to it. To cancel a limit order that you have previously placed, click on the red "X" next to it.

When the alternative, compressed view of the order book is selected (see Figure 3.21), you enter limit orders differently. Select the side by clicking the green "Buy" button to toggle to a red "Sell" Button. Enter the price from the pull-down menu. Note: You cannot enter a limit buy price at or above the lowest offer.

| Limit Order Entry |
| Buy |
| Price: 19.9 ▾ |
| Volume: |
| Submit |

FIGURE 3.21   Limit order entry in compressed view.

Likewise, you cannot enter a limit sell price at or below the best bid. Enter in the volume of the limit order, maximum 99 units, and click "SUBMIT."

Entering a Limit Order—Understanding Your Priority

Once you enter an order, it will be visible in the book. See Figure 3.22. The entry on the left of the screen indicates that you have placed another buy limit order in the book at $19.90. The size (quantity) of your order is 40. As indicated in parentheses, 20 units to buy from other traders have time priority over you, and have to trade (or be withdrawn) before any part of your order can execute. Your order added to all the other orders gives a total bid size of 60.

As shown in Figure 3.23, an incoming market sell order for 22 units arrives to transact against your 30 units limit buy order at $20.00, leaving 8 units on the book.

Canceling your limit orders

There are two ways to cancel a limit order from the order book. Once a limit order is on the book, a red "X" will appear next to the order. Clicking this "X" will cancel your order. Alternatively, you can click "ALL BIDS" or "ALL OFFERS" to cancel all of your buy or sell limit orders with one mouse click.

			Price	Size			Log
			20.40	39		X	[9:45:29] New Limit Bid at 19.90 for 40 units
			20.30	32		X	[9:43:51] New Limit Bid at 20.00 for 30 units
			20.20	60		X	[9:38:38] 19 TAKEN from Book at 20.20
X			20.10			X	[9:38:38] 1 TAKEN from Book at 20.10
X	30 (0)	30	20.00				[9:38:38] Market Purchase Order for 20 units
X	40 (20)	60	19.90				[9:34:34] 25 TAKEN from Book at 20.10
X		51	19.80				[9:34:34] Market Purchase Order for 25 units
							[9:32:15] New Limit Offer at 20.20 for 38 units

FIGURE 3.22   The effect of a new order to buy 40 at $19.90.

			Price	Size			Log
			20.50	115		X	[9:59:25] 22 SOLD to Book at 20.00
			20.40	39		X	[9:59:25] Market Sell Order for 22 units
			20.30	32		X	[9:46:26] 29 TAKEN from Book at 20.20
			20.20	9		X	[9:46:26] 16 TAKEN from Book at 20.20
X			20.10			X	[9:46:26] Market Purchase Order for 45 units
X	8 (0)	8	20.00				[9:44:39] New Limit Offer at 20.70 for 20 units
X	40 (20)	60	19.90				[9:42:49] 3 TAKEN from Book at 20.20
X		68	19.80				[9:42:49] 3 TAKEN from Book at 20.20
							[9:42:49] Market Purchase Order for 6 units
							[9:41:06] New Limit Bid at 19.80 for 17 units
							[9:36:38] New Limit Bid at 19.90 for 40 units

FIGURE 3.23   The effect of an incoming market order interacting with your limit order.

Navigating the OrderBook

As prices move throughout the trading day, it might be necessary to change the view of the order book. By using the navigation button on top of the order book you can adjust the price levels seen in the order book. Clicking the "UP" button will display higher prices in the order book. Alternatively, clicking the "DOWN" button will shift the book down, displaying lower prices. You can also click the "CENTER" button to center the order book prices on the best bid and offer.

Saving Your Simulation Results

At the end of each TraderEx simulation run, the final trading data can be captured to document your performance. By clicking on the "GET DATA" button in the control panel of the simulation, you will generate a zip file. Choose to save this file to your computer, as shown in Figure 3.24. Included in that zip package are three files. The first file contains all the trades that occurred in the simulation. The second file contains all the trade orders that were submitted to the system. Lastly, there is a file that details the changes in the equilibrium price, P*. The file-naming convention is [simulation name][version][date][file description]. We show in Figure 3.24 a sample of the file-naming conventions and file contents. Table 3.1 is an illustration of the contents of the Trades file.

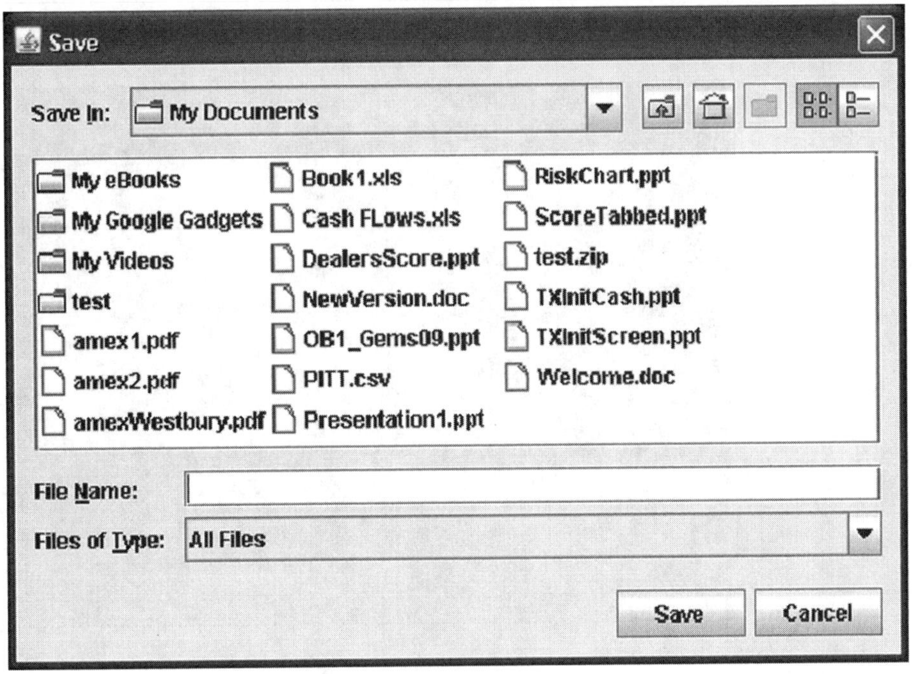

FIGURE 3.24 Saving data from a simulation run.

TABLE 3.1   Sample Data from Trades File

Price	Volume	TradeTime	Vol	Bid	Offer	Buyer	Seller	BuyerID	SellerID
19.95	500	9:30:00	0	20.1	19.8	n/a	n/a	1357	1364
19.85	500	9:30:34	35	19.9	19.8	n/a	n/a	1299	1364
19.85	250	9:30:46	47	19.9	19.8	n/a	n/a	1299	1352
19.85	500	9:30:58	59	19.9	19.8	n/a	n/a	1357	1352
19.85	250	9:31:22	83	19.9	19.8	n/a	n/a	1361	1352
19.85	250	9:31:45	106	19.9	19.8	n/a	n/a	1348	1353
19.85	750	9:31:45	106	19.9	19.8	n/a	n/a	1348	1352
19.85	750	9:31:45	106	19.9	19.8	n/a	n/a	1348	1364
19.85	250	9:32:21	142	19.9	19.8	n/a	n/a	1363	1352
19.85	250	9:32:33	154	19.9	19.8	n/a	n/a	1301	1364

Real-Time Trade Charts

The TraderEx Interactive Charts, shown in Figure 3.25, are available to view by clicking the "CHARTS" button from the control panel in the simulation. A new java window will open. The TraderEx Charts allow for individual performance to be displayed.

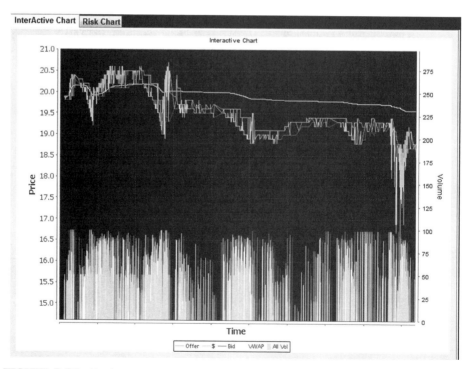

FIGURE 3.25   TraderEx interactive chart data series selection panel.

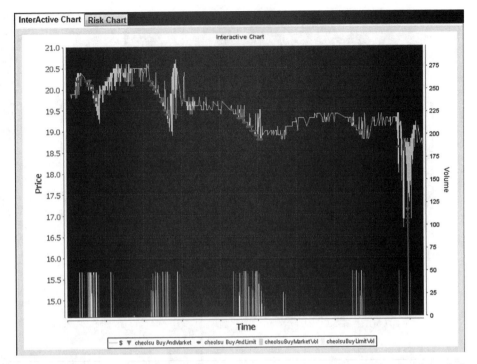

FIGURE 3.26 Chart with market bid and ask, and user's trades highlighted with symbols.

FIGURE 3.27 Adding more information to the price chart.

There are five common data series for all simulations: Price, Bid, Offer, VWAP, and P*. Clicking on the selection box (or deselecting) next to the data series name will show (hide) that series. In the example given in Figure 3.26, we present the bid and the offer data series, which on your computer screen are red and blue continuous lines.

To view your performance, select the details that you wish to display. For instance, Figure 3.27 shows the user's sell trades, which would appear as red triangles. Other options include Buy Trades, All Trades, Limit (orders), and Market (orders).

THE DEALER MARKET

The second market structure TraderEx provides is a quote driven dealer market, shown in Figure 3.28.

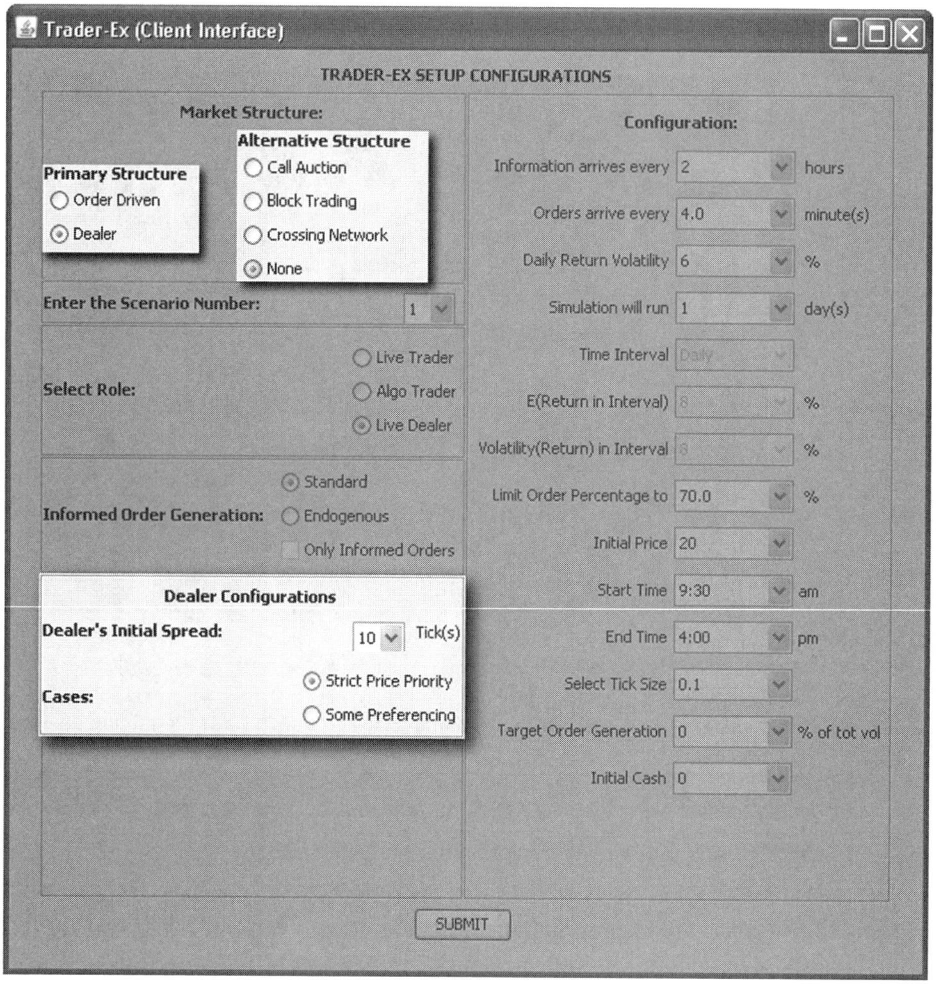

FIGURE 3.28 Launching a dealer market simulation.

To launch the dealer market from the configuration screen, select Dealer. The other relevant parameters in the dealer market structure are:

- **Dealer's Initial Spread:** This is the initial spread on the quotes for the automated dealers.
- **Cases:** Strict Price Priority vs. Preferencing. TraderEx offers the option to allow or prevent preferencing. *Preferencing* means that a customer with an order will send it to a dealer who is not posting the highest bid (if the customer is selling) or the lowest offer (if the customer is buying). Preferencing affects market

maker incentives, and we explore this in simulation exercises later in the book. When there is no preferencing, only the dealer(s) making the lowest offer will sell to incoming buy orders, and only dealer(s) making the highest bid will buy from incoming sell orders.

We refer to the no preferencing environment as *strict price priority*. With strict price priority, if two or more TraderEx dealers are making the best bid or ask quote, they are each equally likely to receive the next arriving order. In the order book market, two limit orders at the same price will be executed in the sequence in which they have arrived at the market—i.e., a first-in first-out, time priority system. Dealer markets in practice do not maintain time priorities and most allow for customer order preferencing.

The dealer market display is presented in Figure 3.29. The screen shows six dealers, each of whom is posting bid and offer quotes that are good for 99 units. On your screen you will see that the dealer(s) with the highest bid is outlined in green, and the dealer(s) with the lowest offer is outlined in red. This particular simulation

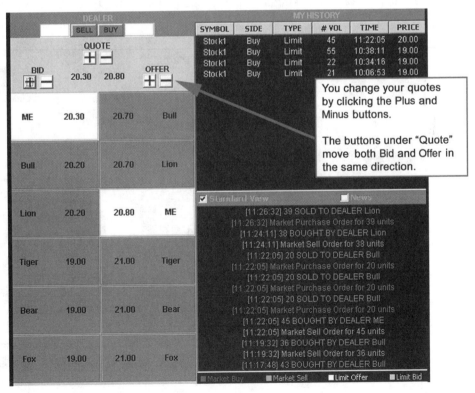

FIGURE 3.29 The dealer market screen—adjusting your quotes.

does not allow for preferencing; only the dealer(s) with the highest bid is eligible to receive an incoming sell order, and only the dealer(s) with the lowest offer will receive an incoming buy order. In the TraderEx Dealer Market environment, you compete against five automated dealers for market share and realized gains.

The dealers, upon receiving incoming orders, buy at their bid quotes and sell at their offer quotes. While trading to "make a market," the dealers must manage their positions so as to avoid becoming excessively long or short. As we have noted, when there is no preferencing, if more than one dealer has the same bid or offer quote, they all have an equal chance of getting the next incoming order. That is, if there are two dealers making the same bid, they each have a 50 percent chance of getting the next order; if there are 3 dealers, they each have 33 percent probability; and so on.

Dealers can trade with each other by using the "SELL" and "BUY" buttons. The maximum order size is 99, and price priority is applied to dealer orders. If you, as a dealer, initiate a trade with an order to sell you will sell at the bid quote. A dealer submitting a buy order to another dealer will buy at the offer quote.

In Figure 3.30, the first trade of the day is a sell order for 35 that trades with ME, who is alone in making the highest bid quote. Having bought, ME is now long

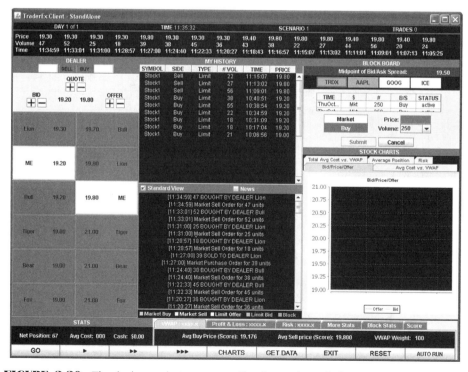

FIGURE 3.30 The dealer market screen—sell order trades at bid with dealer ME.

35 units. In Chapter 4, we will go into dealer performance measures and dealer quote-setting decisions.

CALL AUCTIONS

The call auction batches buy and sell orders at one point in time for a single execution at a single price. The multiple executed orders are reported to the ticker as a single trade. The TraderEx default setting is for call auctions to be held at the market open, midday, and at the market close. You can adjust this to have just one or two calls a day. Figure 3.31 shows the configuration screen for call auctions.

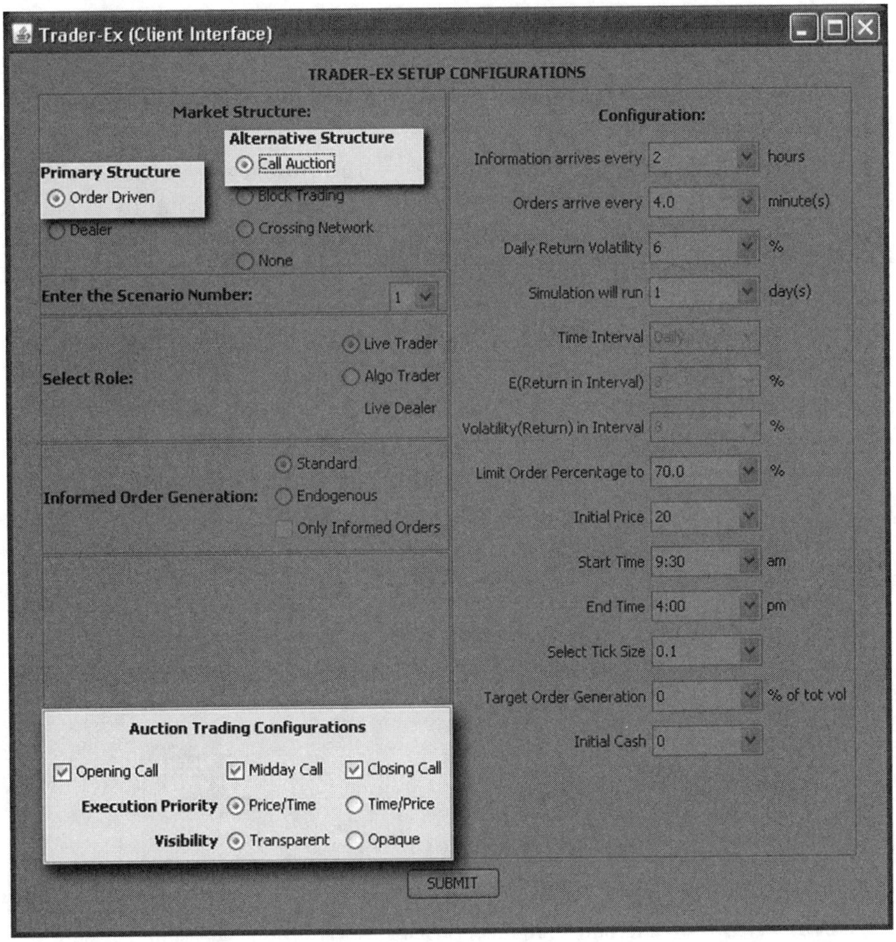

FIGURE 3.31 Configuration screen for call auctions.

Resting orders execute according to a number of execution priorities:

- **Price:** Orders to buy at higher prices, or to sell at lower prices execute ahead of less aggressive orders at the market clearing price.
- **Time:** All orders that are executable at the clearing price are executed according to time priority on a first in, first out (FIFO) basis.

Auctions can also be configured to display all orders, or only some limited information (see Figure 3.32):

- **Transparent:** In this mode, the orders in the call auction are fully visible. One can see where the imbalance is and what volume would trade if the auction were to execute at that time.
- **Opaque:** In this mode, the orders are hidden from the trader. The trader only sees the indicative price.

As orders arrive into the call auction, the volumes are accumulated. The opening screen is shown in Figure 3.33a. Advance the simulation by clicking the "GO" button. You can see in Figure 3.33b that, at the $20.10 price, there are limit buy orders for 21 units. At the next price level, $20.00, there are a total of 57 units sought for purchase.

Now advance the simulation again by clicking the "GO" button. You will see a burst of orders come into the system. Let's get involved in the auction. Put a limit buy order for 30 units at 20.10. Notice that the indicative price went up by one tick, as shown in Figure 3.33c. Once again, advance the simulation by clicking the "GO" button. Enter another limit bid for 60 units at $19.40. Added to the cumulative number of 30 units at $19.50, we now have a total of 90 units at $19.40 (See Figure 3.33d). Advance the simulation by clicking the "GO" button. The Call Auction executes and

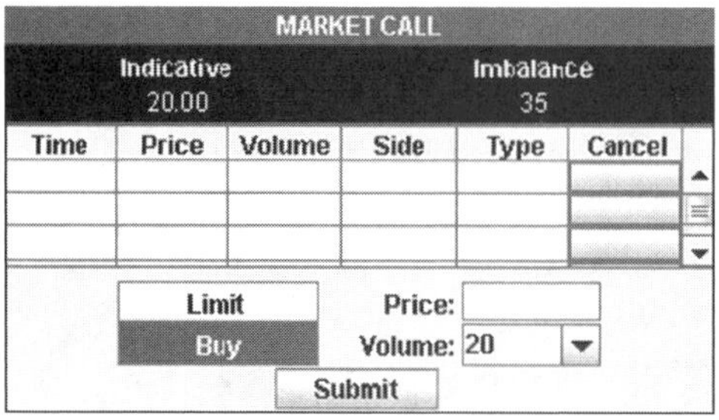

FIGURE 3.32 Alternative, reduced-disclosure view of call auction.

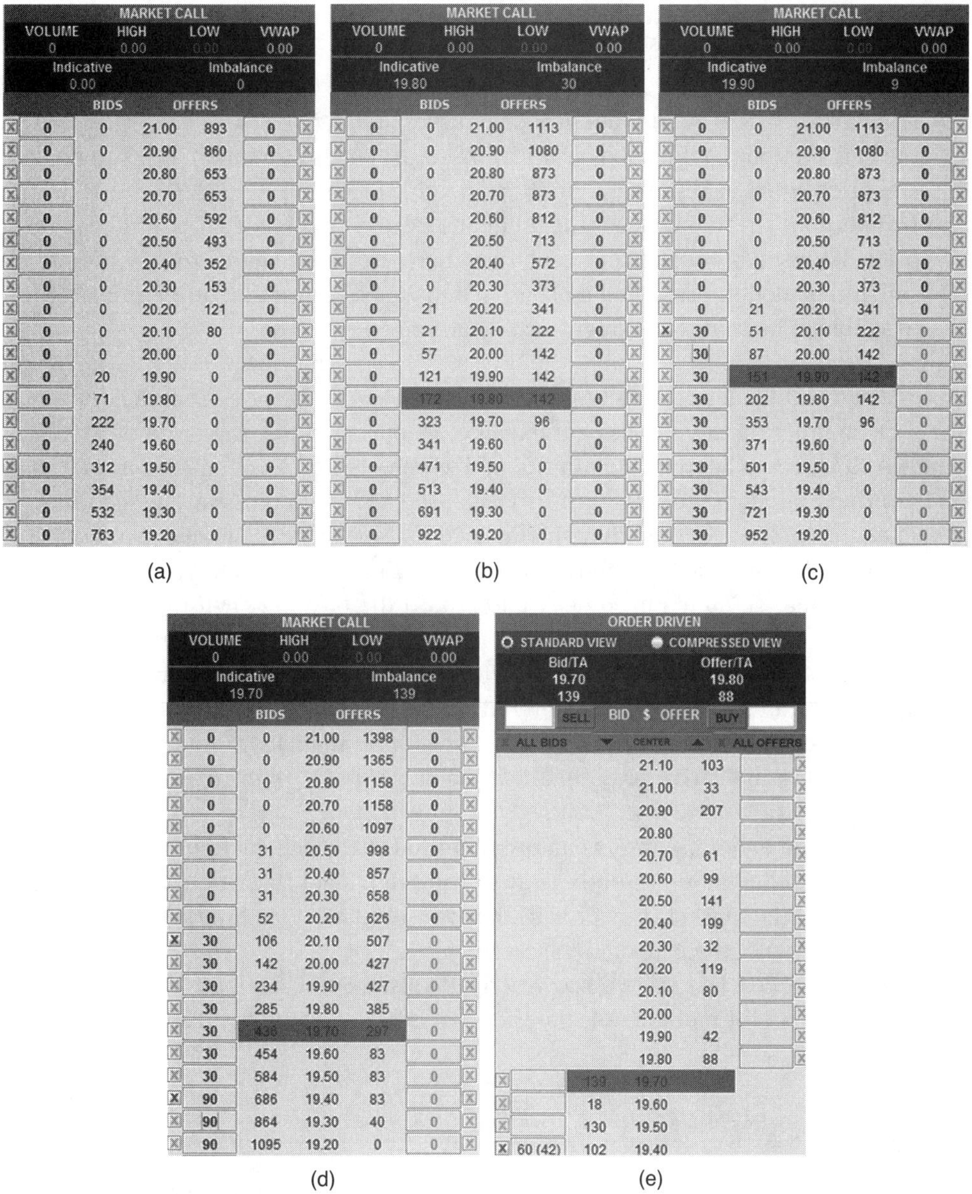

		MARKET CALL				
VOLUME	HIGH		LOW	VWAP		
0	0.00		0.00	0.00		
Indicative			Imbalance			
0.00			0			
	BIDS		OFFERS			
X	0	0	21.00	893	0	X
X	0	0	20.90	860	0	X
X	0	0	20.80	653	0	X
X	0	0	20.70	653	0	X
X	0	0	20.60	592	0	X
X	0	0	20.50	493	0	X
X	0	0	20.40	352	0	X
X	0	0	20.30	153	0	X
X	0	0	20.20	121	0	X
X	0	0	20.10	80	0	X
X	0	0	20.00	0	0	X
X	0	20	19.90	0	0	X
X	0	71	19.80	0	0	X
X	0	222	19.70	0	0	X
X	0	240	19.60	0	0	X
X	0	312	19.50	0	0	X
X	0	354	19.40	0	0	X
X	0	532	19.30	0	0	X
X	0	763	19.20	0	0	X

(a)

		MARKET CALL				
VOLUME	HIGH		LOW	VWAP		
0	0.00		0.00	0.00		
Indicative			Imbalance			
19.80			30			
	BIDS		OFFERS			
X	0	0	21.00	1113	0	X
X	0	0	20.90	1080	0	X
X	0	0	20.80	873	0	X
X	0	0	20.70	873	0	X
X	0	0	20.60	812	0	X
X	0	0	20.50	713	0	X
X	0	0	20.40	572	0	X
X	0	0	20.30	373	0	X
X	0	21	20.20	341	0	X
X	0	21	20.10	222	0	X
X	0	57	20.00	142	0	X
X	0	121	19.90	142	0	X
X	0	172	19.80	142	0	X
X	0	323	19.70	96	0	X
X	0	341	19.60	0	0	X
X	0	471	19.50	0	0	X
X	0	513	19.40	0	0	X
X	0	691	19.30	0	0	X
X	0	922	19.20	0	0	X

(b)

		MARKET CALL				
VOLUME	HIGH		LOW	VWAP		
0	0.00		0.00	0.00		
Indicative			Imbalance			
19.90			9			
	BIDS		OFFERS			
X	0	0	21.00	1113	0	X
X	0	0	20.90	1080	0	X
X	0	0	20.80	873	0	X
X	0	0	20.70	873	0	X
X	0	0	20.60	812	0	X
X	0	0	20.50	713	0	X
X	0	0	20.40	572	0	X
X	0	0	20.30	373	0	X
X	0	21	20.20	341	0	X
X	30	51	20.10	222	0	X
X	30	87	20.00	142	0	X
X	30	151	19.90	142	0	X
X	30	202	19.80	142	0	X
X	30	353	19.70	96	0	X
X	30	371	19.60	0	0	X
X	30	501	19.50	0	0	X
X	30	543	19.40	0	0	X
X	30	721	19.30	0	0	X
X	30	952	19.20	0	0	X

(c)

		MARKET CALL				
VOLUME	HIGH		LOW	VWAP		
0	0.00		0.00	0.00		
Indicative			Imbalance			
19.70			139			
	BIDS		OFFERS			
X	0	0	21.00	1398	0	X
X	0	0	20.90	1365	0	X
X	0	0	20.80	1158	0	X
X	0	0	20.70	1158	0	X
X	0	0	20.60	1097	0	X
X	0	31	20.50	998	0	X
X	0	31	20.40	857	0	X
X	0	31	20.30	658	0	X
X	0	52	20.20	626	0	X
X	30	106	20.10	507	0	X
X	30	142	20.00	427	0	X
X	30	234	19.90	427	0	X
X	30	285	19.80	385	0	X
X	30	435	19.70	297	0	X
X	30	454	19.60	83	0	X
X	30	584	19.50	83	0	X
X	90	686	19.40	83	0	X
X	90	864	19.30	40	0	X
X	90	1095	19.20	0	0	X

(d)

	ORDER DRIVEN			
O STANDARD VIEW		● COMPRESSED VIEW		
Bid/TA		Offer/TA		
19.70		19.80		
139		88		
SELL	BID $ OFFER	BUY		
ALL BIDS ▼	CENTER ▲	ALL OFFERS		
	21.10	103		X
	21.00	33		X
	20.90	207		X
	20.80			X
	20.70	61		X
	20.60	99		X
	20.50	141		X
	20.40	199		X
	20.30	32		X
	20.20	119		X
	20.10	80		X
	20.00			X
	19.90	42		X
	19.80	88		X
X	139	19.70		
X	18	19.60		
X	130	19.50		
X	60 (42)	102	19.40	

(e)

FIGURE 3.33 The progression of the transparent view of the call auction as orders enter into the market.

order book trading starts. Notice that your limit bid from the call auction has been transported to the order book, as shown in Figure 3.33e.

- **Indicative Price:** As the auction progresses, TraderEx shows the price that the call auction would discover if it were to execute at that moment. The final call price could be different than the indicative price.
- **Imbalance:** The imbalance is the number of shares unmatched at the indicative price. A positive imbalance means that there are more shares to buy than to sell at the auction price, and a negative imbalance shows that more orders are available to be sold than bought at the call price.

When the call auction concludes, the system selects the price that maximizes the total number of shares that will execute. In our example, the price of $19.70 enables 297 units to be matched. A total of 436 units to buy were entered at $19.70 or better and, applying the time priority rule, the 297 units that were placed first will execute. After execution, the remaining 16 units to buy remain unexecuted.

If you look one price level above the indicative (which is highlighted in green), you will see that 285 units have been entered on the buy side, and that 385 have been entered on the sell side. This would result in 285 units trading, which is less than the 297 that would execute at $19.70. Or at $19.60, which is one price tick below the indicative, we have 454 entered on the buy side and 83 entered on the sell side, which would result in 83 (which is also less than 489) units transacting. Accordingly, the indicative price is $19.70 because this is the price at which the most units will trade.

Both market and limit orders can be submitted to the call auction. Limit orders are entered by clicking on the box next to the price level that you have selected and the side of the market (buy or sell) that you want to be on. Market orders are entered at the top of the call auction screen.

The call auction is a price discovery mechanism. See Chapter 4 and the exercises in Chapter 7 for more details on price discovery and quantity discovery.

BLOCK TRADING FACILITY

Our dark liquidity pool is based on Pipeline's trading facility (see Chapter 9). It allows large block orders to trade without disclosing their interests to buy or to sell large market-moving quantities of stock.

There are three additional configuration parameters, shown in Figure 3.34, for the block trading facility. "Trade Through Allowed" allows the participants to use the block board to "trade through" contra side orders on the continuous order book. We discuss trade throughs further in Chapter 5. In addition, Exercise 9.6 compares

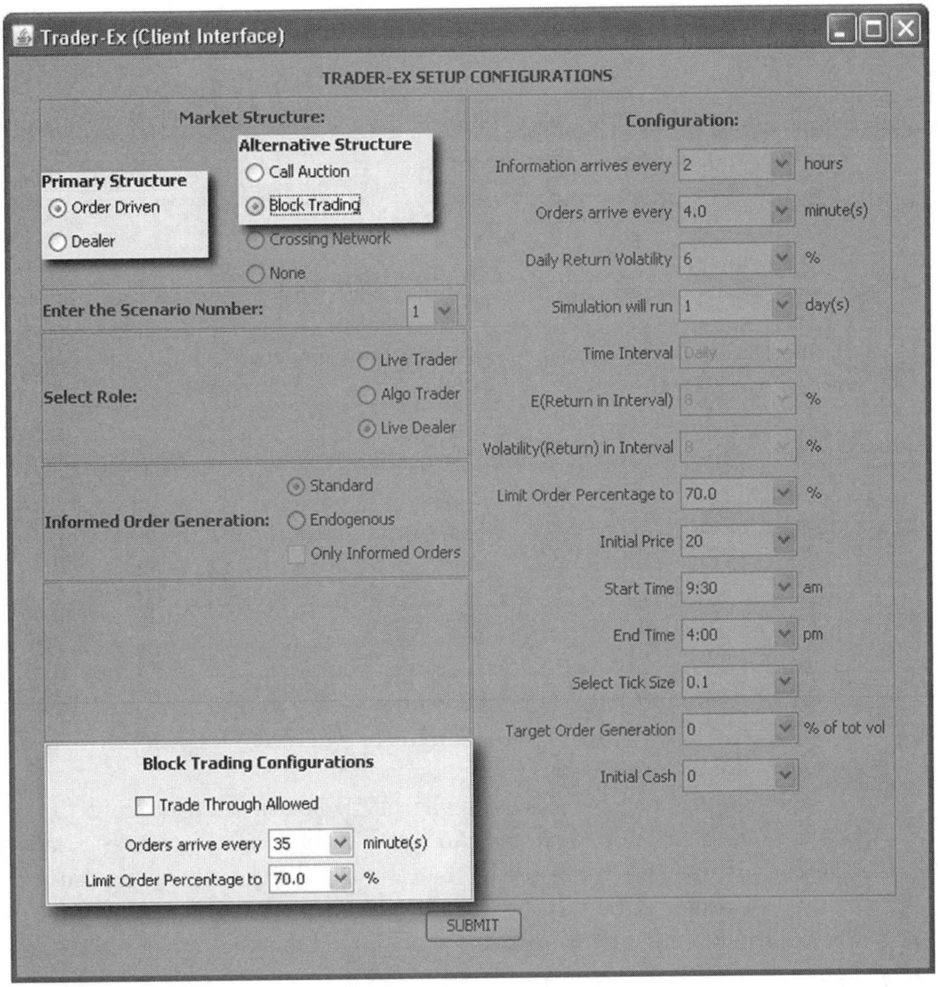

FIGURE 3.34 The initial configuration screen for an order driven market with a block trading facility.

the effect of allowing versus not allowing trade throughs. The order arrival parameter determines how often orders arrive into the dark pool. The limit order percentage determines the liquidity of the dark pool. The higher the limit order percentage, the more liquidity will be in the dark pool.

In the example presented in Figure 3.35, the displayed order book shows that there is a $20.80 limit bid for 187 units and a $20.90 limit offer for 44 units. Accordingly, a trader looking to buy 250 units from the order book would drive the price up in the book. Using the block board, the trader can click on the "Market/Limit" toggle button and the "Buy/Sell" toggle button and place an order in the dark pool.

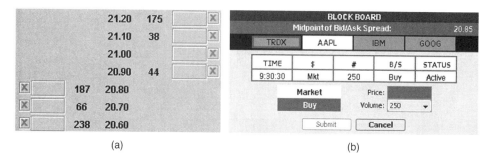

		21.20	175		X
		21.10	38		X
		21.00			X
		20.90	44		X
X	187	20.80			
X	66	20.70			
X	238	20.60			

BLOCK BOARD
Midpoint of Bid/Ask Spread: 20.85

| TRDX | AAPL | IBM | GOOG |

TIME	$	#	B/S	STATUS
9:30:30	Mkt	250	Buy	Active

Market
Buy

Price:
Volume: 250

Submit   Cancel

(a)   (b)

FIGURE 3.35 The continuous order book shows a bid at $20.80 and an offer at $20.90. The block board shows the midpoint of the bid/ask spread as $20.85.

A block board buy market order is available to any counterparty who will sell 250 units or more at the midpoint of the bid–ask spread, which is $20.85 in this illustration.

The TraderEx block board is only for orders with a minimum size of 250 units. Block board orders (see Figure 3.36) are separate from the displayed order book. That is, they are not included in the order book display, and they do not execute against limit orders on the displayed order book. The prices of block board trades are treated with reference to the mid-spread price on the order book. It is possible to trade anywhere at any price within the spread, from the ask price down to and including the bid price.

Limit orders can be placed in the block board in an attempt to achieve a better price than the mid-spread. An order with a limit price that is less aggressive (i.e., worse than mid-spread) is a *Passive Order*. When the mid-spread is $20.85, an order to buy a block at $20.80 is considered passive. A market order or a limit order with a price at or better than the mid-spread is an *Active Order*.

BLOCK BOARD
Midpoint of Bid/Ask Spread: 20.05

| TRDX | AAPL | GOOG | ICE |

TIME	$	#	B/S	STATUS

Limit
Buy

Price:
Volume: 250

Submit   Cancel

FIGURE 3.36 The initial screen of the block board.

The display for stock 1 (TRDX) will show the following colors on your screen:

- Orange: There is a block board order for that stock.
- Orange with Red: You have placed a sell order.
- Orange with Green: You have placed a buy order.
- Yellow with Green: You have placed an active buy order and there is a passive sell order.
- Yellow with Red: You have placed an active sell order and there is a passive buy order.

Example: Passive Limit Order Turning Into an Active Limit Order

In this example (Figure 3.37) we have 2 participants, A (a buyer) and B (a seller). Shown is a snapshot of the current order book. The best bid is at 19.40 for 224 units, and the best offer is at $19.90 for 266 units. The mid-spread is $19.65. Trader A acts

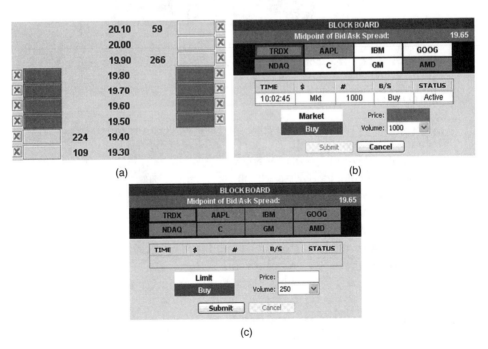

FIGURE 3.37 The continuous order book (a) followed by the block board Trader A sees after entering a market buy order for 1000 units (b). The orange button with the green border is lit up for Trader A. Trader B sees the TRDX button turn orange, signaling interest in the stock (c).

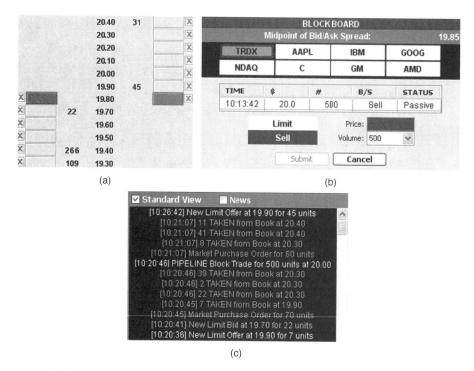

FIGURE 3.38 The continuous order book showing a new limit bid at $19.70 (a). Trader B enters a limit sell order for $20.00 and the TRDX button turns from solid orange to orange with a red border (b). The continuous market changed and a block trade execution is recorded at 10:20 A.M. (c).

first, entering a market buy order for 1000 units in the block board. Trader A will see the TRDX symbol light up orange with a green border.

Trader B sees the TRDX box go from white to orange. B enters a 500 unit sell order into the block board at $20.00. See Figure 3.38. This limit order is Passive.

The market changes. A limit sell order arrives at 10:20:36 for 7 units at $19.90, and it is followed by a limit buy order for 22 units at $19.70, shown in Figure 3.38(c) on the bottom. Next, a market purchase order for 70 units comes in at 10:20:45 that clears out the order book. Now the resulting mid-spread is $20.00 ($19.70 bid, $20.30 offer). The limit passive order becomes active, and it trades with Trader A's market order. So, at 10:20:46 there is a block trade completed for 500 units at $20.00.

Example: How the System Rewards the Aggressive Participant

Next let Trader B place another limit sell order for 500 units at $20.40. The trade-through rule will have an effect (See Figure 3.39a) since the new dark pool sell order is priced above the lowest offer on the displayed order book.

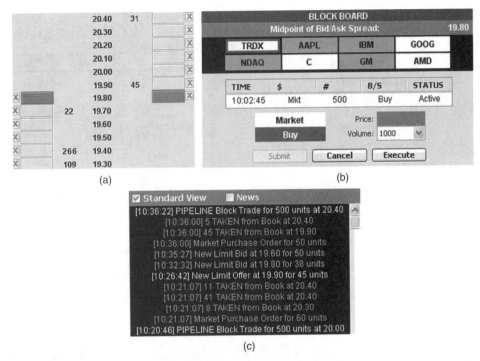

FIGURE 3.39 The continuous order book and block board showing there is a contra order to the market buy order entered. Trade Through Allowed implies that the passive contra order can be at any price, in this case $20.40, above the best offer.

If, at the configuration stage, the default setting was changed to Trade Throughs Allowed, Trader A's button would turn yellow and Trader A would have the opportunity to execute against that passive order. By placing a market order, Trader A is rewarded with information about other orders in the dark pool. If Trader A clicks on "Execute," he will trade through the limit order on the continuous order book at $19.90. As shown in Figure 3.39b, clicking Execute, Trader A accepts the passive contra's offer, not knowing how it has been priced. A trade occurs at the passive order's price (reflected in the event feed in Figure 3.39c.

In the default No Trade Throughs Allowed mode (Figure 3.40), there would be no change to Trader A's block board, since the limit sell order in the block board was priced above the best offer in the continuous market. The market changes again. A market buy order for 50 units arrives on the order book, and it clears out the displayed book (see Figure 3.41a). Trader A's button turns yellow, showing the Execute button, telling him that a limit contra order exists within the posted quotes (see Figure 3.41b). Trader A clicks Execute and we have a trade for 500 units at $20.40 (see Figure 3.41c).

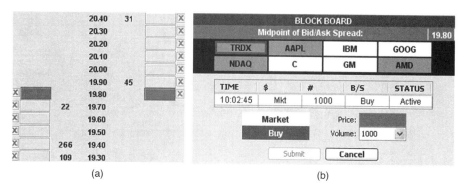

(a)   (b)

FIGURE 3.40 The continuous order book and block board for Trader A when trade throughs are not allowed.

Any time the "Execute" button is visible, there is a contra order that the aggressor can trade with. If trade throughs are not allowed and the "Execute" button is visible, the passive trade is within the posted quotes from the continuous order book, otherwise there is no way to know how the passive order is priced. See Exercises 5.8 and 9.6 for more detail on the impact of the trade-through rule.

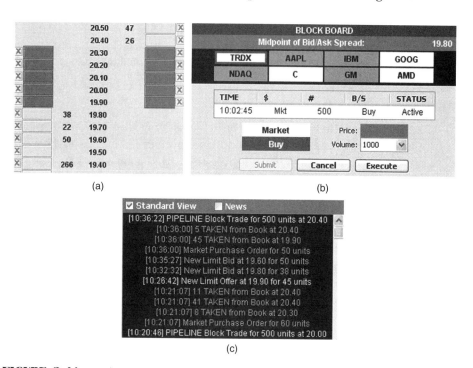

(a)   (b)

(c)

FIGURE 3.41 Trader A clicks Execute and a trade occurs at the limit sell price, as long as it is between the posted bid and offer, if no trade through allowed.

CROSSING NETWORK

In TraderEx, a periodic crossing system can be added to the market structure. Limit and Market orders can be submitted into the Crossing for execution. At each of six different crossing times (10 A.M., 11 A.M., ..., 3 P.M.), buy and sell orders that have been entered into the cross are executed at the midpoint of the bid and ask quotes. See Figure 3.42 for an illustration.

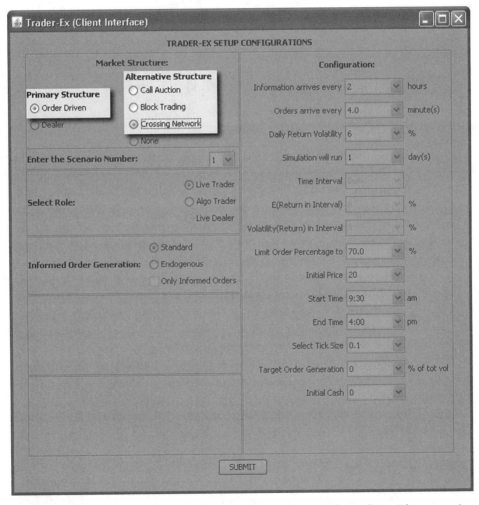

FIGURE 3.42 Initial Configuration Screen for order driven market with a crossing network.

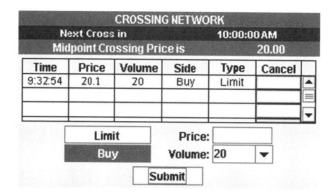

FIGURE 3.43 Order entry for crossing network.

Unlike the call auction, there is no price discovery in the crossing. The orders that can be matched with a counterparty will execute, and any imbalance is cancelled and remains undisclosed. Figure 3.43 illustrates how orders are entered into the crossing network

Other information displayed in the crossing mode is:

- **Next Cross in:** This shows the approximate time of the next cross. The actual time of the cross will be randomly selected around the posted time.
- **Midpoint Crossing Price is:** This is the midpoint of the bid/ask spread from the continuous order driven market. If the cross were to execute at the current time, this would be the crossing price. Buy orders entered into the crossing network above the posted price will execute, providing that there are contra orders that have also been aggressively priced.
- **Entering your order into the cross:** To enter a limit order into the system, make sure the "Limit/ Market" button reads "Limit." Select a side ("Buy/Sell") with the button selector. Enter the price of your order. Note: Limit Buy orders priced below the Crossing Midpoint and Limit Sell orders priced above the Crossing Midpoint will not execute.
- **Viewing your order:** Only your submitted order can be viewed; it will appear in the blotter.

To cancel an order, click the button next to the order in the blotter under "CANCEL."

HYBRID MARKETS

In market centers around the world, trading systems are hybrid combinations of the different facilities that we have focused on thus far. The reason is straightforward. Participants need choice in handling their orders, and a marketplace requires special facilities to open and to close markets (the call auction fits in here), to deal with very large orders (the block trading facilities fit in here), and to focus liquidity for smaller caps, which are more thinly traded issues (call auctions and the dealer market fit in here). Accordingly, TraderEx offers hybrid market structures. You can easily enter a hybrid structure by entering the appropriate instructions in the TraderEx Setup Configurations screen.

As shown in Figure 3.44, you can run a Dealer Market/Call Auction hybrid by clicking on "DEALER" under the Primary Structure and "CALL AUCTION" under the Alternative Structure.

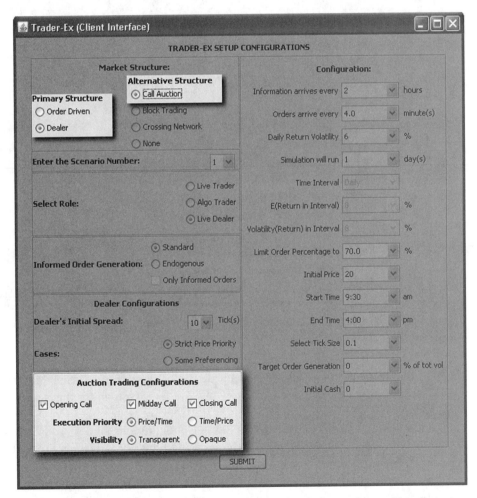

FIGURE 3.44 Configuration screen for order entry for dealer structure with call auctions. The market can also have dealer with crossing network, and dealer with a block trading facility.

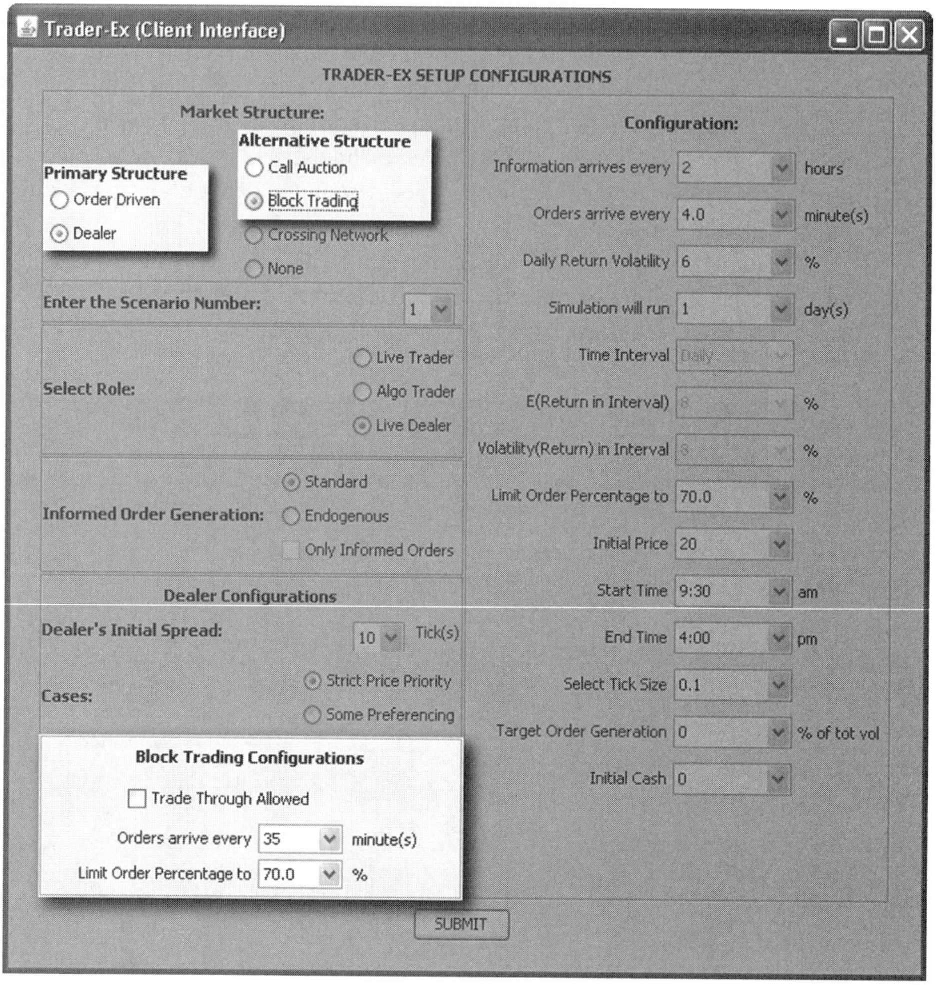

FIGURE 3.45 Configuration for dealer and block board trading.

Figure 3.45 shows how you can alternatively obtain a Dealer Market/Block Trading hybrid, and Figure 3.46 shows the TraderEx screen for this second hybrid structure.

As you can see from TraderEx Setup Configurations screen, you can also run hybrid combinations that include the crossing network. Advancing to include hybrid structures opens up new and interesting possibilities for exercises that reflect real-world situations. These require no further description here because we have already discussed the components. You will be presented with the hybrid market exercises in the ensuing chapters of this book. Before getting to them, however, in

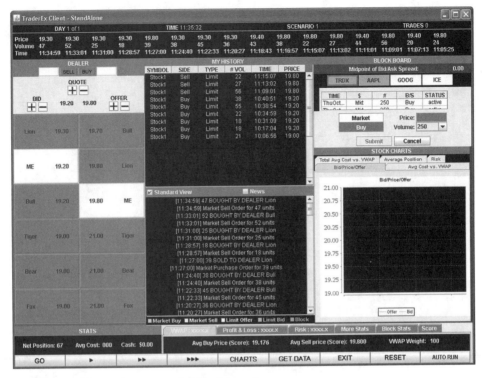

FIGURE 3.46 Dealer quotes and block board.

the next chapter we give you further perspective on the simulation model and the operations of actual participants and real-world market structures.

SUMMARY

TraderEx provides a user with a large number of configuration options and functions. We have described the five market structures here: order book, dealer market, call auction, dark pool, and crossing networks. The next step is to turn to your computer and work through the examples and exercises in the chapters that follow. This is the best way to learn how different market structures function, and to examine how your good trading decisions lead to superior trading (and hence investing) performance.

CHAPTER 4

Introduction to the Trading Exercises

T his is an introduction to the following five chapters that will put you in the role of a trader. As a market decision maker, with profit and loss (P&L) responsibility, you will gain an understanding of how your trading choices in different market structures drive successful outcomes. You will learn how markets function rather than just observing the decisions that were made.

The order book is the first of four different market structures that you will experience via TraderEx simulations. The other three are a call auction, a dealer market, and a market with a dark liquidity pool. You will learn that each market mechanism presents a different set of decision challenges for trading desks.

As a participant in an order book, as in any market system, you want to achieve best execution—the outcome that minimizes trading costs and enhances returns for the investor. To do so, you should be aware of the choices and order types open to you, and you should adjust your orders to the structure and rules of the market. In so doing, a trading desk can operate effectively and contribute to performance while managing its risks.

The roles you will play in the order book will include a trader handling a buy-side investor's instruction to buy or to sell, and a proprietary trader deciding when to "make" liquidity in a market by placing limit orders, and when to "take" liquidity by using market orders to buy and to sell. You will also decide when to trade "in the dark" using a block liquidity pool.

As a buy-side trader you will be assessed on how the average price you pay when buying, or the price you receive when selling, compare to benchmark reference prices. Naturally you want to buy as low as possible, and to sell at prices that are as high as possible. As a market maker and a proprietary trader, you will be seeking to earn a positive profit while managing the risk of the positions that you hold. Each role presents a different set of motivations and risks that we will detail.

In our exercises, three basic questions that you should ask are:

1. How can you assess the quality of the market in different trading mechanisms, and adjust your trading accordingly?

2. How should you handle instructions to buy or to sell large quantities of shares in a market so as to achieve best execution?

3. How can proprietary trading and dealer intermediation be carried out so as to limit risk yet generate profits?

There are no simple answers. Trading decisions should reflect a number of important considerations that we will cover. Moreover, what you learn from one role—say your prop trading experience—will enable you to think more clearly about your trading choices in the other roles.

Let's move on to the roles that traders can have in different market structures. The most important distinction among the roles that you will play is whether you are primarily trading for a buy-side investor seeking to access liquidity and build a position, or are trading as a dealer-intermediary supplying liquidity to the market. We refer to these as the Buy-Side perspective, and the Trading Intermediary perspective.

THE BUY-SIDE PERSPECTIVE

Investment managers tend to fixate on Alpha, and not because they are Greek language scholars. Alpha is the excess positive return a money manager's stock picking generates beyond the return on the overall market adjusted for the level of risk taken. Consider an investor who earns a 10 percent return in a period and has taken risks equal to the overall level of risk in the market, and that the market is up 7 percent; he/she has generated 3 percent in alpha.[*] With an awareness of costs in trading, and armed with decision making skills, a trader should not lower alpha significantly; in some circumstances he/she can actually contribute to the alpha that a portfolio achieves.

---

[*]In the Capital Asset Pricing Model (CAPM), beta measures the non-diversifiable risk of a stock. A portfolio beta is the weighted sum of the individual holdings' betas, and if it is equal to 1.0, the fund is expected to achieve the market rate of return, R_m. In general, a portfolio's expected return is a function of the risk-free return and the portfolio beta: $E(R_i) = R_f + \beta_i (R_m - R_f)$.

How would a trader know if he or she is contributing to alpha? Imagine knowing the precise timing and size of each and every investment decision that a fund manager makes. This knowledge could be used to construct a fictitious "paper portfolio" based on prices at the time of each decision. Call these prices the *decision prices* or *arrival prices* for when the order arrives at the trader's desk. If this "shadow fund" beats the market return by 2 percent in a year, but the real fund as it is implemented through trading only matches the market return, then the costs of implementation and trading that year were 2 percent. Alpha was eroded by trading costs and frictions.

Can you trade in a way that avoids erosion of alpha, or even contributes to alpha? The exercises presented in the next chapters will give you a sense of the extent to which the execution quality achieved by traders impacts investment performance by adding to or subtracting from alpha.

Two basic questions that a buy-side trading desk should ask are:

- How best to operate in an order book system to complete an instruction in its entirety while not receiving poor prices.
- How best to handle instructions to buy or to sell significant quantities of shares, such as 20 percent of average daily volume (ADV), so as to achieve best execution.

Addressing these issues is a challenge, and trading decisions should reflect several important considerations:

- The fund manager's investing style: momentum, value, or growth stocks, etc.
- Liquidity sources available—e.g., an order book, a dealer's capital commitment, and an auction.
- Frequency of trading and the typical holding period for investments.

For a fund manager, trading costs matter. And the more you trade, the more transactions costs can eat into your investment returns. Consider these comments from the head trader of a Chicago-based fund, who explains that his firm's high portfolio turnover rate makes lower transaction costs crucial:

We turn over often, so the transaction costs are much more meaningful to me—a penny to me can translate to as much as one and a half per cent per year in return, so we're very careful about that stuff, and trying to get those costs lower.

"Thinking Outside the Black Box," *Hedge Fund & Investment Technology*, December 2004

Traditionally, money managers have told their brokers what buys and sells they wanted to execute for the portfolio(s) they were managing. Using his or her own judgment, the broker then implemented the trading decisions on behalf of the client. The broker would typically update the client on the progress being made while working an order. After the trading instructions were completed, the broker would report back on the average trade price achieved.

Until recently, few alternative trading systems (ATSs) and multilateral trading facilities (MTFs) were available. Greater technological capabilities and direct market access"(DMA) have changed this:

> *It used to be impossible to not need a broker to do this kind of stuff—we'd give them our orders and they'd work them. Now we have all this capability in-house, because the price of computer connectivity has come down so much . . .*
>
> "Thinking Outside the Black Box," *Hedge Fund & Investment Technology*, December 2004

With new technology and the direct market access (DMA) alternatives that are available today, investors can handle their own orders, entering, updating, and canceling them. In an order driven market, the basic order types are market and limit orders, and a DMA participant sees the full "depth of book." The basic choices a trader has to make are timing, size of order, price of order, and type of order. With DMA available, more participants are taking direct control over trading and the submission of their orders. TraderEx will provide you with a means of understanding how orders can be worked in the different market structures that are available today. We start with the simple order book system.

Buy-Side Trading in "Plain Vanilla" Order Driven Markets

Electronic order book markets are prevalent trading platforms in stock markets today. Order books hold and display limit orders from liquidity suppliers, and execute trades when market orders are entered and matched with the resting limit orders. From the trading desk perspective, simple trading in order book markets requires knowledge of:

A) The rules of the order book, including execution priorities based on

- Order price
- Time of arrival
- Order size

B) How to determine the relative proportions of limit and market orders to use in trading is a challenge. Market orders offer certainty of immediate execution, but a limit order that executes will happen at a more attractive price since the bid-ask spread cost is avoided. We next consider how market entry and exit decisions are made in an order book market structure.

Order Book Dynamics and Trading Performance

Before we start the trading exercises, consider how an order book market operates. Figure 4.1 shows a part of the order book that is similar to what you will see during the exercises. It shows the three best bids to buy and the three best offers to sell.

The bid is $19.90 and the offer is $20.00, and the quantities that can be traded at those prices are 66 and 58 units, respectively. Each unit represents a 100 share round lot. Limit orders to buy are on the left side of the book and (reading from the top down) they are ordered from the highest price to the lowest price. Sell limit orders are offers on the right side of the book and (reading from the bottom up) they are arranged from the lowest price to the highest price.

With respect to the case above, suppose that a trader acquires a position at the offer price of $20.00, and after the market moves up $1 (5 percent) to $20.90 bid and $21.00 offer, he/she sells at the $20.90 bid.

Q: What is the investor's return?
A: (20.90 − 20.00) / 20.00 = 4.5%

What if the trader had entered a limit order at $19.90, and bought at that price? Later, when the market screen shows $20.90 bid and $21.00 offer, he/she sells with a limit order at $21.00.

Q: What is the return?
A: (21.00 − 19.90) / 19.90 = 5.5%

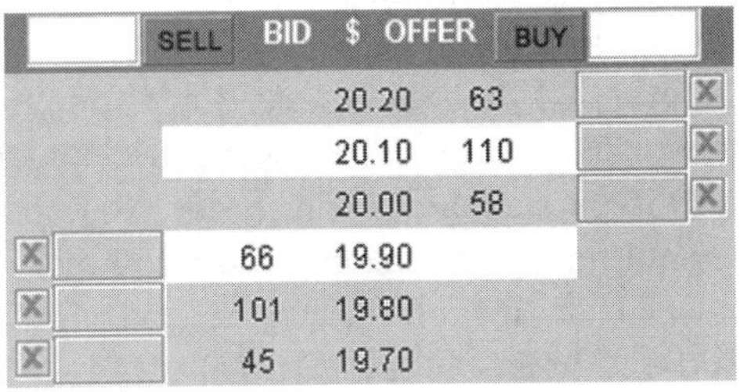

SELL	BID	$	OFFER	BUY
		20.20	63	☒
		20.10	110	☒
		20.00	58	☒
☒	66	19.90		
☒	101	19.80		
☒	45	19.70		

FIGURE 4.1 TraderEx Order Book—19.90 and 20.10 are highlighted as the high and low trade prices of the day so far.

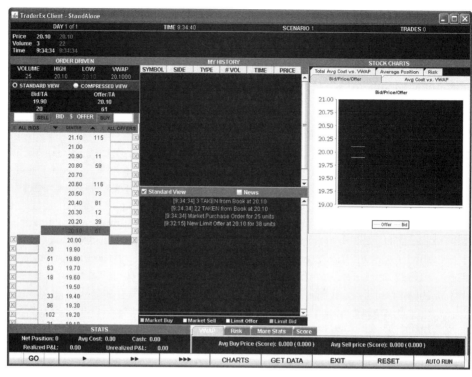

FIGURE 4.2 Full TraderEx market screen in order book market structure. This shows that prices have increased and additional units will be more costly to buy.

As you see, the entry and exit from a position with limit orders increases the investor's return. Q: Is it always possible to enter and exit cost-effectively with limit orders? A: Not always.

Figure 4.2 is a full TraderEx screen. Assume you are seeking to buy for a client at the lowest possible prices. Later in the day, the bid quote is $20.50 and the offer quote is $20.80. The day's high–low range of $19.90 to $20.50 would be given at the top of the screen and by the highlighted prices in the order book. You as the user have bought 119 units so far.

Notice in Figure 4.3 that the user's Buy Order for 25 at $20.50 will execute before the 20 units at 20.40. Also notice the "air pocket" that is in the order book at $20.60 and $20.70, and ahead of your order. No one has a buy order at $20.60. In light of this, should one of the user's orders to buy be re-positioned in the book? Why would we ask that? If the order to buy 25 traded 10 cents higher, that would reduce the return on the investment. You are well positioned at 20.50. How would you respond if orders to buy joined the book at prices of $20.60? Your answers will play a major role in determining the result your trading achieves for the investor.

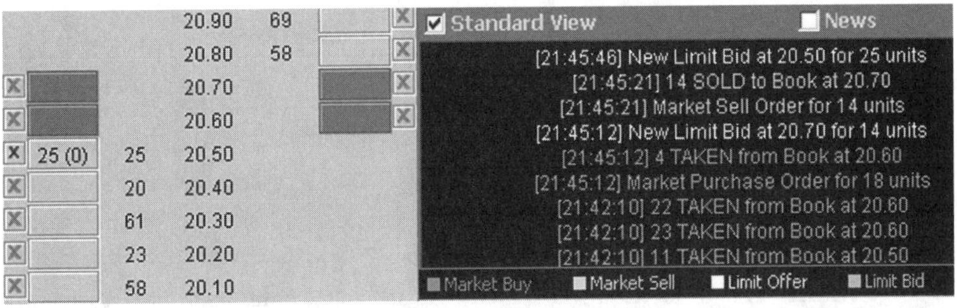

FIGURE 4.3 Event feed showing order events. On screen, market buys and sells and limit bids and offers appear in different color shades.

When the box is checked off, the Standard View of the Event Feed to the right of the order book provides a list of the recent events affecting the order book. The most recent events are on the top. In your simulation software, the list of order events in Figure 4.3 is color-coded, with market buys and sells, and limit buys and sells appearing in different shades. The illustration shows that nearly all recent market events in the past 10 minutes were units TAKEN from the book at the offer price, or a New Limit Order placed. How should a user interpret the preponderance of recent events initiated by buyers? With few signs of selling interest, a buyer may need to be aggressive by using higher priced limit orders, and also market orders to buy. Such momentum information can sharpen your order entry decisions, and enhance your results. Moreover, TraderEx maintains a fundamental value, P^*, for the stock. As Chapter 2 described, when there is information change and P^* shifts away from the current market quotes, the order flow will become imbalanced to the buying or selling side. The Event Feed is one way to see indications of information change in the market.

You'll have a number of chances to answer the questions that we have posed for you thus far in the exercises that follow in Chapters 6 through 9. These will help you become more familiar with market and limit orders, and with how trading decisions are best made.

Exercise: Outcomes from Orders You Place

Your choice of order type will affect your results in the exercises. Launch the TraderEx software (see Figure 4.4). After selecting the Order Book market structure, the parameter screen below will appear. Leave all parameter settings at their default level except for the order arrival rate, which you should change to 2.0. Click on "SUBMIT" at the bottom.

First we will enter market orders, and then compare them with using limit orders. See Figure 4.5.

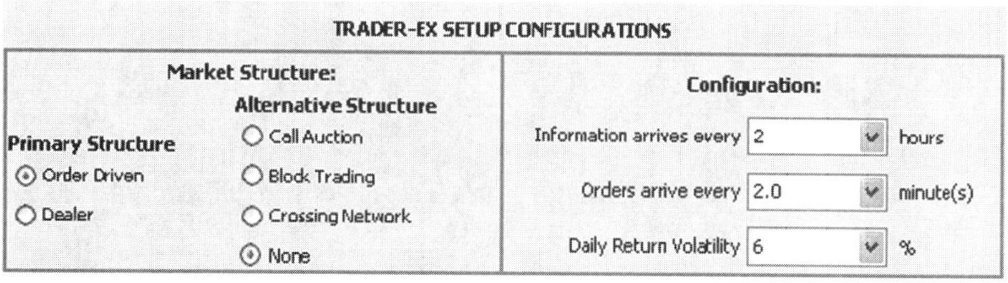
TRADER-EX SETUP CONFIGURATIONS
Market Structure:
Alternative Structure
Primary Structure
Order Driven
Dealer
Call Auction
Block Trading
Crossing Network
None
Configuration:
Information arrives every 2 hours
Orders arrive every 2.0 minute(s)
Daily Return Volatility 6 %

FIGURE 4.4 TraderEx market parameters screen for order book market structure.

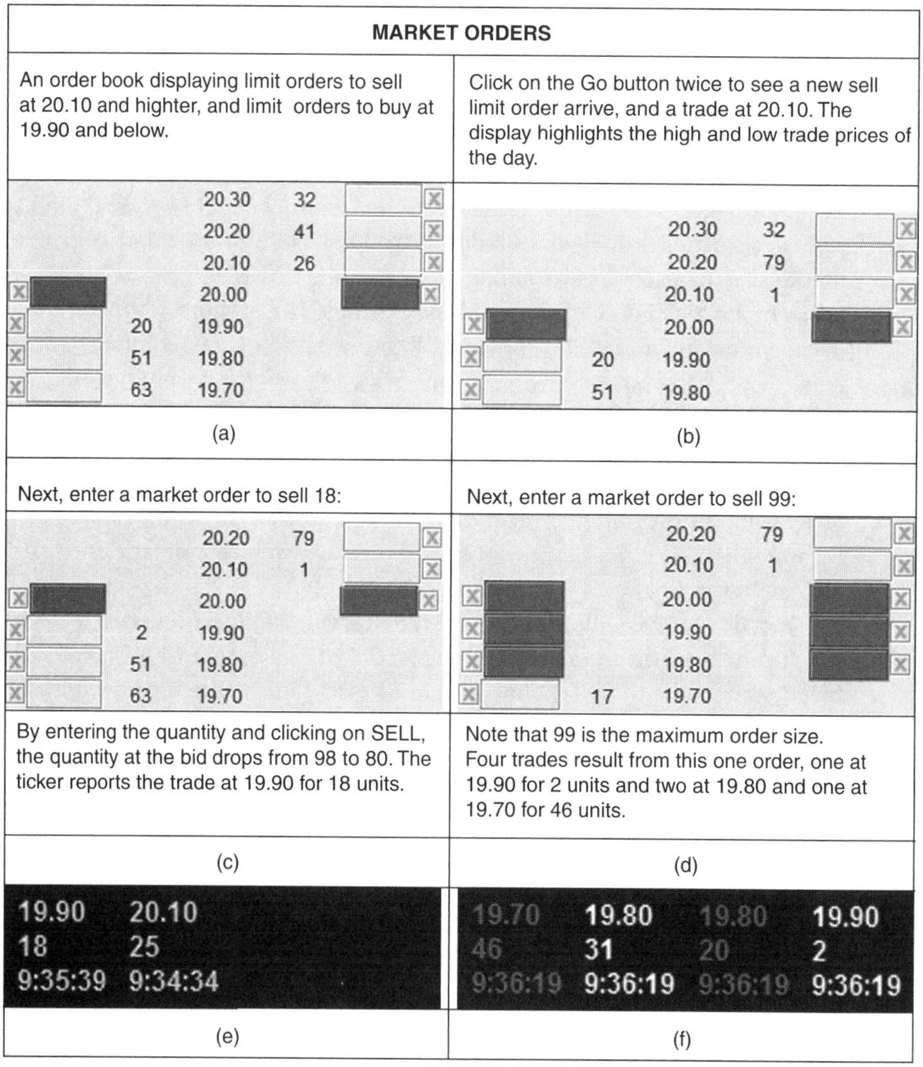
MARKET ORDERS
An order book displaying limit orders to sell at 20.10 and highter, and limit orders to buy at 19.90 and below.
20.30 32
20.20 41
20.10 26
20.00
20 19.90
51 19.80
63 19.70
(a)
Click on the Go button twice to see a new sell limit order arrive, and a trade at 20.10. The display highlights the high and low trade prices of the day.
20.30 32
20.20 79
20.10 1
20.00
20 19.90
51 19.80
(b)
Next, enter a market order to sell 18:
20.20 79
20.10 1
20.00
2 19.90
51 19.80
63 19.70
By entering the quantity and clicking on SELL, the quantity at the bid drops from 98 to 80. The ticker reports the trade at 19.90 for 18 units.
(c)
Next, enter a market order to sell 99:
20.20 79
20.10 1
20.00
19.90
19.80
17 19.70
Note that 99 is the maximum order size. Four trades result from this one order, one at 19.90 for 2 units and two at 19.80 and one at 19.70 for 46 units.
(d)
19.90 20.10
18 25
9:35:39 9:34:34
(e)
19.70 19.80 19.80 19.90
46 31 20 2
9:36:19 9:36:19 9:36:19 9:36:19
(f)

FIGURE 4.5 TraderEx order book market before and after market order arrival.

In the sequence in Figure 4.5, a limit order to sell 38 at 20.20 arrives. Next, our market sell orders for 18 and then 99 trade at 20.00 and 19.90, reducing the size of the buy orders displayed, taking liquidity out of the order book. We sold at an average price less than the initial market bid. Could we have realized more revenue from our sale of 117 units? What are the risks of waiting, and not selling to the orders in the book as above? These questions will be explored in Chapters 6 through 9.

Now that we have sold with market orders, we will consider the use of limit orders to buy. We will compare how the two order types will lead to different results. See Figure 4.6.

In Figure 4.6, we will buy 52 units with a limit order in two separate trades, and paid the bid price. We effectively save the $0.20 spread cost that a market order to buy would have incurred at this point in time. Are there risks to you of buying with a limit order as above? These questions will be explored in Chapters 6 through 9.

These illustrations show that participating in an order book market requires knowledge of the order types permitted in the market (limit, market, or other order types), the rules of the order book (including execution priorities based on order price, time of arrival, order size), how to time the submission of orders into the market, and how to determine the relative proportions of limit or market orders to use.

To recap, the three key characteristics of the order book structure in TraderEx are:

1. In the TraderEx order book, there are two order types: market orders and limit orders.

    As illustrated in Figure 4.6, limit orders are displayed on the book and can execute partially or in full. The 26 units offered at 20.10 in Figure 4.6(e), when a market buy order for 20 arrives, will be reduced to 6 units offered at 20.10. Your order type choice will affect your results, and should depend on your assessment of the short-term dynamics. As actual traders make clear, factors such as the balance between the quantity on the bid side of the book and the quantity on the offer side of the book require consideration when choosing what type of order to place.

2. TraderEx's order book operates with strict price and time priority.

    The most aggressively priced limit orders execute first, and for limit orders with the same price, the earliest to arrive in the order book trades first. In Figure 4.6(b), look at the $19.90 bid for 72. The user has entered a limit order to buy 52 at $20.00, and the (20) figure tells him that because the other orders at that price arrived earlier, he is positioned at the end of the queue, with 20 units to buy ahead of him at that price. His order to buy 52 at $20.00 will execute only after the 20 ahead of him have executed (or have been cancelled by whoever placed them). The orders to buy 51 at 19.80 will not trade until all orders to

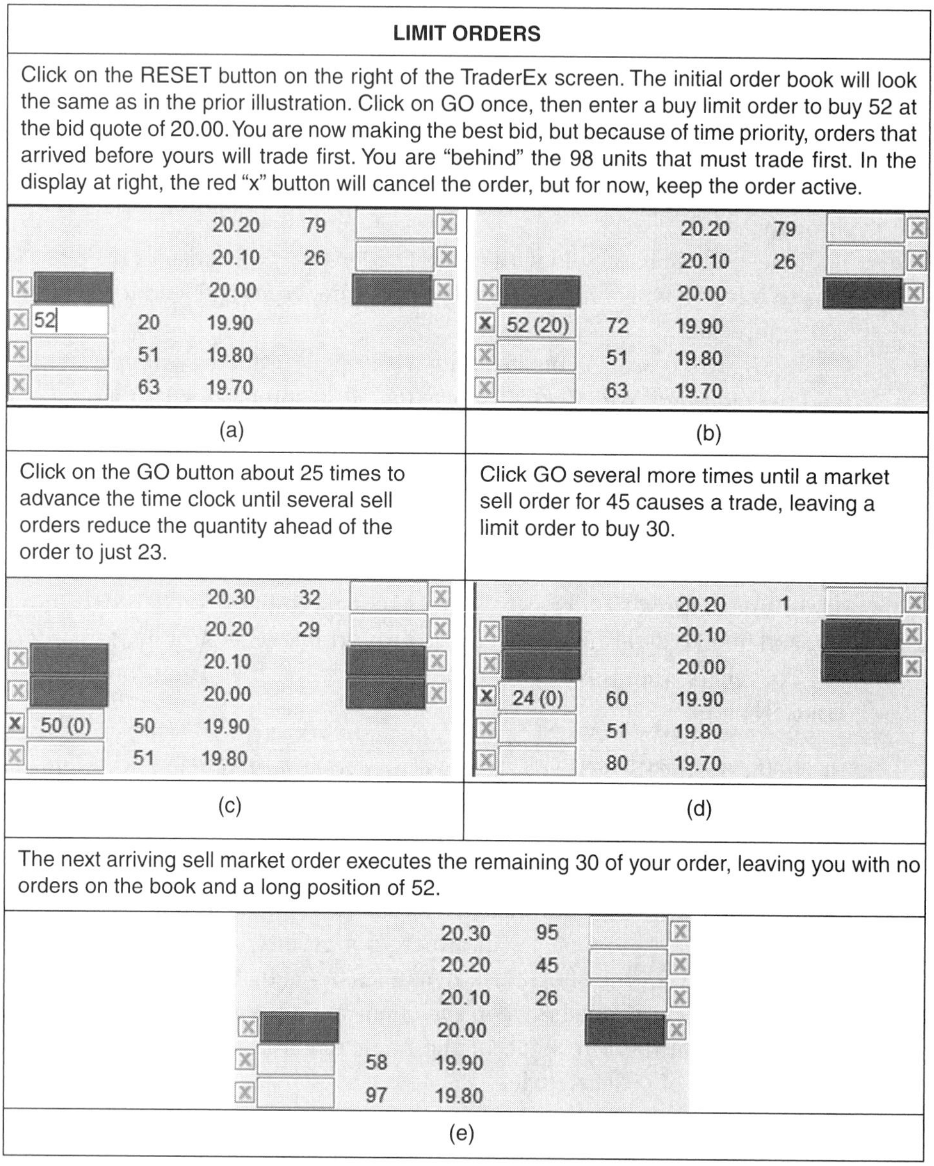

LIMIT ORDERS

Click on the RESET button on the right of the TraderEx screen. The initial order book will look the same as in the prior illustration. Click on GO once, then enter a buy limit order to buy 52 at the bid quote of 20.00. You are now making the best bid, but because of time priority, orders that arrived before yours will trade first. You are "behind" the 98 units that must trade first. In the display at right, the red "x" button will cancel the order, but for now, keep the order active.

	20.20	79	
	20.10	26	
	20.00		
52	20	19.90	
	51	19.80	
	63	19.70	

(a)

	20.20	79	
	20.10	26	
	20.00		
52 (20)	72	19.90	
	51	19.80	
	63	19.70	

(b)

Click on the GO button about 25 times to advance the time clock until several sell orders reduce the quantity ahead of the order to just 23.

	20.30	32	
	20.20	29	
	20.10		
	20.00		
50 (0)	50	19.90	
	51	19.80	

(c)

Click GO several more times until a market sell order for 45 causes a trade, leaving a limit order to buy 30.

	20.20	1	
	20.10		
	20.00		
24 (0)	60	19.90	
	51	19.80	
	80	19.70	

(d)

The next arriving sell market order executes the remaining 30 of your order, leaving you with no orders on the book and a long position of 52.

	20.30	95	
	20.20	45	
	20.10	26	
	20.00		
	58	19.90	
	97	19.80	

(e)

FIGURE 4.6 TraderEx order book market before and after limit order execution.

buy at $19.90 are filled. Therefore, you will see that the actions of others in the market will both compete with your interests, if you are both seeking to buy, and complement or benefit your actions, if they are sellers when you are trying to buy.

3. The TraderEx order book is a level playing field and does not distinguish among the possible sources of orders in establishing the market's priorities for trade execution.

   There is equal treatment of buy and sell instructions from you, and those generated by the simulation to represent orders from public customers, market maker–dealers, proprietary traders, informed participants, and momentum players. Unlike some real-world markets that give priority to orders that are larger, or that are from public participants (rather than dealer intermediaries), the playing field for all orders in the TraderEx book is level.

THE SELL-SIDE INTERMEDIARY PERSPECTIVE

So far, we have discussed the perspective of an investor using the market to build a position and to later reduce it. Now we examine the intermediation activities of traders who are proprietary players or market makers. Market makers generally have a formal designation in a quote driven marketplace to post continuous two-sided quotes during the trading day. Proprietary traders do not have formal obligations, but participate in the market at their own discretion and use their own risk capital to carry out short-term trading strategies in both order driven and quote driven markets. Quote driven, competing dealer platforms are a prevalent trading structure for many options exchanges, and for bond and currency markets, and they are often used for less actively traded equities in some stock exchanges.[*]

Quote driven platforms display bid and ask quotes from multiple competing market makers. Trades occur when customers enter market orders that are routed to a dealer. The dealer receiving an order trades it at the offer price for customer buy orders, and at the bid quote for customer sell orders. The dealers or market makers trade from their own inventory, meaning that, if they start from a flat (i.e., zero) position, they become long when they receive sell orders, and short when they receive buy orders.

---

[*]For instance, in the United States, the OTC Bulletin Board (OTCBB) displays real-time quotes, last-sale prices, and volume information in over-the-counter (OTC) equity securities not listed or traded on Nasdaq or a national securities exchange. The London Stock Exchange's SETSqx supports quote driven market making and four electronic auctions a day, and its SEAQ is a quote driven platform for fixed income and other securities not traded on either SETS or SETSqx.

From the trading desk perspective, effective participation in quote driven markets requires knowledge of:

1. The rules of dealer market making, which include:
   - minimum quote sizes.
   - preferencing of orders to dealers not making the best quotes.
   - inter-dealer trading—when one dealer sells to or buys from another dealer.
2. How a market maker sets quotes in response to long or short positions and the order flow.
3. How market makers control their risk and earn profits from trading the order flow.

Quote Driven Market Dynamics

Before we start doing trading exercises, consider how a dealer market operates. Figure 4.7 shows part of the dealer market screen that is similar to what you will see during the simulation exercises. It shows the three best bids to buy and the three best offers to sell.

The best bid is from you (ME) at$ 20.80 and the best offer is $20.90 from Fox, a competing dealer. Quotes from a third dealer, Lion, are shown but are inferior to the best bid and offer. The quantities that can be traded at those prices are capped at 99 units. Quotes to buy are on the left side, and (reading from the top down) they

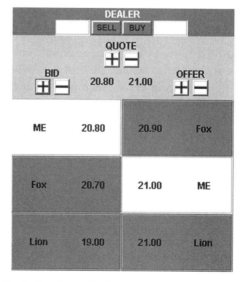

FIGURE 4.7 TraderEx dealer quote display.

are ordered from the highest price to the lowest price. Offers are on the right side of the book, and (reading from the top down) are arranged from lowest price to the highest price.

Based on this screen, a customer entering a Buy Order for 50 would purchase at $20.90 and, without preferencing, Dealer Fox would be the seller.

Based on the screen shown, and with strict price priority, you are the only dealer eligible to buy at $20.80 from incoming sell orders. Assuming that you have a flat position (are neither long nor short), if five large sell orders arrived, how would you want to change your bid quote? Those orders, if they averaged 50 units each, would leave you with a long position of 250, which might be beyond your position limit. What change should you make to your offer quote to reduce your position risk? What market dynamics would enable you to profit or to avoid losses from having taken this inventory position?

With your position at 250 long, what type and size order would you consider sending to another dealer?

You'll have a number of chances to answer these questions for yourself in the exercises that follow. They will help you become familiar with market orders and limit orders, and the setting of dealer quotes.

To recap the quote driven structure in TraderEx:

- In the TraderEx quote driven display, there are only market orders.
- Market orders trade at the best bid quote if selling, and at the best offer quote if buying.
- TraderEx's dealer market can operate with strict price priority, or with preferencing (with preferencing, a dealer who is not making the best quote can nonetheless receive an order).
- TraderEx dealer quotes are good for up to 99 units of stock. After trades of their own or trades involving other dealers, the TraderEx dealers will often change their quotes. Of course, a dealer cannot adjust quotes after he has received an order. He must honor the quotes displayed when the order arrives. Therefore, the positioning of your quotes to buy and to sell will be a key determinant of your P&L and of the success that you will have.

In the Figure 4.7 display, assume that by being on the bid at $20.80 you buy 250 units, and then reduce your bid to $20.60 and lower your offer to $20.90.

1. If you sell the 250 at the offer price, what is your realized profit? What is the return on your initial position?

   Realized P&L = 250 × ($20.90 − $20.80) = $25.00
   Return = $25.00 / (250 × $20.80) = 0.48%, or 48 basis points

2. What is the realized P&L if the dealer sells 100 of the position at $20.90, then lowers his or her offer to $20.80 to sell 100 more?

Realized P&L = (100 × $20.90) + (100 × $20.80) − (200 × $20.80) = $10.00

The dealer still has a position of 50. What is the unrealized P&L on the 50 unit position, if the bid quote is $20.70?

Unrealized P&L = (Mark-to-Market Value of Long Position) − (Cost of Position)
= (50 × $20.70) − (50 × $20.80) = −$5.00

As you see, a dealer capturing the bid–ask spread will earn a profit. Is it always possible for a dealer with a long or short position to earn the bid–ask spread? The answer is "not always."

TRADEREX PERFORMANCE MEASURES

So far, we have focused on investment returns and on P&L as indicators of a trader's success. In real markets and in TraderEx, trading performance needs to be assessed with regard to risk. The applicable risk measures for a trader will depend on the trader's role, time horizon, and trading objective. The three trader roles that are incorporated in TraderEx are a buy-side institutional trader, a market maker, and a proprietary trader.[*] These roles and their associated objectives and risks are shown in Table 4.1.

TraderEx displays three broad measures of how you are performing against the objectives: beat VWAP, control Risk, and generate a good P&L. A fourth objective is *getting the job done*, or completing the trading instruction, whether it is to acquire a 500-unit position, or to trade as a dealer and return to a zero position at the close. The dashboard at the bottom of your TraderEx screen (see Figure 4.8) displays the first three metrics.

Volume Weighted Average Price (VWAP)

VWAP is the Volume Weighted Average Price; it reflects the price that the average share traded at during a day or other time period. It is a common trading benchmark. VWAP is computed as the ratio of the dollar transaction volume to share volume over the time horizon used. To illustrate, if three trades occur in a one hour

---

[*]Outcomes in simulations should always be thought of as samples from a distribution. A better trading result using, say 80 percent limit orders to fill an order, rather than 80 percent market orders, could be a result of the particular "sample path" provided by the Scenario Number used and the chosen parameter settings. On the other hand, the chance of four trials using one trading strategy leading to four outcomes better than an alternative strategy is just one in 16. It is therefore very unlikely that the strategies are equally effective. We can say, at the 94 percent confidence level, that the strategy tested is truly better than the alternative and not a result of random variations in experimental trials.

TABLE 4.1 Roles You Will Play in TraderEx Simulation Exercises

	Trader Role		
	Buy-Side-Handling Institutional Orders	**Market Making**	**Proprietary Trading**
Source of value added	Pricing, timing, and sizing of orders placed	Bid–ask spread, short-term price trends	Short-term price trends, market timing
Trading objective	Minimize transactions cost, contribute to investment alpha Complete trading instructions	Meet market's dealer obligations, positive P&L, control risk, trade to keep position within a limit End the day with a small or flat position	Positive P&L, control risk, trade to keep position within a limit Small or zero position at end
Time horizon	Several hours to several days	Intraday	Intraday

period—1,000 shares at $20.00, 5,000 shares at $20.50, and 10,000 shares at $21.00, we have:

$$\text{VWAP} = \frac{20.00 \times 1,000 + 20.50 \times 5,000 + 21.00 \times 10,000}{1,000 + 5,000 + 10,000} = 20.78125$$

One day, intraday, or multiday VWAP measures are also looked at. VWAP is regarded as a good approximation of the price an average trader with a reasonably small order will achieve in a trading day. Since it reflects a well-understood average, a trader's VWAP performance reflects whether he/she sold for more than the average sale or bought for less than the average purchase. The VWAP score in TraderEx will be greater, the more your average buying and selling prices improve upon the VWAP price.

The VWAP score is calculated as:

$$\text{VWAP score} = \text{your total buy volume} \times (\text{VWAP} - \text{average buy price}) + \text{your total sell volume} \times (\text{average sell price} - \text{VWAP})$$

Buying below VWAP and selling at greater than the current VWAP will contribute to a higher VWAP score.

VWAP	Risk	More Stats	Score			
VWAP: 22.446	P & L: 54.00	RISK: 843700.75	% DONE: 75.00			TOTAL: 76.447
Weight: 100	Weight: 100	Weight: 0%	Weight: 0			

FIGURE 4.8 TraderEx dashboard of performance measures.

Risk

Risk in TraderEx is a function of the target position that a trader has for the end of the day. For instance, a buy-side trader may be seeking to acquire a long position of 500 units in a trading day, while a market maker or proprietary trader wants to end the day with a flat (0) position. The risk a market maker incurs is proportional to the size of the positions they hold during the day. A market maker with a position of 400 long has twice the exposure to a price drop of a market maker who is long 200. Figure 4.9 illustrates the positions held by a dealer over a trading day. The opening position is zero, and he/she later becomes long, holding the largest position sometime after midday. Since risk is the potential for losses, larger positions, either long or short, carry the risk of greater losses from adverse price changes.

TraderEx will measure your risk as the time-weighted average absolute value of the positions you carry during a simulation. Technically, TraderEx takes a snapshot of your position every minute. In the default day length, 9:30 A.M. – 4 P.M., your average position will be based on 390 equally weighted observations. Throughout the day, the average will be computed and displayed based on the number of minutes that have elapsed so far. To illustrate, consider the first 30 minutes of trading for a dealer who kept a flat (0) position for 10 minutes, then bought 50, 70, and 90 units after 10 minutes, 15 minutes, and 20 minutes, respectively, has elapsed. After 25 minutes elapsed, he sold 80. The position was then 130 for the next five minutes. At this point, the risk will be calculated as:

$$
\begin{aligned}
\text{Average Position Risk} &= \frac{\sum_{i=1}^{N} |\text{Position\_at\_i}|}{N} \\
&= \frac{(10 \times 0) + (5 \times 50) + (5 \times 120) + (5 \times 210) + (5 \times 130)}{30} \\
&= 85.0
\end{aligned}
$$

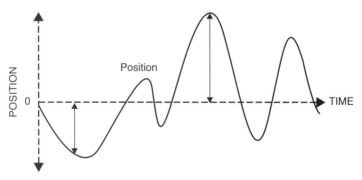

FIGURE 4.9 TraderEx measures dealer risk as the size of the average absolute value of the position.

TraderEx will compute the distance between the position line and the X-axis as the average risk at any point in time, and the average of these distances is the risk level taken over a full simulation.

How can we assess the risk of a buy-side trader who is expected to fill an order to buy 1,000 units over a trading day? Instead of risk measured as the absolute distance of the position from 0 at a point in time, TraderEx computes risk as the size of the gap between the buy-side trader's position and the position that he would have if he paced his buying evenly over the day to reach the target position at the end of the day. Figure 4.10 shows a trader acquiring a 1,000-unit position with three bursts of buying that maintained a position fairly close to the evenly paced line for the 1,000-unit instruction to buy.

Figure 4.11 shows another trader who is also acquiring a 1,000 unit position. This trader took more risk by waiting until the final 30 minutes to complete the bulk of the buy instruction. If the end-of-day prices turn out to be relatively high, this trader will have lost profits relative to a more evenly paced approach to the buy instruction. It is possible, of course, that the lowest price of the day came at the end of trading. But what trader could know ahead of time that this would happen? The advantage such a large late trade provides has to be balanced against the added risk that was taken.

Figure 4.12 shows that TraderEx provides a collar around the evenly paced buying or selling line. Small deviations from the evenly paced line are expected. Your risk score, however, will be worse the more time your position is outside the collars. The tightness of the collars applied to real traders is controllable in the TraderEx software settings, so that tighter collars are placed on a "green horn" than on a more seasoned trader.

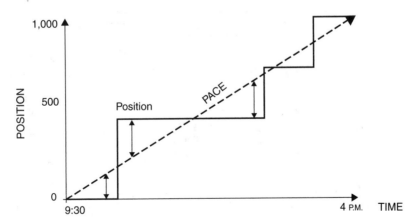

FIGURE 4.10 Buy-side risk as time-weighted distance of actual position from evenly-paced line to reach target position of 1,000.

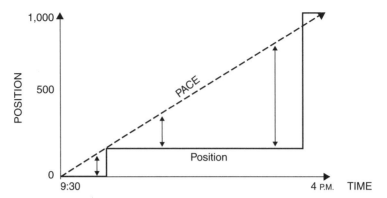

FIGURE 4.11 A buy-side trader acquiring a 1,000-unit position with a greater risk level from acquiring the position unevenly over time.

Figure 4.13 shows the risk collars that TraderEx imposes on a market maker or proprietary trader. This trader has an opening position limit of 2,000 but must return to a flat (0) position by day's end. The risk penalty will cumulate when the position is outside of the collars. The tightness of the collars is controllable by raising or lowering the position limit parameter. Again, smaller position limits and tighter collars are recommended for novice market makers or proprietary traders.

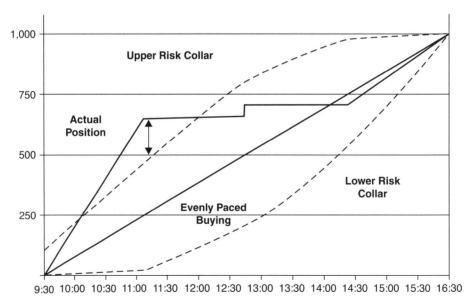

FIGURE 4.12 A buy-side trader instructed to acquire a position of 1,000 long. Risk penalty for time when actual position is outside of the collars.

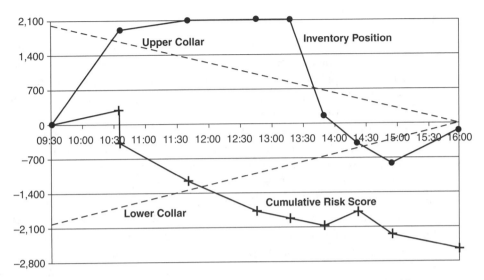

FIGURE 4.13 Cumulative risk penalty for an intermediary with a goal of having a zero position overnight.

When you are outside the collars, the Risk Score is a penalty amount that is the sum of the vertical distances (measured every minute) from the upper or lower risk collars. When you are inside the collar, points are added to the score as a reward, for each minute that you are inside the collar. The even "Pace" amount, and the long and short collars, are shown in the dashboard at the bottom of the TraderEx screen (see Figure 4.14).

When you are within the risk collars, points are added to offset any no risk penalty assessed. In the Figure 4.13 illustration, a small positive bonus is added to the Risk Score for having a position value that is between the low collar value and the high collar value. The risk score is calculated as the points for being within the collar minus the risk penalty.

$$\text{Risk Score} = \sum \text{Max}\,(0, \text{Min}(|\,\text{Position}\,| - |\,\text{Collar LOW}\,|, |\text{Position}| - |\text{CollarHIGH}|))$$

The risk measure will accumulate over the simulation when your position is outside of the position collars. You lower your total score the more often you are outside the position collars and the further out you are.

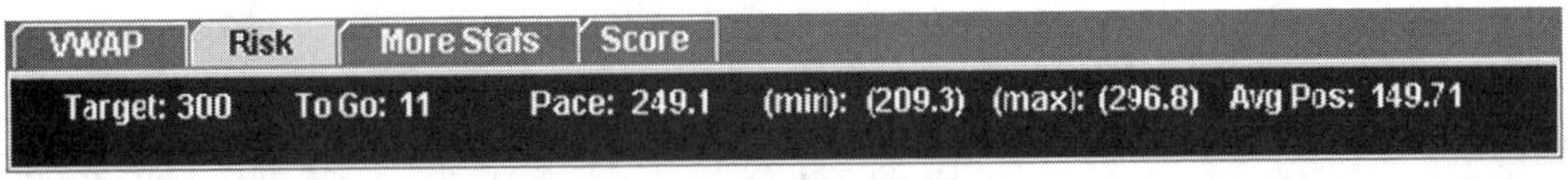

VWAP	Risk	More Stats	Score					
Target: 300		To Go: 11		Pace: 249.1	(min): (209.3)	(max): (296.8)	Avg Pos: 149.71	

FIGURE 4.14 User position of +289 is less than the lower risk collar (209). The upper collar is 296.

Profit

The third measure of performance in TraderEx is the P&L that you achieve. Profits and losses in trading are generated from holding a long position when prices rise, or having a short position when the price falls. Realized P&L is actual money in the bank from buying at prices less than what you sell at. Unrealized P&L is the result of marking a position to market. When you have an open, nonzero share position in TraderEx, it will assess the mark-to-market value of your open position, and your unrealized profit. Trading positions that are long are marked-to-market at the bid price, and short positions are marked-to-market at the offer.

Table 4.2 provides an illustration: start with zero shares and zero cash, buy 80 units at $20.00, next sell 50 at $20.10, and then sell 30 at $19.95. The initial trade cost $1,600, and the two sales generated $1,603.50 in proceeds, leaving the trader with a flat position in the shares, and a cash position and *realized profit* of $3.50.

At 10 A.M. in the example above, the trading position is +30. Assume for illustration purposes that the bid is $19.90. As a result, at 10 A.M., you would have a realized profit of $5 ($0.10 gain per share × 50 units) and an unrealized loss of $3.00 (=$0.10 × 30), for a total mark-to-market P&L of +$2.

TraderEx will show your P&L results in the Stats display and in My History. In Figure 4.15, the trader has bought 88 units and sold 25. Can you account for the $2.41 and $8.59 in Realized and Unrealized P&L?

Here is how you do it. The average paid for the 88 units bought was $20.064, and the 25 units sold were sold at an average price of $20.160. TraderEx values all positions at the average paid or received, so the trader therefore has realized

TABLE 4.2 Example Calculation of P&L for a Sequence of Three Trades

Time	B/S	Units	Price	Cash Position ($0)	Position (0)
9:41:25 A.M.	Buy	80	$20.00	−$1,600.00	80
9:55:49 A.M.	Sell	−50	$20.10	+$1,050.00	30
10:03:01 A.M.	Sell	−30	$19.95	+$598.50	0
				+$3.50	0

STATS			
Net Position:	63	Realized P&L:	$2.41
Cash:	($1,261.60)	Unrealized P&L:	$8.59
My Avg Cost:	$20.06		

FIGURE 4.15 Performance measures in TraderEx screen. Long positions are marked to market at the bid, and short positions are marked to market at the offer.

VWAP		Risk		More Stats		Score				
VWAP:	22.446	P & L :	54.00	RISK:	843700.75	% DONE:	75.00	TOTAL:	76.447	
Weight:	100	Weight:	100	Weight:	0%	Weight:	0			

FIGURE 4.16 Dashboard of performance measures at bottom of TraderEx screen with total score at the right.

$25 \times 0.096 = \$2.41$ in profit. The trader's position of 63 therefore is valued at \$20.20 per share, implying an unrealized profit of $\$8.59 = 63 \times (\$20.20 - \$20.064)$.

$$P\&L \ Score = Realized \ Profit + Unrealized \ Profit$$

Figure 4.16 illustrates the components that go into the user's total score in a simulation.

Job Completion

A final performance measure is the extent to which you completed the trading instruction given to you. The final end-of-game message

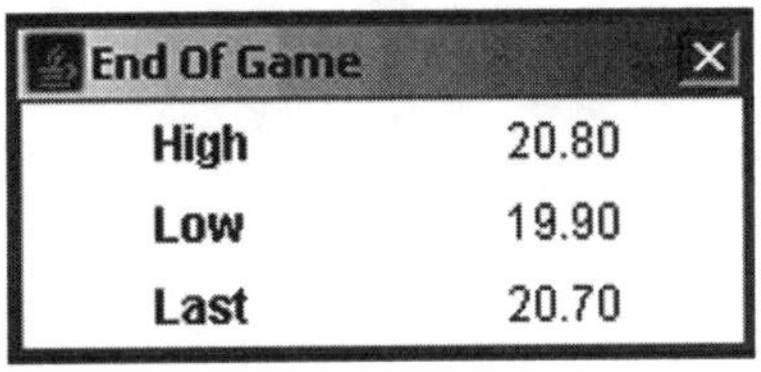

End Of Game	✕
High	20.80
Low	19.90
Last	20.70

will report a completion percentage that will be applied to your final score.

The completion measure is computed as:

$$Completion \ Percentage = 1 - \frac{|Target - Net \ Position|}{|Target|}$$

A trader who is instructed to buy 500, but ends the day long 450 will have his/her final score multiplied by the completion percentage of $1 - (50/500) = 0.90$. In other words, a 10 percent score reduction. Likewise, overshooting the instruction quantity by buying 550 when the instruction was to end the day long 500 will reduce the score by 10 percent.

In TraderEx, a weighted score, Total Score is computed from the four performance measures: VWAP comparison, Risk incurred, P&L generated, and percent completed. The measures can be weighted equally or tilted partly or entirely to one of the metrics. The software will also adjust for the mean and standard deviation of the scores. Our adjustment ensures that each component influences your score depending on whether it is above or below its expected value. As you complete the exercises in Chapters 5 through 9, these measures will enable you to assess your performance, and to reflect on how trading decisions influence outcomes that reward or punish you as a trader according to the weights assigned to each of the performance measures.

SUMMARY

Trading presents a number of decision making challenges, and TraderEx was developed to create realistic market situations for you to respond to. The exercises that follow in the book will put you in different buy-side and sell-side roles. This chapter described the different perspective that each role brings. It also emphasized the need to consider the full set of performance and risk measures that the simulation provides.

PART TWO

TraderEx Exercises

CHAPTER 5

Microeconomics Goes to Market

Microeconomics is about the functioning of a market and the forces that determine prices. With the eyes of a microeconomist, let's look at a particularly important and intriguing market that is the central focus of this book: an equity market where stock shares are traded. Important economic principles can be identified with reference to equity trading, and this chapter will give you a number of exercises that do this. The exercises cover eight topics:

5.1 What a financial market looks like.

5.2 Attitudes toward risk.

5.3 Supply and demand curves as seen in call auction trading.

5.4 The impact of trading costs on participant behavior and market outcomes.

The exercises in this chapter are based on material from Robert A. Schwartz, *Micro Markets: A Market Structure Presentation of Microeconomics*, John Wiley and Sons, 2010.

5.5 Cost and inventory control for a dealer firm.

5.6 Competition between different market venues.

5.7 The dynamic process of finding equilibrium prices.

5.8 The economic effects of a specific governmental regulatory initiative (an order protection rule).

EXERCISE 5.1: THE LOOK OF A FINANCIAL MARKET

The order driven market is a particularly good equity market structure to get started with. You can call up an order driven platform as follows:

1. Go to www.eTraderEx.net. You will see the following screen:

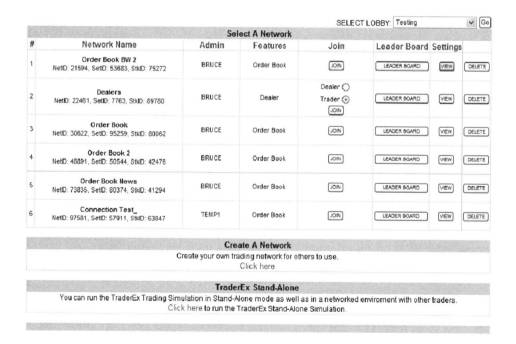

2. To log in, follow the on-screen instructions as stated at the beginning of Chapter 3.

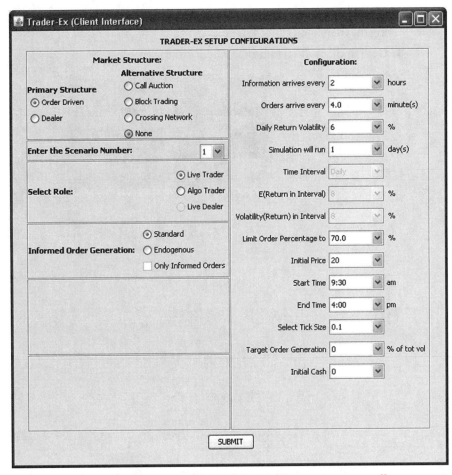

3. Click "Click Here" to launch the standalone. The next screen allows you to configure the simulation:

We refer to this as the "initial configuration screen." This is the starting point for all of the stand alone simulations.

4. The Market Structure, by default, is Order Driven without any alternative trading mechanisms. Click "SUBMIT."

5. Get familiar with TraderEx's limit order:

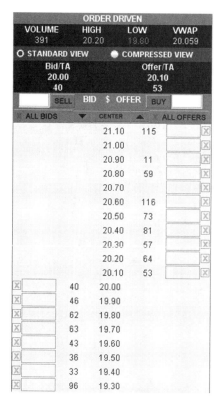

On the TraderEx screen, you will see limit orders that have been placed on the *limit order book*. Recall that a *limit order* means that a price limit has been placed on the order (for a buy order the limit is the highest price that the buyer is willing to pay, while for a sell order the limit is the lowest price that the seller is willing to receive). In this illustration, the highest price any buyer will pay is $20.00, and the lowest price any seller will accept is $20.10.

6. Enter a few buy and sell limit orders simply to get the feel of being part of the market.
   - Do you want to buy? Enter a buy limit at a price of your choosing.
   - Do you want to sell? Enter a sell limit at a price of your choosing.
   - Do you want to do both? Enter both a sell limit and a buy limit—you are allowed to do this, but note that your sell limit must be at a higher price than the best posted bid, and your buy limit must be at a lower price than the best posted offer.

Basic Order Types

There is another way that you can buy and sell: you can enter a *market order*. The order entry boxes for doing this are next to the "SELL" and "BUY" buttons at the top of the limit order book.

- If you buy "at market," you buy at the lowest posted offer (assuming that the quoted size at the offer is large enough to cover the size of your order).
- If you sell "at market," you sell at the highest posted bid (again, assuming that the book at that price has sufficient depth).

Enter several market orders:

- Enter several orders that are larger than the best posted limit orders on the market, and you will see how your own orders can impact market prices.
- Consider what would happen if you enter a market order to buy 50 units. An order of 50 units is larger than the best posted limit orders in the book.

When you click on "BUY," you will see the price impact your relatively large order will have. As you do so, think about whether you would consider the market that you are looking at to be relatively liquid or illiquid.

1. Make a note of your cash position, of the best (lowest) sell quote on the book, and of the best (highest) buy quote on the book.
2. Next, enter a market order to buy one round lot, and then follow it immediately with a market order to sell one round lot.

Have the quotes changed while you have done this? Hopefully (for this demonstration) they have not. In any event, you just made one round trip for one round lot. How did your cash position change? No commission was charged, but did you have to pay something for your purchase and your sale?

Enter two limit orders, one a limit order to buy one tick below the best (highest) bid, and the other a limit order to sell one tick above the best (lowest) offer. Let the market advance for one hour on the machine clock and then stop the simulation.

- Did either or both of your limit orders execute?
- If both of your orders executed, you did a round trip; note what that did for your cash position.
- If one of your orders executed, how do you feel about it given the price that the stock was trading at after one hour, when you ended the simulation run.
- Were you hurt by one (or neither) of your orders executing?
- Did you profit or lose because one (or both) of your orders did execute?

Sell and Buy Orders as Supply and Demand

Buy and sell pressures interact in a marketplace to produce transaction prices and trading volume. You can think of these buy and sell pressures as *demand and supply*. Our basic microeconomic models show how demand and supply jointly determine price and quantity in a marketplace. For now, think about how the limit buy orders on the book collectively reflect the demand propensities (to buy shares) that have been expressed in the market, and how the limit sell orders on the book similarly reflect the supply propensities (to sell shares) that have been expressed in the market.

Note that all of the displayed buy orders are at prices lower than the prices of all of the displayed sell orders. The reason for this is that whenever a buy order matches or crosses a sell order, a trade is made and the two orders are taken off of the book. Note also that the price of the highest priced buy order is discretely below (one or more price ticks below) the price of the lowest priced sell order.

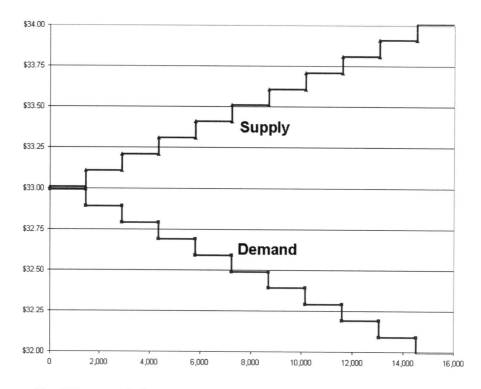

The difference (the lowest sell price minus the highest buy price) is the *bid–ask spread*. When the market is in balance, the equilibrium price for the stock lies within the bid–ask spread.

How do market orders fit into the buy/sell (demand/supply) desires that have been expressed in the market? Until a market order (or any order, for that matter) has been entered, it represents an *unexpressed* propensity to trade. When a market buy order arrives, it can be thought of as part of the buy curve (demand curve) that extends above the current equilibrium price. Similarly, when a market sell order arrives, it can be thought of as part of the sell curve (supply curve) that extends below the current equilibrium price.

A price limit can be placed on a market order, although we do not do this in TraderEx for the machine driven orders or for the market orders that you submit. But you can control the price impact of your market orders by submitting them in pieces that enable you to "walk the book" (walk up, that is, with a large buy order, or walk down with a large sell order) without going further than you wish to go. For now, consider a situation where an array of participants will in effect put price limits on their market orders. Now visualize all of the buy orders (limit and market) being aggregated from the highest priced buy to the lowest priced buy, and all of the sell orders (limit and market) being aggregated from the lowest priced sell to the highest priced sell:

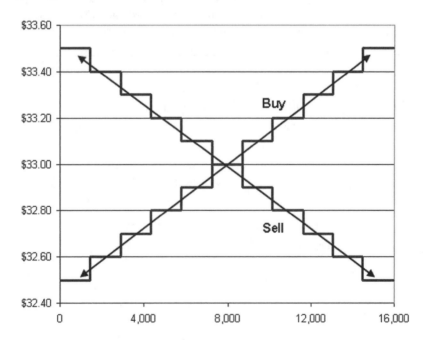

These two aggregates resemble the demand and supply schedules (or, if graphed, the demand and supply curves) that microeconomists like to think about. Together, they establish prices and the size of trades. This is what a market is all about.

EXERCISE 5.2: WHAT ARE YOUR ATTITUDES TOWARD RISK?

Microeconomics pays much attention to the concept of risk aversion as it relates to a decision maker's utility function for income (or wealth), and to risk and return indifference curves. Investing in equity shares certainly is risky, and the greater the risk the greater the expected return that a risk-averse investor will require before acquiring an equity position.

But why are people risk-averse? The microeconomic answer to this question has nothing to do with the pleasure or displeasure per se that a person might get from accepting a risky situation, and it has everything to do with the individual's attitudes toward income and wealth. More specifically, for risk-averse people, marginal utility from income (or wealth) decreases as income (or wealth) increases. A risk-averse person prefers adding $100 to their wealth with certainty, to having a 50/50 chance at $200 or nothing at all being added to wealth.

Perhaps the link between diminishing utility of income (or wealth) and risk aversion is an abstract concept for you. If so, this exercise is designed to sharpen your understanding of your own attitude toward risk. So let's get at it. From the initial configuration screen in Figure 5.1, make sure "Order Driven" is selected for the primary structure and "None" for alternative structure.

1. Set Initial Cash to $10,000.

2. Using the pull-down menu, set the seed number to 1.

3. Set Number of days to 2.

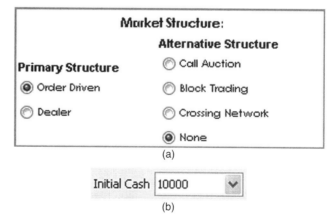

(a)

(b)

FIGURE 5.1 Setting the Market Structure and the initial cash from the initial configuration screen.

- If the number of days is greater than 1, you can set the time interval jumps between the days, and the expected drift and volatility over that time interval (see Chapter 3 for more details).

Enter the Scenario Number:	1 ⌄

(a)

Simulation will run | 1 ⌄ | day(s)

(b)

Time Interval | Daily ⌄ |

(c)

4. Set the Time Interval to Annual from the pull-down menu. Then set the E(Return in Interval) to 5 percent for this first exercise. Set the Volatility to 5 percent.

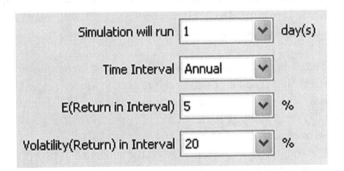

As you see from your cash and shares statistics on the screen, we are starting you off with $10,000 of cash in your simulated account, and with zero shares of the risky asset. Each simulation run for this exercise comprises two trading days that are separated by one year.

- On day 1, which is at the beginning of the year, you are a buyer. By buying, you establish a position that you will hold for one year.
- On day 2, which is at the end of the year, you are a seller. By selling, you liquidate your position and turn your shares back into cash. Hopefully you will have more cash at the end of day 2 than you had at the beginning of day 1.

5. Once you have established your position in the market, click "FF" to advance to the next trading day:

6. Your ending cash position divided by your opening cash position, minus one, is the rate of return, r, that you will have realized for each simulation run.

$$r = \frac{C_1}{C_0} - 1$$

7. Once the simulation parameters have been set, the stock's one-year return from the end of day 1 to the start of day 2 is out of your control. The computer determines this return by randomly drawing from a (lognormal) returns distribution (Figure 5.2 displays a distribution of returns for a risky investment that is expected to rise 5 percent) that has a mean (the expected return) and a variance (the risk). You will see this one-year return virtually instantaneously.

8. For each simulation run, you have five minutes (clock time) on day 1 to establish your stock position, and five minutes on day 2 to trade out of your stock position and see how well you have done. With so little time to trade, you have almost no discretion in how you handle your orders to buy and to sell. You do not have to acquire $10,000 worth of shares in just one purchase, however. In fact, an attempt to do so may result in your buying at an unnecessarily high price. Accordingly, break up your order and trade carefully, both on day 1, when you put on your position, and on day 2, when you liquidate your position. If you buy at relatively high prices on day 1 and sell at relatively low prices on day 2, your one-year return will, accordingly, be relatively low.

In this exercise, however, we focus on the investment return and deemphasize the effect that trading costs can have on the longer period return. We achieve this focus by giving you very short trading periods (just five minutes of clock time on each day) and a highly liquid market (a speedy execution of a $10,000 order should have a minimal impact on your one-year return).

For this exercise, you set two parameters at the start of each simulation run: the expected return [E(r)] and the standard deviation [SD(r)]. Use these four combinations:

E(r)	SD(r)
.05	.20
.20	.05
.05	.05
.20	.20

For each of the four combinations, run the simulation enough times so that you get some high returns (above the mean) and some low returns (below the mean). Then do the following:

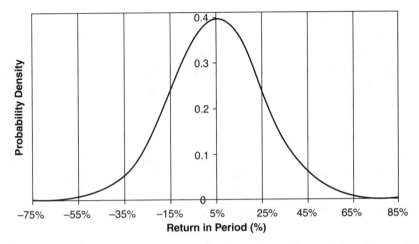

FIGURE 5.2 Normal curve showing a distribution of annual returns in a time period. Expected return is 5 percent and the standard deviation of returns is 20 percent.

1. Make note of the high return, the low return, and the average return realized for each combination, and rank the combinations according to your preference.

2. For each of the four combinations, explain whether the expected return was high enough (in your opinion) to compensate you for the risk involved.

3. If you are particularly satisfied or dissatisfied with a specific risk–return combination, explain why.

4. Try a couple of other E(r), SD(r) combinations in an attempt to locate two combinations that you would be indifferent between (that is, which in the terminology of microeconomics would put you on the same indifference curve).

By the end of this exercise, you should better understand how your attitude toward risk is related to your utility function for income (or wealth) rather than your tastes or distastes for any risk-taking activity itself.

EXERCISE 5.3: CALL MARKET TRADING

The primary purpose of this exercise is to demonstrate price and quantity determination in a market that comprises a large number of traders. The trading facility that is used for this exercise is the call auction. Call auctions are being widely used today in equity markets around the world to open markets at the start of each trading day, and to close markets at the end of each trading day. In call auction trading, orders are brought together for simultaneous execution at a single (predetermined) point in time, at a single price, in one big multilateral trade. This is in contrast with continuous trading where a trade is triggered at any moment in continuous time that a buy order matches or crosses a sell order in price. We get you started with a call auction in this exercise, and then focus in more depth on this trading facility in Chapter 7.

In the TraderEx call, like in most real-world call auctions, buy and sell orders are entered during a pre-call, order entry period. During this period, an indicated clearing price is displayed. The indicated clearing price is determined by cumulating the buy orders from the highest priced orders to the lowest, cumulating the sell orders from the lowest priced orders to the highest, and by then matching the two cumulated order columns to find the price that maximizes the number of shares that trade.

At the time of the call, the book is frozen and, following the procedure we just described for determining the indicated clearing price, the final clearing price is set. All buy orders at the clearing price and higher are executable, as are all sell orders at the clearing price and lower. If executable buys do not equal executable sells exactly, the heavy side of the market is rationed according to the time priority rule (the first orders placed execute first). If two different prices result in the same maximum number of shares that would execute, the clearing price that is selected is the value that minimizes the absolute size of the buy–sell imbalance.

With the call auction environment that we have just described, we can see how buy and sell orders are integrated together to set the common market clearing price and the exact set of orders that execute. You can think of the market clearing price as the equilibrium value that microeconomists like to model. Sorting and cumulating buy orders, starting with the highest buy limit price and moving down to successively lower values, gives us a schedule that resembles a demand schedule. Sorting and cumulating sell orders starting with the lowest sell limit price and moving up to successively higher values, gives us a schedule that resembles a supply schedule. If you were to graph these two schedules, you would essentially be looking at a demand curve and at a supply curve.

What price maximizes the number of shares that trade? The value where the demand curve intersects the supply curve. Perhaps when you see this you will agree that a call auction is a microeconomist's dream.

With this as background:

1. Open the initial configuration screen and select "Order Driven" for the primary structure and "Call Auction" as the alternative structure.

2. Make sure that all three call check boxes (opening, midday, and closing) are selected, that the execution priority is "Price/Time," and that the visibility is

set to "Transparent." Your initial configuration parameters should look like this:

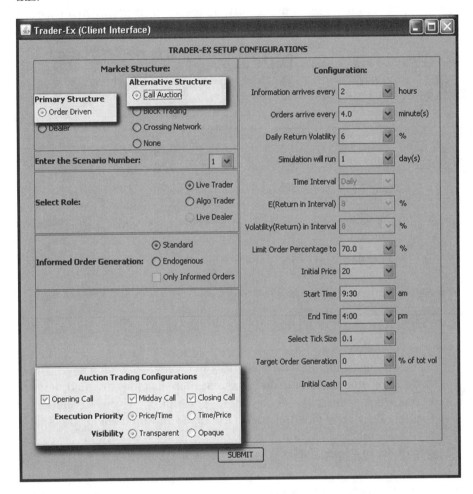

3. Set the scenario to 1. Make sure that the tick size is set to $0.10 for this simulation.

4. Click on "Submit." You will see a book of orders that have already been submitted. Note the following:
   - Price is a discrete variable (we have set the tick size at 10¢).
   - The buy orders and the sell orders are rank ordered. In accordance with the cumulation procedure that we have just described, the TraderEx screen shows at each price the total number of shares that have been entered at that price and at all prices that are more aggressive (i.e., at higher prices for the buys and at lower prices for the sells).

- The screen shows that shares are being offered for sale at prices that are equal to and lower than some of the prices at which shares are being sought for purchase. Consequently, trades will be made when the market is "called."

MARKET CALL					
Indicative 19.80			Imbalance 484		
	BIDS		OFFERS		
X	0	113	20.30	2051	0	X
X	0	172	20.20	1794	0	X
X	0	260	20.10	1523	0	X
X	0	427	20.00	1189	0	X
X	0	823	19.90	963	0	X
X	0	1337	19.80	853	0	X
X	0	1752	19.70	569	0	X
X	0	1869	19.60	417	0	X
X	0	1904	19.50	255	0	X
X	0	1978	19.40	146	0	X
X	0	1978	19.30	127	0	X

In this simulation, we will give you a last mover advantage. You can advance the simulation a bit more and see some more machine driven orders come in. Then the process will stop. When it does, you can enter your orders and, in so doing, affect the market clearing price. Of course you would not get this special treatment in an actual call auction, but for our purposes it is a useful device for showing a number of things. This is what we would like you to do:

1. Before you enter any orders of your own, identify the clearing price that will maximize the number of machine entered shares that will trade. As you do this, keep in mind the following. At each price, the number of shares that will trade is the minimum of two numbers: the number of shares sought for purchase and the number of shares offered for sale. The clearing price that you are looking for gives you the maximum of these minimums.

2. With price being a discrete variable, we generally do not have a clean cross, which means that the number of shares to buy does not exactly equal the number of shares to sell. This being the case, a secondary rule of order execution is needed. In TraderEx (and in most call markets), time priority is the secondary

rule (orders that have been entered first execute first). Noting this, and with the clearing price established, identify which orders will execute and which orders will not execute when the market is called.

3. Determine the maximum number (if any) of buy orders that can be entered at the clearing price or higher without raising the clearing price.

4. Determine the maximum number of sell orders (if any) that can be entered at the clearing price or lower without lowering the clearing price.

The cumulated buy column and the cumulated sell column as shown in Figure 5.3a, can be graphed as shown in Figure 5.3b. When graphed, we refer to the cumulated columns as "buy and sell *curves*." The intersection of the buy and sell curves establishes a price that we can consider an equilibrium price. Note that the equilibrium price in the graph will generally differ from the clearing price that is based on the orders that have been submitted. What explains this?

The answer lies in the discreteness of prices and order sizes. The clearing price is generally not determined by a clean cross, while the equilibrium price in the graph appears to be at a value where a clean cross is identified. Actually, it is not. The buy and sell curves may look continuous, but we get them by plotting the cumulated buy and sell points and then connecting the points with straight lines. The point where the buy and sell curves cross is generally at a value where two linear connecting lines cross, and this value is generally not at a price that actual trades can be made at. Nevertheless, the graphs are useful.

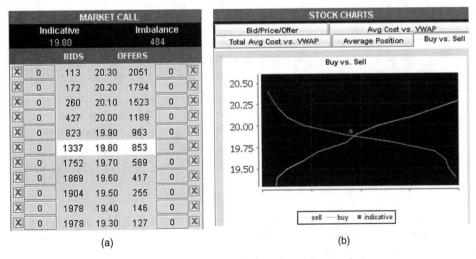

(a)   (b)

FIGURE 5.3 Snapshot of the buy versus sell chart from the simulation screen.

5. As a pedagogical exercise, you can effectively shift one of the curves while keeping the other curve constant by entering a sufficiently large market order to buy or to sell. Do so by entering a large market order to buy and see what happens to the clearing price. Then compute the arc elasticity of the sell curve as the percentage change in transaction volume divided by the percentage change in price[*].

6. You can effectively shift the sell curve to the right (while keeping the buy curve constant) by entering a sufficiently large sell order as a market order. Do so, and see what happens to the clearing price. Then compute the arc elasticity of the buy curve as the percentage change in transaction volume divided by the percentage change in price.

7. Following up on questions 5 and 6, which is greater—the size of your order or the increase in the number of shares that trade? What explains the difference? For question 5, the answer depends on the elasticity of the sell curve; for question 6, the answer depends on the elasticity of the buy curve. Do you see the effect that your sell and buy orders have on the market clearing price?

8. Verify that the less elastic the sell curve is in the neighborhood of the clearing price, the more the clearing price changes in response to the large buy order that you have entered at a high price. Similarly, verify that the less elastic the buy curve is in the neighborhood of the clearing price, the more price changes in response to the large sell order that you have entered at a low price.

9. Large buy and sell orders placed in the neighborhood of the clearing price make these portions of the buy and sell curves more price elastic; they also make the market more liquid. Do you see that, in this context, elasticity and liquidity are essentially one and the same?

10. Enter orders into the call to verify that the buy and sell curves are more elastic when more orders are placed in the neighborhood of the equilibrium price, and that they are less elastic when more buy orders are entered at higher prices and more sell orders are entered at lower prices.

11. If some participants are very optimistic (bullish) about a stock, they would be expected to place higher priced buy orders in the call. Similarly, if some other participants were very pessimistic (bearish) about the stock, they would be expected to place lower priced sell orders in the call. How would a greater

---

[*]The term "arc elasticity" is used when the elasticity is measured using discrete price and quantity changes. With infinitesimal changes, the term "point elasticity" is used. To compute the percentage changes of price and quantity, for both price and quantity sum their initial values and their new values and divide each sum by two.

divergence of expectations between the bulls and the bears affect the elasticity of the buy and sell curves in the neighborhood of the market clearing price?

12. Envision a sequence of calls, and consider the volatility of the clearing price from call to call. How might this volatility be related to the divergence of expectations between the bulls and the bears?

EXERCISE 5.4: TRADING COSTS IN ACTION

This simulation exercise is designed to show you how trading costs can negatively impact portfolio performance.

Trading costs may be thought of as the flip side of the same coin that liquidity (or the lack thereof) is on. Liquidity is a difficult term to define, but we typically know it when we see it. Trading costs, on the other hand, may be easily seen if they are explicit (commissions and taxes, for instance), or they may be difficult to see if they are implicit (market impact, for instance). The bid–ask spread is a trading cost that can be seen if you have access to a transparent trading screen (as you do with TraderEx), but which you will not see on the confirmations that your broker might send you.

Whether visible or not, trading costs can be substantial, but through careful trading they can be controlled. Good trading, in fact, is all about controlling trading costs. This exercise is designed primarily to give you a feel for the importance of trading cost. Other exercises in this book will give you more insight into how trading costs can be kept under control by good trading.

The framework for this exercise is similar to the one that we used for Exercise 5.2. While Exercise 5.2 was designed to make the link between a participant's utility of income (or wealth) and his/her risk aversion more concrete, the current exercise should sharpen your understanding of the impact that trading costs have on longer-run returns. As in Exercise 5.2:

- You start each simulation run with $10,000 of cash in your simulated account and zero shares of a risky asset.
- The simulation will run for two trading days that are separated by one year. On "day 1," which is at the beginning of the year, you buy to establish your position. On "day 2," which is at the end of the year, you sell to liquidate your position and turn your shares back into cash.
- Your ending cash position divided by your opening cash position, minus one, is the percentage return that you will have realized for the simulation run. Once the simulation parameters have been set, the stock's one-year return from the

end of day one to the start of day two is out of your control. The computer determines this return by a random draw from a (lognormal) distribution that has a mean (which is an expected return) and a variance (which is risk).

- From the initial configuration screen, select "Order Driven" and "None" for alternative structure.

Set the initial cash and days as shown in Exercise 5.2. Set the time interval to Annual, the E(Return) to 10 percent, and the Volatility to 30 percent.

For Exercise 5.2, you were given a five-minute period (clock time) on day 1 to establish your equity position, and a five-minute period on day 2 to liquidate your position and see how well you have done. In that previous exercise, on both days, the limit order book was relatively deep (that is, the stock was relatively liquid). These two conditions are changed for this current exercise. The day 1 and day 2 trading periods are considerably longer (approximately twenty minutes of clock time), and the book is considerably thinner. With these two changes, we can redirect your attention from utility curves and risk, to trading costs and returns.

For each simulation run, set both the expected return and the standard deviation of returns equal to 10 percent. At the start of each simulation run, we ask you to set two parameters: the average time between order arrivals measured in minutes [E(ORDERS)], and the average percentage of orders that are limit orders [E(LIMITS)]. Run the simulation for each of the following two markets:

Market	E(ORDERS)	E(LIMITS)
A	3.5 minutes	80 percent
B	6.5 minutes	55 percent

- Set the E(Order) using the pull-down menu to "Orders arrive every 3.5 minutes."
- Set the E(Limits) using the pull-down menu to "Limit Order Percentage to 80%." For instance,

For each market, run the simulation enough times to get a sense of the distribution of returns that you might realize from that market. Then respond to the following:

1. Calculate the one-year return using the day 1 and day 2 closing prices.
2. Which of the two markets is more liquid, A or B?

3. Did you get some high returns in either of these two markets (e.g., greater than 10 percent)? If so, was this because the underlying, one-year return for the stock was high, or because you traded well on day 1 and/or on day 2?

4. Did you get some low returns in either of these two markets (e.g., less than 10 percent)? If so, was this because the underlying, one-year return for the stock was poor, or because you traded poorly on day 1 and/or on day 2?

5. For each of the two markets, what was your average return across the set of simulations that you ran? How does your average return for each market compare with the 10 percent expected return that you set as a parameter for the simulation runs? What might explain any difference?

6. Which was the easier trading environment for you to work your orders in—market A or market B?

7. What thought did you give to each of the following while working your orders in these two markets?:
   - The bid–ask spread
   - Market impact
   - Intra-day price volatility
   - Pressure to invest your $10,000 fully on day 1, and then to sell all of your shares on day 2?

8. Do you now understand better the impact that trading costs can have on realized returns and, in the presence of these costs, that trading requires making strategic decisions?

EXERCISE 5.5: DEALER COSTS AND INVENTORY CONTROL

This exercise will show you the challenge that a dealer firm faces keeping its inventory of shares in reasonable balance as it swings between long and short positions. A dealer firm's main inventory control mechanism is its quote setting. The dealer firm will raise its quotes to work off an excessively large short position, and it will lower its quotes to work off an excessively large long position. The dealer firm's second control mechanism is to trade with other dealers: it will buy in the inter-dealer market to re-liquefy after having acquired an unduly large short position, and it will sell in the inter-dealer market to re-liquefy after having acquired an unduly large long position.

A dealer firm that is willing to accept larger inventory swings will 1) have a larger expected trading volume and 2) operate at a higher level of expected costs.

In this exercise, we would like you to experience these realities by trading as a dealer in our simulated environment. Here is what you can do:

- You will start each simulation run with zero cash and zero shares of the risky asset for which you will be the market maker.
- There are no explicit trading costs in the simulation. You can borrow cash at no cost to buy shares, and you can also sell shares short and pay no stock borrowing costs. In other words, all of the costs in the simulation exercise are implicit.
- You are one of five dealers: you, plus the four machine dealers who are your competitors. You can trade with these dealers (inter-dealer trading), or you can sell shares to the public when customer buy orders arrive, and buy shares from the public when customer sell orders arrive.
- The simulation will run for one trading day.
- Your primary decision is how to set your quotes in light of your inventory position, which itself, in turn, is affected by the flow of orders that you are experiencing. And as noted, you may also trigger trades with the other four dealers.
- Your performance will be assessed according to two alternative metrics: 1) your closing profit and loss (P&L), and 2) a risk measure that is described in Chapter 4.
- Make every effort to bring your share position back to zero by the end of each trading day so that you avoid taking any undue overnight risk.
- From the initial configuration screen, select "Dealer" as the primary market structure and "None" for the alternative structure:

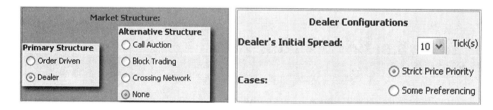

Set the expected order arrival in the pull-down menu to "Orders arrive every 3.5 minutes." Set the SD(Returns) in the pull-down menu to "Daily Return Volatility 10%":

For each simulation run, you will set two parameters: the average time between order arrivals measured in minutes [E(ORDERS)], and the standard deviation of annual returns [SD(RETURNS)]. Run the simulation for each of the following two market settings:

Market	E(ORDERS)	SD(RETURNS)
A	3.5 minutes	10 percent
B	6.5 minutes	5 percent

For each market, run the simulation enough times to get a sense of the distribution of returns that you might realize from that market. Then respond to the following:

1. Which of the two market settings did you prefer to be making a market in, A or B? Be sure to explain the reason for your selection.

2. For the set of simulations that you have run, what was your largest inventory position in absolute value? How did you respond as this position was being reached? Do you think that your response kept you from realizing an even larger imbalance?

3. Contrast your two performance measures for the two different markets, A and B. For which market were your performance measures better?

4. Contrast your P&L measure over successive simulation runs. Do you feel that you did a bit better with experience? Explain why or why not.

5. Contrast your risk measure over successive simulation runs. Do you feel that you did a bit better with experience? Explain why or why not.

6. Were your realized transactions in volume and market share related to the size of your inventory fluctuations?

7. For which measure, P&L or Risk, did your performance improve the most? Can you explain why?

8. On the basis of your simulation experience, did you sense that accepting larger inventory swings was costly to you as a dealer? In standard microeconomic models of a competitive firm, a firm's average cost of doing business is expected to rise after a certain output rate has been reached. Based on this simulation exercise, can you see why a dealer firm's expected average cost of trading can be higher when, by allowing its inventory to fluctuate more widely, it operates at a higher expected transaction rate?

9. How easy was it for you to control your inventory positions? Did you succeed in bringing your inventory positions back to the neighborhood of zero by the end of each simulation run?

10. Do you feel that your P&L results were attributed largely to the bid–ask spread, or was some other factor involved?

11. In the initial configuration screen, click on "Some Preferencing" and run another simulation of your choosing. What effect does preferencing have on your ability to control your inventory positions?

EXERCISE 5.6: INTER-MARKET COMPETITION FOR A STOCK EXCHANGE

In this exercise, we look at markets not from the trader's perspective but from the perspective of a stock exchange or a market operator that is in competition with other market venues to provide trading services. The existence and nature of inter-firm competition is a key microeconomics topic. While clearly of much importance, price is not the only competitive variable. Other variables such as product quality, service, and advertising also matter. In this simulation exercise, we place you on the management team of an equity market operator that is competing with another equity trading market for public order flow. Your actions in the exercise will involve the trading of shares. The questions that we ask you involve the advice that you would give your firm concerning how best to strengthen your firm's competitive position, and how to profitably gain more order flow. Here is the setting:

- You are on the management team of the National Stock Market (NSM). The Exchange has just one trading platform: an electronic limit order book. NSM is facing intense competition from MegaPipe (MP), an alternative trading system that delivers block executions to its institutional customers.
- MP is a dark pool trading venue (the price and size of orders in the system are not displayed to the market) that enables institutions to trade with each other whenever their orders match or cross in price, as long as the crossing price is at or between the quotes posted on the public limit order book of the National Stock Market, where the stock is listed.
- Being on the management team at NSM, you want to experience trading in both venues to get a better understanding of how each system operates, to identify the advantages that each system offers, and to think more clearly about your firm's competitive responses to MP's growing success. Fortunately, you can trade in a simulated environment and thus do not have to put real capital at risk.
- Start each of your simulation runs with a single objective: purchase 2,000 units of a stock in the course of one trading day. Assess your purchase prices against VWAP, the volume weighted average price that the stock has traded at over the course of the day.

- Employ three different strategies: 1) your trades are made entirely on NSM's open limit order book, 2) your trades are made predominantly in MP's dark pool, block market, and 3) your trades are made in roughly equal proportions in both venues. For each of these three strategies, run the simulation enough times to get a feel for how your average buying prices compare with VWAP for each of them.

To get started, select "Order Driven" and "Block Trading" from the market structure panel. Make sure "Trade Through Allowed" is not selected. Orders arrive every 35 minutes, and a Limit Order Percentage of 70 percent is selected. Figure 5.4 shows these default settings.

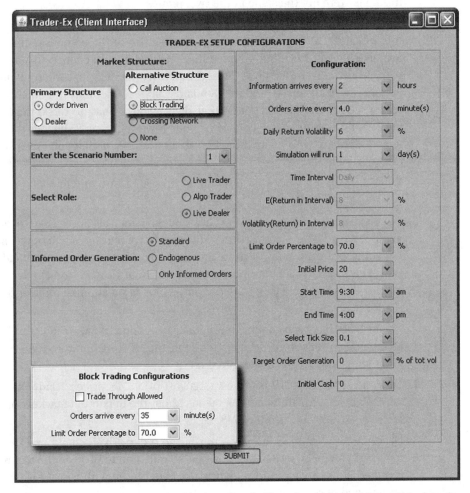

FIGURE 5.4 Order driven with a block trading facility selected with additional block trading configurations shown.

Enter the target on the simulation screen by clicking on the "Target" button on the bottom of the simulation screen. Enter your target (in this case 2000) in the white text area, and then click "Return."

Please respond to the following:

1. Assess your VWAP performance for each of your trading strategies (mainly NSM trading, mainly MP trading, and a fairly even balance of the two). Which strategy worked best for you?

2. No commissions were charged for trading in either venue. If commissions had been charged, would you have directed your order flow differently if the commissions were not the same in the two venues?

3. Assume that each of the two trading venues is charging a 2¢ per share commission and that the order flow is price sensitive to the commission rate. You are considering lowering your commissions at the Exchange in an attempt to capture more order flow. Two competitive models that microeconomists commonly use are the Kinked Demand Curve model and the Nash Equilibrium (see *Micro Markets* for further discussion). What do these models suggest would be the consequences of your lowering your Exchange's commissions? Present your own thoughts about the desirability of lowering your commissions.

4. What did you like and what did you not like about trading in each of the two venues?

5. Having traded in both markets, how do you feel as an executive at NSM about having MP as a competitor? The alternative market is, of course, attracting some order flow away from the Exchange, but on the other hand, MP's presence might have some positive effects. What do you think? (Remember, large orders are not easily traded in large blocks on an open limit order book platform.)

6. Because MP has been gaining appreciable order flow, NSM would certainly like to take steps that would make it difficult for MP to gain more market share. What steps might you consider taking?

7. Do you realize that MP is "free riding" off of NSM's prices? Can you explain why? Can you explain what this means about the maximum market share that MP may attract away from NSM?

8. Describe how competition plays out in the order driven equity markets. How much do you feel that competition can be relied on to provide the desired carrots and sticks that keep the equity markets on the path to robust economic growth and performance?

EXERCISE 5.7: FINDING AN EQUILIBRIUM VALUE

Finding equilibrium values is an important function for any marketplace, and the accuracy of price formation is a measure of the efficiency of a market. This simulation exercise deals with price discovery in an equity market. To this end, we contrast the process of price discovery under two different scenarios:

- The underlying equilibrium price, because it is not sensitive to the incoming order flow, is relatively stable.
- The underlying equilibrium price, because it is sensitive to the incoming order flow, is relatively unstable.

Here is the setting:

- You submit your limit and market orders to a transparent, plain vanilla limit order book.
- Each simulation run will be for one trading day (roughly 10 minutes of clock time).
- Run several simulations in each of the two environments as a day trader. Toward the end of each run unwind your inventory position and close the trading day with zero shares (or as close to zero as you can get).
- Your objective can be to maximize your trading profits, but achieving this goal is not the reason for running the exercise. Rather, pay attention to the prices that are set in the simulation run during the trading day. To this end, record the mid-spread of the bid–ask quotes for each hour on the hour, from 10:00 A.M. through 4:00 P.M.
- Take your recorded mid-spread prices for each of the runs and, for each of the two environments, assess their distributions for each of the seven hours of the trading day.

To get started, select "Order Driven" and "None" from the market structure panel. Next, set the Informed Order Generation to "Endogenous":

(a)   (b)

Click on "Submit" to launch the simulation.
Now respond to the following:

1. For each of the two environments, A and B, contrast the dispersion of the mid-spread prices across your simulation runs for each of the seven different hours of the trading day. Do you see any pattern?

2. Contrast the dispersion across your simulation runs for the A vs. B environments as of 10:00 A.M., as of 12:00 noon and as of 4:00 P.M. For which environment is the dispersion greater? If you do not observe a clear difference, run the simulation a few more times to increase the size of your sample.

3. The two simulated environments have been structured so that the variability of prices from one run to another, at any specific hour of the trading day, is expected to be greater in environment B than in environment A. This is because the equilibrium price is sensitive to the order flow in environment B, while it is not sensitive to the order flow in environment A. You might question what makes the equilibrium sensitive to the order flow in environment B. Here is the reason: 1) the computer generated order flow reflects a divergence of expectations across investors (some investors are relatively bullish about the stock and others are relatively bearish), 2) the proportion of investors who are bullish is revealed as trading progresses, and 3) the computer generated order flow reflects the fact that some individuals switch between being bulls and bears upon learning the valuations of others. Can you see the effect that this switching behavior has on price formation in the data that you have collected?

4. In some of your simulation runs, acquire a large long position by bunching your buy orders in the morning, and then work your inventory position off by bunching your sell orders in the afternoon. Did this bunching action affect the closing prices and, if so, in which environment did it have a bigger effect, A or B?

5. How would you rate the quality of price discovery in the two different simulation environments?

EXERCISE 5.8: ECONOMIC EFFECTS OF AN ORDER PROTECTION RULE

The U.S. Congress and the U.S. Securities and Exchange Commission (SEC) have taken a number of regulatory initiatives since 1975 to strengthen the U.S. equity markets. These regulations can have far ranging impacts, unintended consequences can occur, and mistakes may prove to be very costly. Thus the Commission has proceeded with great care, seeking much advice and counsel, including formal requests for comments from the public.

In this simulation exercise, we focus on one of the SEC initiatives, the trade-through rule, which was instituted as part of the SEC's 2005 Reg NMS release. Our purpose is to give you further insight into how the rule can affect the placement of orders in an order driven equity market. The trade-through rule can be described as follows:

> *When a transaction occurs at a price that is higher than the best posted offer or lower than the best posted bid and orders at these better prices are not included in the transaction, a trade-through is said to occur. Alternatively stated, the better priced orders have been "traded through." For example, if a sell limit order on the book at 50.10 remains unexecuted after a trade takes place at 50.12, the 50.10 sell order has been traded through. Since 2007, trade-throughs have not been allowed in the U.S. equity markets.*
>
> Robert A. Schwartz, *Micro Markets: A Market Structure Presentation of Microeconomic Theory*, John Wiley & Sons, 2010, Chapter 8.

Here is the setting for the simulation exercise:

- Two trading venues are used in this exercise: 1) a transparent limit order book, and 2) a block trading facility.
- Each simulation is run for one trading day (roughly 10 minutes of clock time).
- Your task for each run is to execute a 3000 unit buy order. Your success will be assessed by: 1) how completely you have filled your order (did you buy all 3000 units?) and 2) your average buying price relative to VWAP (did you beat the stock's volume weighted average price over the course of the simulation run?).
- Run your simulations for each of three settings:
  - limit order book only,
  - limit order book and block trading facility with no trade-through rule, and
  - limit order book and block trading facility with the trade-through rule enforced.
- For each of the three settings, run the simulation a few times so that you get an idea of the distributional properties of your results.
- Keep count of the number of trades that you have made in each simulation run and of the number of limit orders that you have placed.

To get started:

1. Open the initial parameter configuration screen.

2. Select "Order Driven" and "Block Trading" from the market structure panel. You'll then see the Block Trading Configuration Options:
   - For setting B below, make sure the "Trade Through Allowed" check box is checked.
   - For setting C, make sure it is not checked.

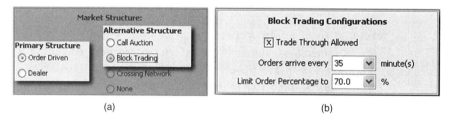

(a)   (b)

3. Click "Submit" to launch the simulation.

Respond to the following:

1. Contrast setting A (a limit order book only) with setting B (a limit order book and the block trading facility without a trade-through rule). How did the inclusion of the block trading facility affect your order placement? How did it affect your two performance measures?

2. Contrast settings B and C (a limit order book and the block trading facility with and without a trade-through rule). How did the inclusion of a trade-through rule affect your order placement strategy? How did it affect your two performance measures?

3. Did any trade throughs occur when the trade-through rule was not enforced? If so, how do you feel about it?

4. What are your thoughts now about 1) the desirability of having the block trading facility, and 2) the desirability of having the trade-through rule enforced?

5. Run the simulation again for settings B and C, with your task being to fill a 6,000 unit order. Does increasing your order size change your thoughts about the effect of having a trade-through rule?

CONCLUSION

This chapter presented eight exercises motivated by microeconomic issues that arise in financial markets. Using the TraderEx simulation, textbook concepts such as risk aversion, supply and demand curves, and inter-market competition were examined in the context of equities trading. Public policy questions concerning government regulation of equities can also be studied using simulation and, to this end, we focused on the trade-through rule recently imposed by the U.S. SEC. Building on these microeconomic underpinnings, the next four chapters will provide further exercises in trading in different markets.

CHAPTER 6

The Order Book Market Structure

T his chapter puts you in the role of a trader in an order driven market structure. Different trading challenges will be described, and you will make decisions under a range of market conditions. Measures of your performance will be displayed, showing you how you did.

You will see a variety of market structure and trading environment settings that can be adjusted. For now, accept all of the initial parameter settings, and click on "SUBMIT":

Click twice on the "GO" button at the lower left of the screen, and you will see the first trades of the day take place at $20.10:

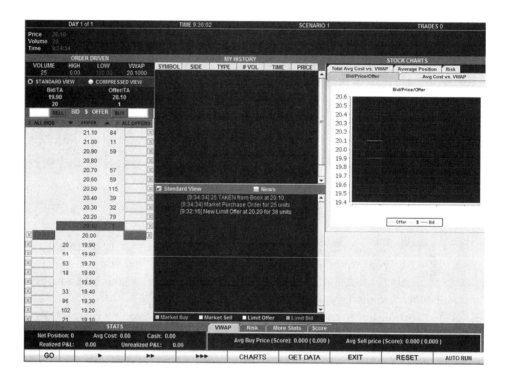

In Chapter 3, you saw how to enter market and limit orders, and buy and sell orders. Enter several orders of each type for practice, notice how the position value and P&L measures update as trades occur and market prices change. Click on the "EXIT" button. Again, select the "Order Driven" market structure, which will return you to the initial parameter screen.

EXERCISE 6.1: ENTERING LIMIT ORDERS

At the Setup screen, enter an Order Arrival rate of 3.0 minutes between orders for all runs in Exercises 6.1 and 6.2. For your initial run, set the Scenario Number to 7. Otherwise accept all of the default settings. The market open and close times define a $6\frac{1}{2}$ hour trading day. Click on "SUBMIT", and begin the simulation. The opening order book contents will be similar to those shown above.

1. Once the market opens, use **only limit orders** to buy 300 units ($\pm$ 25) to achieve a position in the range 275–325.
   - Once you have entered a limit order at a price, you can later enter additional limit orders at that price. The individual orders remain in time priority order, but only the aggregated total quantity is displayed.
   - You may need to reenter your buy orders at more aggressive prices if the price moves away from your order price.
   - Remember to cancel the old order.
   - When you have built your position to 300 or so, make a note of the time in the simulation day:

     Completion Time: _____:_____

2. Once your Net Position is +300, examine your statistics for trading done so far. In this illustration, the cost of the purchases is $5,990.10, and the average price paid is $19.97.

STATS			
Net Position:	300	Realized P&L:	$0.00
Cash:	($5,990.10)	Unrealized P&L:	$9.90
My Avg Cost:	$19.97		

   - By buying 300 so far in this example, the user has accounted for a potentially large percent of the total trading volume. Participating as a limit order buyer in such a percentage of market activity reflects an aggressive approach to buying. Without the user's limit orders at $20.00 and $19.90, the market bid could have dropped to $19.80 or lower. Recall that in TraderEx, you can affect the market.
   - What was your percent Market Share once you acquired the 300 unit position? Answer: _____ percent
   - Notice that there is no "Realized P&L" at this stage. The positive Unrealized Profit of $9.90 in the illustration means that the current long position of +300, when marked-to-market at the bid quote at the time ($20.00), shows a profit. Once you begin to sell the shares, you will see the realized profit change to values other than zero.

3. Now, sell the position of 300 with limit orders only. When you have returned to a flat position (inventory = 0), write the time you finished and your realized profit. You can click on the "EXIT" button to end the simulation before the market close.

   Time: _____
   Realized P&L: _____

Buy Low, Sell High

TraderEx's performance board at the bottom of the screen shows your trading volume was 600. What percentage of the total trading volume did the 600 account for? Realized and Unrealized P&L are also displayed. As covered in Chapter 3, profits are realized when a trader returns a long or short position back toward zero.

Realized P&L will be positive when you have sold shares at a higher price than you paid to get them. In the example below, a Realized P&L of $7.60 can be considered money in the bank:

STATS			
Net Position:	0	Realized P&L:	$7.60
Cash:	$7.60	Unrealized P&L:	$0.00
My Avg Cost:	$0.00		

The performance board also tells you the average selling price and the average buying price that you have achieved. Clearly, when your position returns to 0, you will have a positive Realized P&L only if your average selling price is greater than your average buying price. In this example, the selling price is 2.5¢ (= $19.992–$19.967) greater than the buying price, which will lead to a positive P&L (profits) and a positive P&L score.

- Did it take more time to complete the buying or the selling?
- Why do you think one took longer than the other?
- What pattern of trade prices speed up or slow down the execution of your limit orders?

Repeat steps 1 through 3 three more times, using for each trial a different Scenario Number (2 through 90, but not 1 or 7). At the initial parameter screen, enter 3.0 minutes between orders. You will encounter different environments and see a distribution based on your four outcomes (an admittedly small sample).

Question: As a limit order trader, were you able to complete the full instructions in all four runs?

Answer: _____

What pattern of orders from the computer, and what short-term price changes enabled you to complete the limit order trading instructions most successfully?[*]

Answer: _____

EXERCISE 6.2: ENTERING MARKET ORDERS

Repeat Exercise 6.1 using only **market orders** this time:

1. Use Scenario Number 5 in the initial run. Pace your submission of market buy orders to reach a long position of 300 at about the same time as in Exercise 6.1, Part 1, above.

   Completion Time: _____

2. Once your position is Long 300, sell with market orders and attempt to finish selling at about the same time as in Part 1 of this exercise. When you have returned to a flat position (inventory = 0), write down the time you finished and your Realized Profit. You can click on the "EXIT" button to end the simulation before the market close.

   Time: _____
   Realized P&L: _____

3. Compare your outcomes in Exercises 6.1 and 6.2. In the initial run with Scenario Number 7, did you generate a better outcome with strictly limit orders or with strictly market orders? Why do you think this is so?

   Answer: _____

4. Repeat steps 1 through 3 three more times. Choose different Scenario Numbers in the range 1 through 90 that you have not used yet. You will encounter different environments and see a distribution for the four outcomes. Based on four runs with strictly limit orders and four runs with strictly market orders, would a combination of orders have done better than strictly one order type or the other? Why?

   Answer: _____

_____

[*]Chapter 2's discussions of mean reversion, accentuated volatility, and two-sidedness are applicable here.

EXERCISE 6.3: ADJUSTING LIMIT ORDERS

Order book systems provide several ways to remove unexecuted limit orders from the book, including "Straight Cancel" and "Cancel/Replace" functions. The first takes a working order you no longer want filled out of the order book. A cancel/replace order changes the size or price of an existing order, and re-enters it in the book. In most order books (including TraderEx), cancel/replace results in the order's time being set to the present time, which means the loss of its time priority on the book (i.e., the replacement order goes to the end of the queue at its limit price).

In Figure 6.1, the user has limit orders at $20.00 to buy 50 and at $19.80 to buy 90. To perform a cancel/replace, click on the red "X" next to the order to cancel and immediately click the rectangle to enter the new buy order.

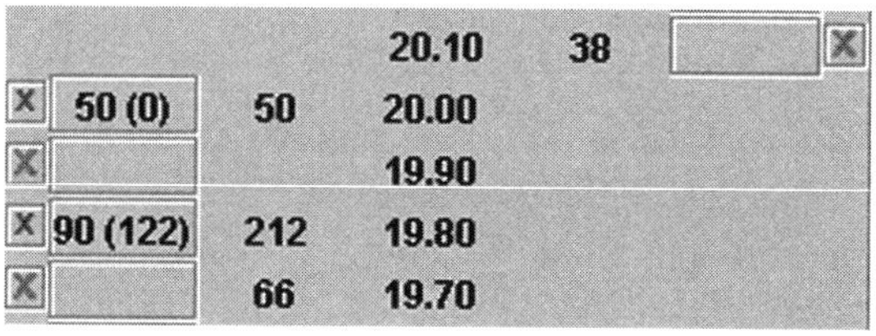

			20.10	38		X
X	50 (0)	50	20.00			
X			19.90			
X	90 (122)	212	19.80			
X		66	19.70			

FIGURE 6.1   User's two limit orders to buy with cancellation buttons (red x's) on the left.

In Figure 6.2, the user is offering to sell 50 at $20.10. Another 98 is for sale at $20.10 also, and these have arrived before the user's order. Therefore, the quantity ahead is "(98)." It will take five mouse clicks/keystrokes to cancel/replace your order with a limit sell of 50 at $20.00:

- "X" to cancel
- click on the rectangle to the right of $20.00
- <5>
- <0>
- <Enter>

Part 1: Limit order only selling tactics

1. You are to **sell 300** using **limit orders** and making adjustments when a price moves away from your orders.

2. Submit sell limit orders at the best offer price to begin with. In Figure 6.2, the user has entered an order to sell 50 at $20.10.

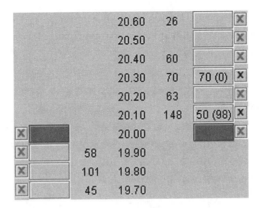

FIGURE 6.2 User's limit orders to sell with active cancel buttons on the right.

3. When new offers come in at lower prices, first cancel and then submit a limit order at the new offer price. For instance in the illustration above, if an order to sell at $20.00 arrives, cancel the order to sell 50 at $20.10 and replace it with an order to sell 50 at $20.00.

4. Sell until you reach a short position of –300. Record the following:

   Average Selling Price: _____
   Completion Time: _____

5. Now that your position is short, buy the same quantity following the same strategy. When you have returned to a flat position (inventory = 0), write down the time you finished and your realized profit.

   Time: _____
   Realized P&L: _____

Part 2: Limit order and market order tactics

1. You are to **sell 300** using **limit orders** and making **more aggressive** adjustments by using market orders **when the prices move away** from your orders.

2. As in the prior exercise, begin by submitting a sell order at the best offer price.

3. When new offers come in at lower prices, cancel and submit a market order to sell. In Figure 6.2, if an order to sell at $20.00 arrives, cancel the order to sell 50 at $20.10 and replace it with a market order to sell 50. It will trade at $19.90.

4. Sell until you reach a short position of –300. Record the following:

   Average Selling Price: _____
   Completion Time: _____

5. Buy back all of the shares sold short following the same strategy. When you have returned to a flat position (inventory = 0), write down the time you finished and your realized profit.

Time: _____

Realized P&L: _____

Questions:

- In Exercise 6.3, did you generate a better outcome with the strategy in Part 1, or with the more aggressive cancel/replace strategy in Part 2? Why?
- Would a combination of order adjustment approaches have done better than strictly one type or the other? Why?

EXERCISE 6.4: SIZING YOUR ORDERS—MARKETS AND LIMITS

In the TraderEx simulations, orders can be any size up to 99. In this two-part exercise you will use only (5) orders of size 60 to complete an instruction to sell 300.

Part 1

1. In the first part of this exercise you are to buy using **limit orders** of size 60 only. They will not always execute, or may only execute partially, so you may need to cancel and re-enter them.

2. Buy until you have reached a long position of +300. Record the following:

Average Buying Price: _____

Completion Time: _____

3. Once your position is Long 300, sell 300 with the same strategy. When you have returned to a flat position (inventory = 0), write down the time you finished and your realized profit.

Time: _____

Realized P&L: _____

Part 2

1. In Part 2 of this Exercise you are to buy 300 using five **market orders** of 60 only.

2. Buy until you reach a long position of 300. Record the following:

Average Buying Price: _____

Completion Time: _____

3. Once your position is Long 300, sell 300 following the same strategy. When you have returned to a flat position (inventory = 0), write down the time you finished and your realized profit.

Time: _____

Realized P&L: _____

Answer these two questions based on Exercise 6.4:

1. Compare the two results in Part 1 and Part 2. Was 60 the optimal order size? How would you adjust your order sizes up or down from 60 to generate better outcomes in:

Part 1 (limit orders)? _____

Part 2 (market orders)? _____

2. In most order book systems, the average limit order size is twice to five times as large as the average market order size. What do you think explains this size difference?

Discussion for Exercises 6.2 to 6.4

In Exercises 6.2 to 6.4, you gained experience with placing limit and market orders in an order book structure. Under some circumstances, limit orders enhance outcomes for a trader. The adjustment of limit order sizes and prices, and decisions about cancelling and replacing orders require careful consideration.

An insight for order handling comes from splitting market price changes into two parts: permanent changes and temporary changes. Permanent price changes generate price shifts that do not systematically reverse themselves, which is disadvantageous for limit order users. Consider the simplified illustration in Figure 6.3. In it, a sequence of three trades has occurred along with some negative information about the company.

In the chart, negative news comes out and three market sell orders arrive. A limit order to buy, which participated in Trade #1 will suffer ex-post regret. The order was picked off by someone with better information who, much to the limit order placer's chagrin, sold at the higher price before the price dropped. The limit order buyer's loss is equal to the permanent price change. Trade #2's price turns out to be at the post-mean reversion price, which reflects only the permanent impact of the information. The traders in #2 have neither lost nor gained from these price dynamics. In the diagram, the price overshoots and the buy limit order that executes in Trade #3 benefits from the temporary component of the price change that occurred. The limit order buyer's gain from Trade #3 is equal to the temporary price change.

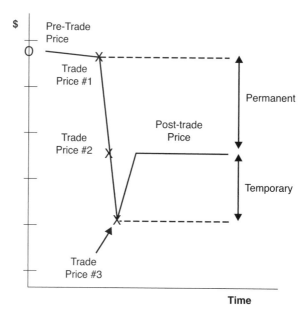

FIGURE 6.3 Price impact and three seller-triggered trades—temporary and permanent components.

The main benefits of limit orders can be summarized as follows:

- Temporary, non-permanent price changes are advantageous for limit order users.
- Limit orders generate a positive return for the investor when they execute due to liquidity events and temporary price impact.
- After temporary price shocks, the market mean reverts, returning to earlier levels.
- Under these circumstances, returns have negative serial autocorrelation and limit orders generate greater returns than market orders.
- Limit orders also profit from the bid—offer spread (i.e., from the negative auto-correlation in returns that occurs when prices bounce between the bid and the offer).

The primary costs of limit orders include:

- Permanent price movements occur when information changes in a market and this can disadvantage traders who have placed limit orders.
- When prices shift to a new level, it is better not to have placed limit orders.
- If the price moves through your limit order, your order executes and you regret the trade.
- Also problematic for the limit order user, information change can move the price away from his/her limit order.

- The trader later buys for more or sells for less than he would have, had he/she used a market order initially.

Having identified a number of the determinants of a successful trade, we next analyze how a set of trades can be analyzed, and how the positive and negative contributions of each can be identified.

EXERCISE 6.5: POST-TRADE ANALYSIS

In this exercise, you will conduct a post-trade analysis. During each simulation, TraderEx keeps a record of your decisions and the market's evolution over the time of the simulation run. After you have completed one run of Exercise 6.4– Part 1, click on "CHART" next to the "EXIT" button. A chart similar to the one shown in Figure 6.4 will appear.

Charts

The trades that you have made are displayed in Figure 6.4. In this illustration, the user sold early in the simulation, and bought toward the end of the day. The eight

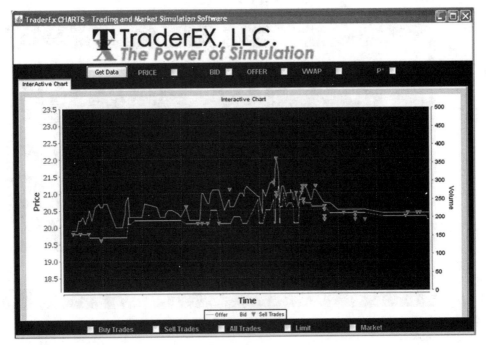

FIGURE 6.4 TraderEx price chart with midday volatility and users' trades shown.

sell orders (triangle shapes) were mainly executed with limit orders at the offer price. In total, 10 buy orders executed, some at the bid as limit orders, and others (the diamond shapes) at the offer as market orders. The lines graph the bid and offer quotes and the trade prices, and the smooth line shows the evolution of VWAP over the day.

Figure 6.5 shows a larger number of trades to buy (diamond symbols) and to sell (triangles). The market became more volatile late in the day.

Can you identify the good and bad trades from these charts? Not all trades will be good in retrospect. How can you enhance the outcomes you achieve on average? Recall the discussion of permanent and temporary price impacts in the previous section. Here are three identifiers of poor outcomes in trading:

- Buy trades may have occurred just before a permanent price move to the downside.

    If so, you were a "sitting duck" and got "bagged," as traders say. Economists call it "adverse selection." Someone with superior information sold to you at a price that turns out to be overly valued once the adverse news comes out.

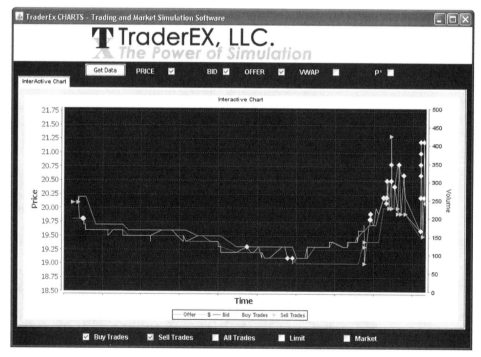

FIGURE 6.5   TraderEx price chart with a late day reversal of a downtrend and users' trades shown.

The same reason for a bad result occurs if your sell trade occurs just before a permanent price increase.

- A second category of bad trades identifiable on the TraderEx chart is a trade that occurs on the "wrong" side of a temporary price change.

  If the price rises and you buy, and the price mean reverts back to a previous level that was lower, you will consider it a bad trade. Temporary price changes, or liquidity shocks, create the chance for inopportune trades.

- Another type of poor outcome occurs in trading when you are seeking to buy and you miss an opportunity to complete the order before the price move you were anticipating occurs.

  Traders often have orders that go unfilled because market conditions are not sufficiently liquid to enable them to complete the full trading instruction. An investor may have a price target for a stock 10 percent above its current level, for example. The trader is instructed to buy a large block, but few sellers are offering shares, and the buyer does not want the price driven up against him. The trader buys what is available and waits for sellers to appear, but they do not. The price reaches a level 10 percent above the price when the instruction arrived, but only half of the order was complete. The trades that were realized are good, but an opportunity cost from the lost profit on the shares not purchased was incurred.

Data

TraderEx stores a record of your decisions and the market's development. After examining the charts, click on "GET DATA" to access the three files containing:

- All orders arriving in the order book
- All trades that occurred
- The P* price during the simulation

Chapter 3 provides instructions for creating and saving these files to your computer.

Open these three CSV files in Excel to see the changes in P* during the simulation run, the orders that arrived in the order book market, and the trades that occurred.

EXERCISE 6.6: A REALLY BIG ORDER

So far the exercises have asked you to buy and to sell based on a fund manager's instructions to increase or to decrease a position by 300 units. In this case study, you will receive large buy or sell instructions, and measure the quality of the

Target Order Generation [20   ▼] % of tot vol

FIGURE 6.6 Target order generation.

outcomes that result from your trading decisions. At the end, your execution prices will be compared to a few performance benchmarks. You might then consider the impediments to more effective trading, and better identify the factors that lead to good trading outcomes.

In this exercise, assume that as a fund manager you planned to significantly alter a stock's weighting in the fund. In TraderEx, the Stand Alone | Order Driven mode, select "Scenario Number = 2," and "Target Order Generation" set to 20 percent. You will be given a buy instruction that will require you to trade a quantity that will make up about 20 percent of the total volume in the market. Odd numbered Scenarios (1, 3, 5, . . .) will generate trade instructions to sell. Even numbered Scenarios (2, 4, 6, . . .) will generate trade instructions to buy. In trader's terms, at approximately 20 percent of volume, you are the "ax" in the stock with the dominant interest in buying or selling this particular trading day. See Figure 6.6.

In this example, at the open, you are given an instruction to buy 1,000 units. In the "Target Order Generation" mode, the order size that you will receive in the simulation could be different. Look at the amount below the "Target" label on the bottom row in Figure 6.7. This will be a large quantity, about 20 percent of the average daily trading volume of the stock. Before the fund manager walks away from your

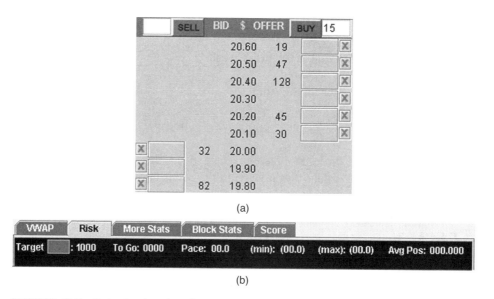

(a)

(b)

FIGURE 6.7 Order book and trading instructions to buy 1,000.

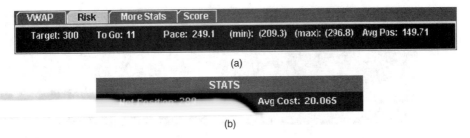

(a)

(b)

FIGURE 6.8 The user is long 289 and has nearly completed an instruction to buy 300, paying an average price of $20.065 per share so far.

trading desk, he/she adds. *"I don't want to overpay, and I may have more to buy in the afternoon after I speak to an analyst."*

The bottom row of the TraderEx screen shows you your current position and your target position, and the prices paid or received so far. In Figure 6.8, the instruction is to buy 300.

Consider how you could have come to the market with a buy instruction for 300. In Figure 6.9, the opening order book indicates that you could buy up to 30 at $20.10 with a market order. For illustration, say you decide to buy half that amount. The most aggressive buyer(s) in the order book is willing to pay $20.00.

The first trade at 9:30:39 is yours for 15 units, which was done at $20.10 and is shown on the far right of Figure 6.10.

The My History trade blotter in Figure 6.10 shows that, using market orders to buy, and a buy limit order on the bid side of the book, this user has accumulated a position of 45 (30 by limit order and 15 by market order), and needs to buy 255 more. In the illustration, the user has bought with a market order at $20.10, and

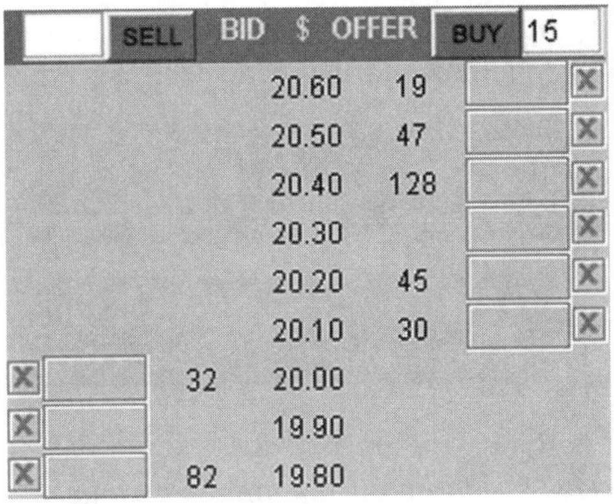

	SELL	BID $ OFFER	BUY	15
		20.60	19	X
		20.50	47	X
		20.40	128	X
		20.30		X
		20.20	45	X
		20.10	30	X
X	32	20.00		
X		19.90		
X	82	19.80		

FIGURE 6.9 Order book at the open.

	DAY 1 of 1					10:24:57				2
Price	20.10	19.90	19.90	20.00	20.00	20.30	20.20	20.20	20.10	20.10
Volume	47	9	30	14	18	5	22	23	15	15
Time	10:21:21	10:18:30	10:18:30	10:18:30	10:07:20	09:39:24	09:39:24	09:33:58	09:33:58	09:30:39

ORDER DRIVEN		MY HISTORY					
○ Standard View ● Compressed View		SIDE	TYPE	# VOL	TIME	PRICE	SYMBOL
Bid/TA 19.90 14	Offer/TA 20.10 19	Buy	Limit	30	10:18:30	19.90	Stock1
		Buy	Market	15	09:30:39	20.10	Stock1

FIGURE 6.10 Ticker with reports of first 10 trades of the day.

placed a limit order that traded at $19.90. You should continue to buy over the course of the next 3–4 simulated trading hours (about 15–30 minutes in real time).

Performance in Handling the Really Big Order

Once the instruction to buy 300 is fully completed, *how have you done as a buy side trader?* You should consider the following metrics to assess your results.

VWAP The volume weighted average price (VWAP), a common benchmark, is described in Chapter 4. VWAP is regarded as a good approximation of the price an average trader will achieve in a day. As we have previously noted it is, literally, the price at which the average share has traded over the course of the day. You must be careful to at least stay near VWAP if you are on the wrong side of it. This is more difficult to achieve when you use market orders because, with each market order, you incur a spread cost. It is also difficult if your trading is concentrated in time and you fail to participate later in trades that turn out to be attractive given the side of the market you are on.

Pace of Trading You will begin the simulation with an instruction from TraderEx. This is your "Target Shares." You have an instruction to buy 300 and, so far, you have built a position of +139 and therefore have 161 units left to buy. The average price paid for the shares acquired so far is $20.10.

Based on how far you are into the trading day, TraderEx will compute how many shares *you should own* to be on an even pace of trading so as to complete the order by 4 P.M. As shown in Figure 6.11, at this point in the day, 161.6 units would be the amount that would bring us to a final position of 300 with evenly

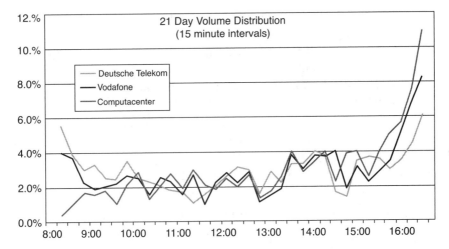

FIGURE 6.11 Distribution of trading volume in three European stocks averaged over 21 days for 34 fifteen-minute intervals in an eight-and-a-half hour trading day. Market activity is not evenly distributed. It is higher near the close, and for two of the three stocks is also above average in the opening periods.

paced trading. *The user's position is 136, so he is within the collar and there is no undue risk at this point.*

The TraderEx risk measures will track whether you are sufficiently close to the Pace number of shares to complete the instructions without taking a large price risk. What is risky? Executing a big part of the order in just one narrow time slice within the day is risky. The prices at that time could turn out to be very unattractive.

Profit & Loss   Of course, P&L is an important outcome from trading activities. When a trader is given a buy or sell order, however, a positive P&L outcome is largely a result of the investor's stock selection. Even if a trader outperforms VWAP and takes minimal pace risk, P&L for a trader who is buying can be negative if the stock falls in price. A stock could open at $20 and close at $19 in one day, and have a VWAP of $19.50. A trader who buys for the client at an average price of $19.45, however, has reduced the loss to $0.45 per share from the –$0.50 P&L per share that average trading would have generated. A stock that rises from $20 to $21 with a one-day VWAP of $20.50 will create a P&L of $0.50 per share or 2.5 percent (=0.50/20.00) on average, but a trader who has bought at $20.40 has contributed an additional $0.10 to the P&L and has added about 0.50 percent to the fund's "alpha."

Now that the three primary performance metrics have been covered, let's begin. In TraderEx, the Stand Alone | Order Driven mode, enter "3.0" as the Order Arrival Rate, and select "Scenario Number = 4," and "Target Order Generation = 20%." You will be given a buy instruction that will require you to trade a quantity that will make up about 20 percent of the total volume in the market.

1. Run the simulation for a full day up to the close of trading at 4 P.M. (at 16.00). During the run consider and write down the following:
   - What is your trading strategy? At any point did you change your trading strategy? When and why?
   - Explain why you are ahead of or behind the VWAP.
   - What positive or negative effects did the market's price changes have on you?

2. When you reach the market's closing time, compare your average cost to VWAP. Which of these resulted?:
   - Average Buying Price < VWAP (good)
   - Average Buying Price > VWAP (not so good)
   - Average Buying Price = VWAP (okay)

3. Did you complete the full order? Yes, or if no, why not?

4. Is the day's closing above or below your average buying price?

5. Did your trading "add alpha" to the fund's performance, or did it detract?

6. What is the P&L at the end? Do you understand why the P&L is what it is?

7. Can you attribute the position P&L, at the close, to the trading desk or to the stock selection? Did the trading performance you generated contribute to or detract from the fund manager's returns?

8. Using the "GET DATA" tool, review the TradeOrders.csv file—
   - What percentage of your trading was done by limit order and what percent by market order?
   - Do you feel this was an optimal split between the two types of orders?

9. Using the "GET CHART" function or the "GET DATA" function, graph the market's trade prices, your trades (select the option to display limit and market orders), and an end-of-day VWAP line, shown here:

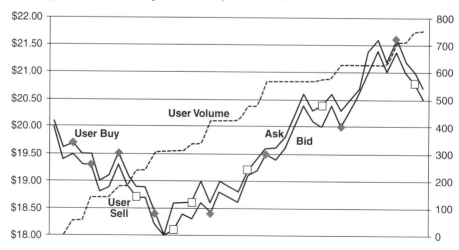

Identify your best and worst trades of the day.

10. Looking at your chart, how did the timing of your order placement and your trades affect your performance? Was your timing a positive or a negative factor for you?

11. What post-trade analyses could a market participant use to improve his/her order placement decision making in the future?

12. Repeat the simulation three more times using in each trial an *even* Scenario Number other than 4. Set "Target Order Generation" to 20 percent, and also in the initial parameter screen, enter "5.0" as the interarrival time. This will reduce the number of computer generated orders and decrease the depth of the book. As you encounter varied environments, you should reflect on the distribution of results from your four outcomes.

Discussion of Exercise 6.6

You just completed an exercise that asked you to buy a quantity large enough for your trading to be about 20 percent of the total market volume. While not under your control as the trader, the fund manager selected an attractive investment if the closing price is greater than the price you bought the shares for. In assessing your results we suggested that, as of the end of the day, you did well if you paid less than VWAP for the shares.

We also asked you to attribute the P&L to its two contributors: stock selection and trading. How did you do that? Consider this example: you are given an order to acquire a long position, say 1,000 units, in a stock. The stock has opened at $25.00, and the day's VWAP is $25.60. As a trader, you acquire the desired position at an average purchase price of $25.50. The stock closes at $26.00. The money manager's position is up 50 cents a share, or 2 percent. Average trading would have lowered that by 10 cents. We can therefore attribute about 20 percent (= 10¢/50¢) of the return to successful trading. Did you use a similar approach? If a trading desk consistently contributes to alpha, it can improve an investment fund's results very impressively indeed.

Not everyone in the markets believes that VWAP is a good benchmark. How can it be misused? What would you do as a trader if your bonus were a function of the amount by which you beat a daily VWAP measure?

To be more concrete, in an actual market, what if you have 100,000 more shares left to buy at 3:45 P.M. The market closes in 15 minutes, and the price in the market is $0.50 over VWAP. Do you buy the entire 100,000? How will the fund manager react if you have bought only 200,000 out of a total instruction to buy 300,000? Can the last 100,000 wait until the next day?

In Table 6.1, Trader 1 completes the instruction, but overall pays 15 cents, or 63 basis points, *more than the Day 1 VWAP*. Trader 2 asks for more time to fill the

TABLE 6.1   VWAP Gaming Example

Trader 1	Day 1		Total
VWAP	$24.00		
Quantity bought	300,000	→	300,000
Price paid (average)	**$24.15**	→	$24.15
VWAP Comparison	−0.63%		

Trader 2	Day 1	Day 2	Total
VWAP	$24.00	$25.00	
Quantity bought	200,000	100,000	300,000
Price paid (average)	$23.95	$24.95	**$24.28**
VWAP Comparison	+0.21%	+0.20%	

Two traders with an instruction to buy 300,000. Trader 1 completes it in one day and Trader 2 finishes it in two days and pays 13 cents more

order, and the final 100,000 are completed the next day at $24.95. Trader 2 winds up buying shares *below VWAP* in Day 1 and *below VWAP* in Day 2. However, Trader 2's total per share price paid for the 300,000 shares is $24.28, or *13 cents higher*! The investor's returns will be reduced by 55 basis due to Trader 2's delay.

By carrying the unfinished amount over to the next day, it is possible for the trader to pay more overall, yet still beat VWAP in Day 1 and VWAP in Day 2. Often traders will use a time interval VWAP, measuring VWAP from 10 A.M. to 12 noon, for instance. Similar gaming strategies are possible by changing the time window or extending the time to complete the order.

By stretching the time period of an order's execution, VWAP can be gamed to make a trader look good at the expense of the fund's investors. Consider the following two comments from senior traders:

> *The biggest firms … think their trading operations are their competitive advantage, that their traders can beat VWAP. Those firms are less inclined to use algorithms.*
>
> *Though we always compare the VWAP of the market to the executing price, that's not what's most important. For us, we look at pure market impact—the price we manage to reach on the execution compared to the price at the beginning of the execution.*
>
> "Thinking Outside the Black Box," *Hedge Fund & Investment Technology*, December 2004

While VWAP benchmarking has its detractors and shortcomings in actual practice, it is a sensible benchmark in TraderEx. Our TraderEx exercises are usually runs of one day only, so multiday gaming is not possible. But, if you do see a way to game it, make note of it. VWAP comparisons are commonplace, and are part of understanding how continuous markets work. Also note that the daily VWAP is a tough criterion if you are given an order after the start of a trading day. The reason is that the full day VWAP would not match the period over which you are working your order, and a VWAP for just part of the day could also be affected by trades that your own orders are triggering. The upshot is that any benchmark that can be affected by a participant is not a good benchmark.

EXERCISE 6.7: ANOTHER REALLY BIG ORDER

You have handled a large buy order in the order book market, now try to sell at attractive prices. In TraderEx, the Stand Alone | Order Driven mode, enter "5.0" as the Order Arrival Rate, and select "Scenario Number = 5," and "Target Order Generation = 20%." You will be given a sell instruction that will require you to trade a quantity that will make up about 20 percent of the total volume in the market.

1. Run the simulation for a full day up to the close of trading at 4 P.M. (at 16.00). During the run consider and write down the following:
2. At the market's closing time, compare your average cost to VWAP. Which of these resulted?:
   - Average Selling Price > VWAP (good)
   - Average Selling Price < VWAP (not so good)
   - Average Selling Price = VWAP (okay)
3. Did you complete the full order? Yes, or if no, why not?
4. Is the day's closing above or below your average selling price?
5. What is the P&L at the end? Do you understand why the P&L is what it is?
6. Did the trading performance you generated in selling contribute to or detract from the fund manager's returns?
7. Using the "GET DATA" tool, review the TradeOrders.csv file—
   - What percentage of your selling was done by limit order and what percent by market order?
   - Do you feel this was an optimal split between the two types of orders?

EXERCISE 6.8: ILLIQUIDITY

So far, we have examined trading decisions in fairly liquid markets. We will now change the simulation parameters to create a relatively *illiquid* market. In

TraderEx's Stand Alone | Order Driven mode, select "Scenario Number = 3," and "Target Order Generation" set to 20 percent. You will be given a sell instruction that will require you to trade a quantity that will make up about 20 percent of the total volume in the market. In the initial parameter screen, reduce the average number of minutes between orders to 9.0. Rather than 12 or more orders per hour on average, there will now be just 7:

1. Run the simulation for a full day, up to the close of trading, at $16.00. What was the impact on the market of the reduced rate of order arrival and the reduced liquidity?

2. How did your trading strategy change? Explain why you are ahead of or behind the VWAP.

3. When you reach the market close time, compare your average cost to VWAP. Which of these resulted?
   - Average Buying Price < VWAP
   - Average Buying Price > VWAP
   - Average Buying Price = VWAP

4. Was beating VWAP more difficult? Less difficult? Why?

5. Did your trading add alpha to the fund's performance, or did it detract?
   - Added. Why? _____
   - Detracted. Why? _____

6. Using the GET DATA tool, review the TradeOrders.csv file—
   - What percentage of your trading was done by limit order and what percentage by market order?

     Limit orders _____ percent Market orders _____ percent

   - How does this compare with the more liquid market environment that you faced in Exercise 6.8?

     A: _____

   - Repeat the simulation three more times using an **odd** Scenario Number in each trial. Set "Target Order Generation" to 20 percent and, at the initial parameter screen, enter 9.0 minutes between orders. You will encounter varied environments and should reflect on the distribution of results from your four outcomes.

7. How did this exercise differ from the previous one, which called for working a really big order?

EXERCISE 6.9: HEIGHTENED VOLATILITY

The volatility level of prices will affect the trading decisions you make in ways we will examine in this exercise. In TraderEx, the Stand Alone | Order Driven mode, select "Scenario Number = 4," and "Target Order Generation" set to 20 percent. You will be given a buy instruction that will require you to trade a quantity that will make up about 20 percent of the total volume in the market. Odd-numbered scenarios (1, 3, 5, ...) will generate trade instructions to sell. As we have said, in trader's terms you are the "ax" in the stock, with the dominant interest in buying or selling this particular trading day. For this run at the configuration screen, return to the more active rate of order arrival (2.0 minutes between orders), and increase the daily returns volatility to 10 percent. This means a 10 percent standard deviation of daily returns, which means that 10 percent price swings are not at all unexpected.

Figure 6.12 shows the influence of the volatility parameter. The three price paths have daily returns volatility of 10 percent, 5 percent, and 2.5 percent, respectively. The stocks are subjected to the same valuation shocks, however the shocks are amplified by a factor of two and four for the more volatile stocks. In this realization, the most volatile path's high-low difference is $3.55, or four times larger than the $0.89 for the most stable stock.

As volatility increases, how should you alter your trading decisions and order handling? Assuming you have a large sell order, what are the risks in trading the most volatile stock? How can these volatility risks be mitigated? As in Exercises 6.8 through 6.9, TraderEx will give you an instruction to buy or to sell a quantity that will be a substantial percentage of the day's trading volume.

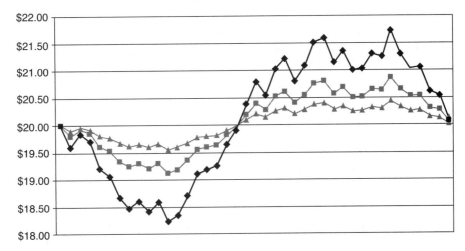

FIGURE 6.12 Three stock prices with high, medium, and low volatility levels.

1. Run the simulation for a full day, up to the close of trading at 16.00. What was the impact on the market of the heightened volatility?

2. How did your trading strategy change? Explain why you are ahead of, or are behind the VWAP.

3. When you reach the market closing time, compare your average cost to VWAP. Which of these results have you achieved:
   - Your Average Price < VWAP
   - Your Average Price > VWAP
   - Your Average Price = VWAP

4. With increased volatility, was beating VWAP:
   - more difficult?
   - less difficult?
   - Why? _____

5. Did the extra volatility and your trading add alpha to the fund's performance, or did it detract?
   - Added. Why? _____
   - Detracted. Why? _____

6. Using the GET DATA tool, review the TradeOrders.csv file—What percentage of your trading was done by limit order and what percent by market order?

   Limit orders _____ percent

   Market orders _____ percent

   How does this compare with the less volatile market environment that you faced in Exercise 6.6? A: _____

Repeat the simulation three more times using an **even** Scenario Number other than 4 in each trial. Set "Target Order Generation" to 20 percent and, at the initial parameter screen, set the daily returns volatility to 10 percent. You will encounter varied environments and should reflect on the distribution of results from your four outcomes.

Discussion of Exercise 6.8

You just completed an exercise that asked you to buy or to sell a substantial quantity in a market that had about twice the underlying P^* volatility of the prior exercises. What adjustments should traders need to make to respond best to the heightened volatility?

Because limit orders in a displayed order book take on some properties of options, options analysis provides useful insights. An option is the right, but not the obligation, to do something. In options trading, the seller extends the option (and is compensated for doing so), and somebody else acquires it (and pays something). A standardized, exchange traded option is the right to either buy or to sell shares under certain pre-specified conditions. The right to buy shares is a call option, and the right to sell shares is a put option.

An exchange traded option specifies the stock the option is written on (the underlying asset), the time to expiration (the length of time the option is good for), and a strike price (the price at which the option can be exercised). For instance, the option might be a call on BlueChip Corp. with a strike price of $20.00. If the underlying stock is currently trading at $21.10, the premium for the call might be $2.20. Say you buy the option. If, in three months, BlueChip is trading at $24.00, you will exercise the option (buy the shares) at the strike price of $20.00, sell the shares received from the option at $24.00 and, after subtracting the $2.20 you have paid for the right to do this, you walk away with a profit of $1.80 per share. On the other hand, if the option expires with the stock trading below $20, you will have paid $2.20 for something that has wound up being worthless.

By placing a 50 unit (5,000 shares) buy order at $21.00, you are extending the right to anyone in the market to sell you up to 50 at $21.00 at any time until the order is cancelled by you or until it trades. The analogy is not perfect; there is no fixed expiry (expiration) point for the option—you can withdraw it whenever you want. Nevertheless, while your order is on the book, it is a live option that can be exercised by anyone who wants to sell shares. Effectively, you have written a put option. Similarly, if you place a 70 unit limit order to sell at, say, $21.50, you are extending the right to anyone in the market to buy 7,000 shares from you at $21.50. Effectively, you have written a call option.

Options have prices and sellers of options expect to be compensated. Nobody paid you to place a limit order, so how do you get compensated? Unlike exchange traded options, the compensation is implicit. You receive payment when a short-term liquidity imbalance causes your limit order to execute (i.e., the option is exercised), and the price of the underlying reverts back toward a previous level (the process is called *mean reversion*). The temporary price impact therefore triggers the execution of your limit order, and the return to a previous price level generates a positive return for the limit order trader. If the price impact is permanent, meaning valuation has truly changed; then the limit order has been bagged, and suffers a loss. In equilibrium, limit order placers will find that the losses from information change will be offset by gains from temporary price impact.

In valuing options, increases in a stock's volatility level increase the price of its options. Similarly, a limit order placer will require added compensation for placing limit orders in the book for a volatile stock. A limit order user in a volatile stock, like an option writer, is providing something of more value to the market, and for which he expects to be compensated somehow. The incentive to place a limit order is sufficient only if the bid–ask spread is reasonably wide. A narrow spread will induce more traders to trade with certainty of an execution by submitting a market order rather than, say, leaving a limit order to buy one tick below the offer quote. We refer to this "attraction to certainty of execution" as a "gravitational pull," and it is part of the TraderEx program. Gravitational pull in an order book market causes many orders to be entered at market rather than as limit orders, and those limit orders that are entered on the book are apt to be placed further away from the contra-side orders (which accounts for the spread being wider).

Greater volatility in TraderEx results from *more frequent* P* changes, as well as from *larger* P* changes, which is the volatility parameter that we can control. Volatility and its associated opportunities also come from "noise" traders, and the overshooting that is caused by you as a user, as well as by the machine driven momentum orders. This overshooting is a source of positive returns for limit order placers because it leads to mean reversion.

How did you adjust your use of limit order to reflect their greater value in the order book of a volatile stock?

EXERCISE 6.10: NEWS AND CHANGING EXPECTATIONS

In this exercise, TraderEx will provide news stories that are sometimes associated with P* changes, and increases or decreases in fundamental valuations as represented by changes in P*. Positive news will appear at the time of a P* increase, and negative news will be linked to a P* decline. Some news stories may be neutral, and may contain no meaningful information except to warn you that an important news release is imminent.

Recall that informational efficiency means that a stock's price fully incorporates the entire information set. If this were not the case, you could use the public information set and generate profitable trades. In TraderEx, the market will adjust to reflect the news releases, but there will be some lag in the response. In fact, your participation in the market will impact the speed of the response to the news.

When you receive a piece of news about the company that you are trading in TraderEx, how should you react to it? Economists generally assume that a stock's price, at any moment in time, properly reflects the full information set available to investors. Therefore, a stock's price change in the future cannot be attributed to the current information set. For informational efficiency to hold, a stock's price will change only because of the advent of new information (news). The news needs to be unexpected because any possible anticipation is part of the current information set.

If the news is totally unanticipated, its effect on the share price cannot be predicted and the stock, therefore, follows a random walk (our information driver, P^*, itself follows a random walk in our simulation runs that do not involve news stories). This exercise will provide you with news releases that need to be interpreted. Only news that is unanticipated will have a meaningful impact on prices. But, as you will see, prices do not adjust to the news (to the new value of P^*) instantaneously. This is very important for you—it gives you a small but critical window of opportunity to beat the market.

To start the exercise, enter 94 as the Scenario Number, and set the arrival rate to an order every three minutes on average:

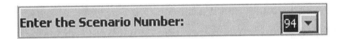

The role you will play in the simulations with news is that of a proprietary trader. Prop traders take long and short positions to generate a positive P&L. They buy and sell based on short-term price movements that they anticipate on the basis of trends, price charts, news releases, or other indicators. You will have no initial position but should respond to the news that arrives with orders and trades. During the run, TraderEx will release news, such as:

As each news story comes in, you will need to assess its value relevance, and its probable impact on P^*. You should take a position that will profit from the price change you anticipate. While the news shown in the News Wire comments shown above reflects neither pessimism nor optimism, it makes clear that the subsequent releases will have an impact. Assume that a position limit of 750 is imposed on you, meaning you should not exceed that many units, short or long. As a proprietary trader you do not carry overnight positions, and thus must return to a flat (zero) position by the close.

1. Run the simulation for a full day up to the close of trading at 4 P.M. (at 16.00). During the run, consider and write down the following:
   - Once news was released, what was your strategy for trading?
   - What positive or negative effects did the news and the market's price changes have on your proprietary trading?
   - How did your order handling differ as a result of receiving news stories?

2. Did you return to a zero position? What was your average position? What was your largest position at any point in time?

3. What is your P&L at the end? In a proprietary trading role, do you understand what led to your P&L result?

4. Using the GET DATA tool, review the TradeOrders.csv file—
   - What percentage of your prop trading was done by limit order and what percent by market order?
   - Do you feel this was an optimal split between the two types of orders?

      A: _____

5. Using the GET CHART function or the GET DATA function, graph the market's trade prices, your trades (indicate limit and market orders), and show your position. Identify your best and worst trades of the day.

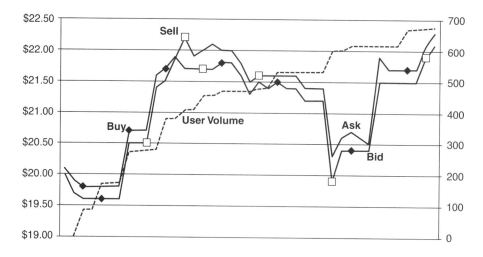

6. What post-trade analyses could a prop trading participant use to improve his/her order placement decision making in the future?

Repeat the simulation three more times using other Scenario Numbers of your choice in the range 92 to 99. These will contain other news stories and different P* paths. After three runs of the simulation, examine the three P&L results you achieve in each trial.

EXERCISE 6.11: ENDOGENOUS EXPECTATIONS

All of the simulations so far have assumed that there is a background P* path that you and your orders did not affect. While you may have had an impact on the price levels in the short term by entering limit or market orders, any P* changes were exogenous. In this exercise, we will take an alternative perspective and make a different assumption about how P* changes occur.

With endogenous expectations, the orders that you and the computer place on the book will influence expectations of the simulation's trading agents, and alter the order flow that comes from the computer. In other words, a rash of sell orders can lead to a drop in P*, and evidence of strong buying interest in the order book can raise the value of P*. In the Stand Alone | Order Driven mode, select "Target Order Generation," and enter 20 percent, then select the "Endogenous" option for Order Generation and put the Order Arrival Rate at 3.0 minutes between orders on average (See Figure 6.13). Otherwise, keep all of the simulation settings at their default level.

1. Run the simulation for a full day up to the close of trading at 16.00. What was the impact on the market of the endogenous source of P* changes?

2. Since your orders influenced the flow of the simulation's orders, how did your trading strategy change? Explain why you are ahead of or are behind the VWAP.

3. Was beating VWAP more difficult? Less difficult? Why?

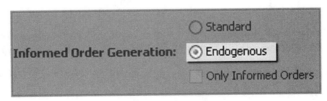

FIGURE 6.13 Selecting an alternative source of Informed Order Generation and P* changes.

4. Did the endogenous P* changes and your trading add alpha to the fund's performance, or did it detract?
   - Added. Why? _____
   - Detracted. Why? _____

5. Using the GET DATA tool, review the TradeOrders.csv file—
   - What percentage of your trading was done by limit order and what percentage by market order?

     Limit orders _____ percent
     Market orders _____ percent

   - How does this compare with the market environment that you faced in Exercise 6.6?

     Answer: _____

Repeat three more times. At the initial parameter screen, enter "Target Order Generation," and enter 20 percent, then select the "Endogenous" option for Order Generation, enter 3.0 minutes between orders, and choose a different Scenario Number (from 1 to 90). You will encounter different environments and see a distribution based your four outcomes.

EXERCISE 6.12: A ONE-YEAR HOLDING PERIOD

The simulations so far have asked you to trade over a one-day period. In this exercise, you will do two days of trading, but the trading days will be separated by a year in the market. Prices will change over the one-year period according to a distribution with an expected return and a standard deviation that can be adjusted. See Figure 6.14.

For our discussion here, we will use the default setting of 8 percent for both values. With this setting, the price is expected to increase by 8 percent, but with dispersion around that value. As a trader, you will be seeking to add to the return through effective trading decisions.

1. Run the simulation for a full day up to the close of trading at 16:00, and build a long position but do not let the market share of your trading exceed 20 percent.

2. What is your closing position at the end of the day? What is the closing price, and what is your average buying price?

3. What do you expect the order book to look like at the opening of the market on the day a year from now?

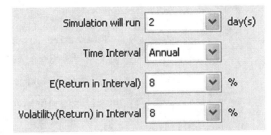

FIGURE 6.14 Selecting a 2-day simulation and "annual" as the time interval between the days.

4. Advance to the trading day for a year from now. Over the course of this second trading day, reduce the position to zero. What is the P&L? What was your average selling price?

5. What is the close-to-close return on the stock? For instance, if the first day close was $10 and the second day close was $11, there was a $1 return, or 10 percent.

6. Compare the close-to-close return in the market to the return you achieved based on the difference between the average buying price in Day 1 and the average selling price in Day 2.

EXERCISE 6.13: CROSSING NETWORKS

Crossing networks have been a feature of institutional trading in the U.S. equities markets since the late 1980s. Crossings are matching sessions that take place periodically (e.g., every hour), and put together submitted buy and sell orders at the midquote of the reference market, usually the NYSE or NASDAQ. If the NYSE bid and offer are $20.50 and $20.56, then offsetting orders to buy and to sell in a crossing system will be matched at $20.53.

1. Select Order Driven as the primary market structure, and Crossing as the alternative structure. See Figure 6.15. Every hour on the hour (10 A.M., 11 A.M., 12 noon, 1 P.M., 2 P.M., and 3 P.M.), TraderEx will average the order book's bid and offer quotes and match the buy and sell orders that were submitted at the midquote price. You will see the crossing trade appear on the ticker, but you will not learn what the submitted but unmatched quantities were.

2. Select Scenario Number 10, and Target Order Generation to 30 percent of total volume to receive a large-buy trading instruction from TraderEx.
   Entering orders into the crossing—Market orders will execute at the midpoint of the bid and ask quotes. A limit order in the cross also trades at the common crossing price, but gives the user protection against executing at a

FIGURE 6.15 Selecting an order book and crossing system market.

midpoint price that moves to a higher level than the buyer is willing to pay, or a lower level than the seller wants to accept:

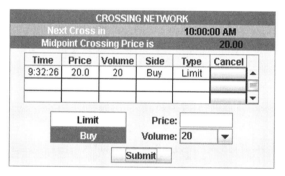

3. Run the simulation for a day. What was the size of your instruction? Did you complete it? How much of it was completed in the hourly crossing sessions?

4. How much did you use the crossings? What percentage of your submissions to the cross was matched?

5. Did you outperform VWAP? Did you reduce or increase your Pace risk when crosses were available? Was your performance improved with the crossing system?

6. Replay with the Scenario Number set to 11 and play the role of a seller. Again assess your performance relative to VWAP and the level of Pace risk. Was your performance improved with the crossing system?

EXERCISE 6.14: A NETWORKED SIMULATION

A multi-user version of TraderEx is in use in the courses of a number of leading business schools. It networks the users' computers together to form networked markets. What makes the networked version of TraderEx exciting is the competition that it generates between live users like yourself, and the performance comparisons that are possible at the end.

This material is for those who have access to the networked version of the software. We give further instructional material for the networked software on our web page (www.etraderex.net).

After a simulation run, the leader board is the focus of the group's attention. In the following example, 12 teams of two traders each were given instructions to buy or to sell 1,500 units. The top of the leader board shows the day's high–low price range, VWAP, and volume:

LEADER BOARD - OrderBook_G, Version#: 2					
HIGH: 22.00	LOW: 19.60	LAST: 20.20	VWAP: 20.64	VOLUME: 11379	TRADES: 349

Clicking on "Show All Details" will expand the Leader Board so that you can see the details of the participants' performance.

Net Pos - Show Details	VWAP - Show Details	PNL - Show Details	RISK - Show Details	Show All Details

In this run, two of the five sellers completed or nearly completed the instruction, and sold for average prices ($21.014 and $20.993) greater than the $20.64 value of VWAP. Only four of the seven buyers completed the instruction to buy 1,500 and of those only two bought for less than VWAP. Outperforming market benchmarks is difficult, but it can contribute to the returns an investor achieves.

OrderBook_G, v.2 ▼ | Submit | GET DATA | LAUNCH CHARTS

CHANGE SCORING WEIGHTING: Risk Weight: 0 | P and L Weight: 0 | VWAP Weight: 100 | Job Completion: ☐ | Submit Changes

LEADER BOARD - OrderBook_G, Version#: 2					
HIGH: 22.00	LOW: 19.60	LAST: 10.00	VWAP: 20.64	VOLUME: 11379	TRADES: 349

Net Pos - Hide Details	VWAP - Hide Details	PNL - Hide Details	RISK - Hide Details	Hide ALL Details

RANK	TRADER	TOTAL SCORE	NET. POS	NET. POS :am / :pm	AVG. BUYING PRICE (SCORE)	AVG. SELLING PRICE (SCORE)	VWAP SCORE	REALIZED / UNREALIZED P&L	P&L SCORE	RISK SCORE	AVG. POS.	TARGET	% MKT SHARE	TOTAL VOL	MKT ORDER VOL	TRADES
SELLERS:																
1	TEMP20	-362.3	-1550	-466/ -1346	0.000 (0.000)	20.410 (-362.320)	-362.3	0.00 / 14.70	14.70	0.00	321.96	0	13.62	1550	1550	43
2	TEMP2	-185.6	-1215	-140/ -440	0.000 (0.000)	20.490 (-185.635)	-185.6	0.00 / 109.90	109.90	0.00	450.27	0	10.68	1215	815	45
3	TEMP1	-147.3	-1652	-297/ -705	0.000 (0.000)	20.554 (-147.328)	-147.3	0.00 / 254.50	254.50	0.00	615.05	0	14.52	1652	423	35
4	TEMP5	503.7	-1360	-181/ -1063	0.000 (0.000)	21.014 (503.697)	503.7	0.00 / 834.50	834.50	0.00	570.62	0	11.95	1360	407	43
5	TEMP4	524.9	-1499	-265/ -1142	0.000 (0.000)	20.993 (524.885)	524.9	0.00 / 889.50	889.50	0.00	349.30	0	13.17	1499	0	41
BUYERS:																
1	TEMP7	-606.8	1500	0/ 928	20.974 (-545.356)	20.233 (-61.486)	-606.8	-111.06 / -1310.63	-1421.70	0.00	598.07	0	15.82	1800	1294	47
2	TEMP11	-430.5	1784	0/ 1295	20.885 (-430.463)	0.000 (0.000)	-430.5	0.00 / -1399.60	-1399.60	0.00	237.99	0	15.68	1784	1595	45
3	GREG	-55.8	10	-40/ 0	21.604 (-48.038)	20.450 (-7.729)	-55.8	-46.16 / -15.04	-61.20	0.00	17.35	0	0.79	90	50	4
4	TEMP6	115.2	1500	451/ 1645	20.628 (27.037)	21.000 (88.120)	115.2	91.94 / -791.64	-699.70	0.00	380.95	0	17.52	1994	1089	52
5	TEMP9	215.3	808	100/ 258	20.377 (215.337)	0.000 (0.000)	215.3	0.00 / -223.60	-223.60	0.00	254.46	0	7.10	808	100	23
6	TEMP10	231.7	1500	1550/ 1550	20.496 (228.819)	20.700 (2.838)	231.7	10.22 / -593.42	-583.20	0.00	867.33	0	14.06	1600	1600	52
7	TEMP8	300.4	1104	185/ 290	20.371 (300.435)	0.000 (0.000)	300.4	0.00 / -299.30	-299.30	0.00	309.16	0	9.70	1104	367	44

The following screenshot is from a larger simulation with 25 participants. The Leader Board for the sellers and the buyers is shown below. The instructions were to sell or to buy 2,000 units. Can you identify the top performers?

CHANGE SCORING WEIGHTING: VWAP Weight: 100   P and L Weight: 0   Risk Weight: 0   Job Completion: 0   [Set Weighting]

UNREALIZED P&L TYPE: ● LAST (18.50)   ○ BEST BID/BEST OFFER (18.50/18.80)   [Set P&L Type]

LEADER BOARD - TS5, Version#: 2

| HIGH: 20.70 | LOW: 14.90 | LAST: 18.50 | VWAP: 19.57 | VOLUME: 99844 | TRADES: 2617 |

☑ NET POS Details   ☑ VWAP Details   ☑ PNL Details   ☑ RISK Details   [Set View]

RANK	TRADER	TOTAL SCORE	NET. POS	NET. POS 11am / 2pm	AVG. BUYING PRICE (SCORE)	AVG. SELLING PRICE (SCORE)	VWAP SCORE	REALIZED / UNREALIZED P&L	P&L SCORE	AVG. POS.	TARGET	RISK SCORE	% MKT SHARE	TOTAL VOL	MKT ORDER VOL	TRADES
SELLERS:																
1	ZACHARY	2270.1	-2000	-2041/-914	19.196 (661.661)	19.998 (1608.460)	2270.1	1415.92/3006.69	4422.61	1274.30	0	0.00	5.54	5532	693	135
2	BRIAN	1611.4	-1168	-8182/-3553	19.562 (112.996)	19.675 (1498.430)	1611.4	1489.72/1372.49	2862.21	3913.13	-2000	23732.70	27.64	27592	16028	698
3	IAN	1430.7	-1950	-1986/-1961	18.721 (211.548)	20.125 (1219.150)	1430.7	349.60/3169.30	3518.90	1764.93	-2000	23885.70	2.45	2448	273	57
4	AZER	1340.1	-1850	-1849/-1849	19.352 (63.353)	20.167 (1276.730)	1340.1	236.37/3084.83	3321.20	1464.04	-2000	27023.70	2.43	2430	628	70
5	VANDITA	1269.7	-2000	-1941/-2000	19.945 (-389.159)	20.117 (1658.830)	1269.7	177.98/3233.44	3411.42	1833.87	-2000	14204.50	4.08	4078	535	88
6	UFLA1	722.4	-2667	-1807/-1807	0.000 (0.000)	19.842 (722.375)	722.4	0.00/3578.39	3578.39	1576.39	-2000	13751.30	2.67	2667	251	56
7	ALEX	432.6	-2000	-789/-771	19.566 (2.954)	19.735 (429.696)	432.6	105.01/2469.38	2574.39	884.03	-2000	22409.30	3.25	3246	842	80
8	KENNETH	364.1	-2000	-1487/-207	19.295 (711.227)	19.495 (-347.163)	364.1	515.86/512.22	1028.08	680.93	-2000	31579.70	7.16	7148	758	184
9	JARED	333.7	-2000	-1338/-1543	0.000 (0.000)	19.738 (333.652)	333.7	0.00/2475.40	2475.40	1217.00	-2000	10627.70	2.00	2000	396	39
10	ZACHARYM	-153.1	-1038	-479/-746	0.000 (0.000)	19.423 (-153.064)	-153.1	0.00/958.50	958.50	488.66	-2000	16812.70	1.04	1038	571	38

CHANGE SCORING WEIGHTING: VWAP Weight: 100   P and L Weight: 0   Risk Weight: 0   Job Completion: 0   [Set Weighting]

UNREALIZED P&L TYPE: ● LAST (18.50)   ○ BEST BID/BEST OFFER (18.50/18.80)   [Set P&L Type]

LEADER BOARD - TS5, Version#: 2

| HIGH: 20.70 | LOW: 14.90 | LAST: 18.50 | VWAP: 19.57 | VOLUME: 99844 | TRADES: 2617 |

☑ NET POS Details   ☑ VWAP Details   ☑ PNL Details   ☑ RISK Details   [Set View]

RANK	TRADER	TOTAL SCORE	NET. POS	NET. POS 11am / 2pm	AVG. BUYING PRICE (SCORE)	AVG. SELLING PRICE (SCORE)	VWAP SCORE	REALIZED / UNREALIZED P&L	P&L SCORE	AVG. POS.	TARGET	RISK SCORE	% MKT SHARE	TOTAL VOL	MKT ORDER VOL	TRADES
BUYERS:																
1	MICHAELP	2428.9	2000	-2449/104	19.493 (710.304)	19.813 (1718.580)	2428.9	2272.68/-1095.57	1177.11	1755.76	2000	13021.40	16.22	16190	7425	414
2	STEVEN	1181.8	230	-1454/140	19.321 (860.527)	19.671 (321.270)	1181.8	1124.36/-188.87	935.49	718.80	2000	16968.10	6.67	6662	1483	156
3	UFLA5	1141.5	2000	831/1552	18.925 (1612.220)	18.620 (-470.682)	1141.5	-150.82/-849.39	-1000.21	1153.93	2000	4512.15	2.99	2990	515	67
4	UFLA3	418.7	2000	29/29	19.159 (974.992)	18.051 (-556.339)	418.7	-405.52/-1317.58	-1723.10	203.09	2000	9823.15	2.74	2732	1506	55
5	BLAKE	289.7	2038	1275/1544	19.429 (353.004)	19.433 (-63.260)	289.7	1.51/-1894.21	-1892.70	1287.99	0	0.00	2.96	2954	278	77
6	CHEOLSU	254.8	2050	1190/1890	19.335 (539.305)	18.385 (-284.510)	254.8	-227.99/-1712.51	-1940.50	1355.55	2000	8455.79	2.53	2530	200	73
7	ALFREDA	228.9	2000	135/1224	19.570 (1.438)	19.824 (227.414)	228.9	227.86/-2004.98	-1777.12	919.29	2000	13641.90	3.81	3800	2270	93
8	PHILIPPE	91.5	2160	948/1996	19.602 (-75.212)	20.296 (166.699)	91.5	159.46/-2381.06	-2221.60	1327.95	2000	11010.10	2.62	2620	314	84
9	DANIELLE	-24.5	2000	1242/1126	19.459 (335.928)	19.212 (-360.384)	-24.5	-248.18/-1918.02	-2166.21	960.86	2000	12699.90	4.01	4006	2726	85
10	MICHAEL	-129.5	2190	1574/2130	19.559 (31.539)	19.195 (-161.034)	-129.5	-155.88/-2318.83	-2474.71	1629.54	2000	10019.10	3.05	3046	299	68

A number of performance measures are displayed after a group trading simulation. The participants can see how they did compared to the overall market outcome, and to each other. These are the metrics used to compare individual results after a simulation:

- **Net Pos A.M./P.M.:** This column shows each participant's position at 11 A.M. and again at 2 P.M.
- **VWAP Score**: This metric reflects whether a user outperformed the volume weighted average price for the market (VWAP) in his/her buying and selling activities in the simulation. It is calculated as the total value of a trader's outperformance relative to VWAP:

$$= \text{Trader's Total Buy Volume} \times (\text{VWAP—Trader's Average Buy Price})$$
$$+ \text{Trader's Total Sell Volume} \times (\text{Trader's Average Sell Price—VWAP})$$

If a trader's average buying and selling price are the same as VWAP, this score will be zero. A negative score indicates buying for more than VWAP and selling for less than VWAP.

- **Avg Buying Price (Score):** There are two components to this column. The first is the Average Buying Price, which is the average price paid for all shares purchased. The second is the buying part of the VWAP Score calculated with reference to the VWAP.
- **Avg Selling Price (Score):** There are two components to this column. The first is the Average Selling Price, which is the average price received for all shares sold. The second is the selling part of the VWAP Score calculated with reference to the VWAP.
- **P&L Score:** Is the sum of the Realized P&L and Unrealized P&L. Unrealized P&L is the current inventory of shares marked to market. We use the convention of marking long positions to the bid quote and short positions to the offer without taking the size of a position into account.
- **Risk Score:** The Risk Score, as detailed in Chapter 4, reflects how evenly paced (low risk) you bought or sold the trading instruction given to you. Risk collars around the pace position give the traders some leeway within which no risk penalty is assessed. Having a position vastly different than the pace position is risky, and the risk score is calculated as:

$$\text{Risk Score} = \sum \text{Max} (0, \text{Min}(| \text{Position} | - | \text{CollarLOW}, | \text{Position} | - | \text{CollarHIGH} |) |)$$

In other words, risk points accumulate when the size of the user position is less than lower collar value or greater than the higher collar value. The risk score reduces your total score the more often your position is outside the position collars, and the further out you are.

- **Avg Pos:** This is the average position the trader had throughout the trading day. It is computed as the average of the N minute observations of the trader's position. For a trader or a dealer seeking to close the day with a flat or zero position, higher average position levels create greater risk.

$$\text{Average Position} = \frac{\sum_{i=1}^{N} |\text{Position\_at\_Minute\_}i|}{N}$$

CONCLUSION

In this chapter, you played a number of roles in a continuous order book market structure. In some exercises, you were a trader handling a buy-side investor's instruction to buy or to sell a quantity of shares. Such position traders seek to trade without paying overly high prices, or receiving prices that are too low. In other exercises, you were a proprietary trader deciding when to "make" liquidity in an order book market by placing limit orders, and when to "take" liquidity by using market orders to buy and sell. Proprietary traders seek to earn a positive profit while managing the risk of the positions they hold. Each role presented a different set of motivations, and each involves its own risks.

CHAPTER 7

The Call Auction Market Structure

This chapter includes trading exercises in a call auction facility that operates in conjunction with a continuous order book market structure. The exercises will teach you about the decisions traders make when call auctions are available, and the effects of a call auction on traders in their various roles in a stock market.

Most major stock exchanges open and close trading with a call auction, and some have a midday auction. The rest of the day, a continuous market for trading operates. A call auction batches orders and discovers a price for multilateral trades in which buyers and sellers collectively arrive at a single clearing price. In the simulations, you will see the price formation process of a call auction, and participate in it. You will be handling large buy or sell orders as a buy-side trader, and can choose to participate in any of three daily auctions (at the open, at 12:45 P.M., and at the close). You will seek to trade profitably using both the call and continuous market structures.

By batching many transactions together, a call auction concentrates liquidity and, in so doing, can significantly decrease transaction costs for participants. As an alternative market structure, call auctions affect order flow, handling decisions, price discovery, and market transparency.

As you turn to the exercises that include this new market structure, you should address these questions:

- How do the operations of the market change when a call auction is added to an order book system?

- How can you compare the quality of the call auction market to other, different market systems?
- What changes should you make to your tactics for buying or selling large quantities of shares when a call auction market structure is available?
- Does the new call auction structure alter the way you carry out proprietary trading by limiting risk or by increasing profit opportunities?

There are no simple answers to these questions. Trading decisions in call auctions should reflect a number of important considerations that we will cover.

Orders put into TraderEx's call auctions are typically *priced* orders. In other words, nearly all orders are limit orders in our calls. You can enter a market order into the call to ensure its execution, but there is a risk the price will be unattractive. A critical feature of the call auction is that the limit price of an order in the call auction is typically not the price at which the limit order executes in that facility. For instance, a buy order in a call may have a maximum price it is willing to pay of $20.50, but it will execute at $20.40 if the clearing price at the call is $20.40. This limit order has received a *price improvement*. Similarly, a seller in the same auction may have a price limit of $20.30, below which it will not execute. In the call, however, the seller also receives $20.40 a share as that is the clearing price. In contrast, during *continuous* trading in an order book, as we examined in Chapter 6, a limit order executes *at its limit price*.

THE PRICE SETTING MECHANISM IN TRADEREX CALL AUCTIONS

Two important operational details of any call auction are the pricing mechanism used, and how any buy-sell imbalances at the call auction price are handled. The most common pricing mechanism in a call auction is to choose the price that maximizes the number of shares that trade.

Table 7.1 shows the accumulated orders on the book of a call auction. Buy orders accumulate from the high price to lower prices on the left. Sell orders accumulate from the low price to higher prices on the right. For instance, the order to buy 20 priced at $19.60 is added to the order placed to sell 20 at $19.50 or higher. The cumulative quantity to sell at $19.60 therefore is 40. Anyone willing to sell at $19.50 is surely willing to sell at $19.60 or higher. Moving up to $19.90, the 50 units at that price are added to the 85 units that could be sold at $19.80. In total, 135 units can be sold at $19.90. Likewise, the call auction buyers who would pay $20.00 per share would certainly be willing to buy at $19.90. At the price of $19.90, there are orders in the call auction to buy 10, and these are added to the buy orders for 130 at $20.00, leaving a total buy interest of 140 units at the price of $19.90.

TABLE 7.1 Price Determination Based on Orders in TraderEx Call Auctions

BUYS			SELLS		
Orders at Price	Cumulative	Price	Cumulative	Orders at Price	Cumulative-Minimum
0	—	$20.60	250	20	—
5	5	$20.50	230	0	5
10	15	$20.40	230	45	15
20	35	$20.30	185	5	35
15	50	$20.20	180	10	50
45	95	$20.10	170	20	95
35	130	$20.00	150	15	130
10	140	$19.90	135	50	135
20	160	$19.80	85	35	85
30	190	$19.70	50	10	50
10	200	$19.60	40	20	40
25	225	$19.50	20	20	20
20	245	$19.40	—	0	—
10	255	$19.30	—	0	—
			Maximum of the Minimum Cumulative Sizes =		135

Inspection of the order book in this illustration shows that the call auction's maximum trade quantity is 135 at 19.90. Embedded in the software for the call auction is an algorithm that finds the price that, scanning across prices, **maximizes the minimum of the buy and sell aggregate order quantities** at each price. At $20.00, only 130 can be traded (130 is the minimum of the aggregated buy and sell quantities at that price), while at 19.80 only 85 would trade (85 is the minimum of the two quantities at that price). Therefore the unique price for the auction is $19.90, at which the minimum of the buy and sell quantities is maximized. At $19.90, 5 out of the 140 units to buy will not be matched with a seller, and the call auction must prioritize the orders on the "heavy" side of the imbalance to determine which of the set of buy orders in this case will be executed.

There are several sensible ways to prioritize among the orders on the heavy side of the auction. One is to order them by size and execute the largest orders first. In this example the 5 units to buy that would not be matched would be from the smallest orders submitted. This encourages larger order submissions and could make the auction deeper and more liquid. A second approach would be to first match orders on the heavy side that have the most aggressive limit prices. In this illustration, all of the buy orders with limit prices of $20.00 or higher will trade, and only 5 of the 10 units to buy entered with a limit price of 19.90 will trade. The 5 selected for execution from among the 10 would be those that arrived first. If the

10 units are all from one order, that order will receive a partial execution. The third approach is to take all of the orders on the heavy side and rank them by time of arrival. They would be matched and traded according to a first-in first-out (FIFO) discipline. TraderEx provides a choice of either a price/time rule or a time priority rule for selecting which orders execute on the heavy side of the book at the call auction price. At the initial configuration screen, when the call auction is chosen, you will be able to select price–time priority or time priority.

Below is a list of the steps that TraderEx goes through to set the call auction price, including the tie-breaking criteria when more than one price leads to the same, maximum trading quantity. You must know the rules of auction price setting in order to determine how best to price and size your orders in a call auction.

Price-setting rule #1—Select the price that maximizes trade quantity. In Table 7.2, the price of $20.00 maximizes trade quantity.

Price-setting rule #2—If there is more than one price that maximizes trade quantity, select the price with the smallest surplus, or imbalance, between the buying and selling quantities. In Table 7.3, two prices generate the same maximum trade quantity; the price $20.10 will be selected because its imbalance quantity of $330 - 280 = 50$ is the least of the two candidate prices.

After the call, the unexecuted orders can roll into the continuous order book, which will appear as in Table 7.4. The call auction imbalance of 50 now appears as the low offer in the order book.

The call algorithm, as described earlier, can handle the buy–sell imbalance at the auction price in several ways. In this illustration, the auction system left unexecuted 50 of the 330 units for sale at $20.10.

With price–time priority, the call auction gives priority to the sellers who placed orders with the most aggressive, or lowest selling prices. In this case, the sell orders for 50 placed with the price limit of $20.10 will not

TABLE 7.2 Price Determination Based on Maximum Trade Quantity

BUYS			SELLS	
At Price	Cumulative	Price	Cumulative	At Price
70	100	$20.30	640	180
45	145	$20.20	460	100
65	210	$20.10	360	80
70	280	$20.00	280	70
80	360	$19.90	210	65
100	460	$19.80	145	45
200	660	$19.70	100	80

TABLE 7.3 Price Determination ($20.10) Based on Minimum Imbalance

BUYS		Price	SELLS		Imbalance
At Price	**Cumulative**		**Cumulative**	**At Price**	
70	100	$20.30	630	200	−530
45	145	$20.20	430	100	−285
135	280	$20.10	330	50	−50
70	350	$20.00	280	70	70
80	430	$19.90	210	65	220
100	530	$19.80	145	45	385
200	730	$19.70	100	80	630

execute while all of the sell orders priced at $20.00 or less will execute. In time priority, the 330 units to sell will be ranked by time of arrival into the call auction, and will be executed on a first-in, first-out basis.

Price-setting rule #3—If there is more than one price that has the same trade quantity and the same buy–sell imbalance, select the price that conforms with market pressure. In Table 7.5, the maximum trade quantity (330) and minimum imbalance (20) are evident at both $20.10 and $20.20. Since the imbalance is –20 (negative), and therefore tilted toward the selling side, the call auction will take place in the direction of market pressure at $20.10.

Price-setting rule #4—Although it is very unlikely, it is possible for more than one price to yield the same maximum turnover, with equal imbalances and market pressure. For this to happen, one of the prices will have an imbalance on the buying side, and one will have a heavy selling side, as illustrated in Table 7.6. In this unusual case, whichever of the candidate

TABLE 7.4 Continuous Order Book Market after Call Auction in Table 7.3 Executes at $20.10

BIDS		Price	OFFERS	
At Price	**Cumulative**		**Cumulative**	**At Price**
		$20.30	350	200
		$20.20	150	100
		$20.10	50	50
70	70	$20.00		
80	150	$19.90		
100	250	$19.80		
200	450	$19.70		

TABLE 7.5 Price Determination ($20.10) Based on Market Pressure

	BUYS		SELLS		
At Price	**Cumulative**	**Price**	**Cumulative**	**At Price**	**Imbalance**
70	100	$20.40	550	100	−450
100	200	$20.30	450	100	−250
130	*330*	$20.20	350	0	−20
0	*330*	$20.10	350	70	−20
70	400	$20.00	280	70	120
80	480	$19.90	210	65	270
100	580	$19.80	145	45	435
200	780	$19.70	100	80	680

Excess selling at the two candidate prices leads the algorithm to select the lower of the two prices.

call prices, $20.10 or $20.20, is closest to the most recent "reference" price is selected. If the last trade before the auction shown below was at $20.20 or greater, for example, the call auction price will be $20.20. If the last trade was at $20.15, the call auction randomly selects from the possible prices.

The auction price setting rules were illustrated with static auction order books shown at the moment the call executes. Next, we show how indicative call auction prices evolve as orders accumulate on the book. Again, buy orders accumulate from high to low prices on the left, and sell orders accumulate from low to high prices on the right.

Call auctions progress over time as orders arrive. In Figure 7.1, the call auction is shown in three stages as the book builds. On the left, the call auction is in an early stage and there are only three prices at which buy and sell orders overlap in

TABLE 7.6 Price Determination ($20.00) Based on Least Change from Last Trade Price

	BUYS		SELLS		
At Price	**Cumulative**	**Price**	**Cumulative**	**At Price**	**Imbalance**
70	100	$20.40	550	100	−450
100	200	$20.30	450	100	−250
130	*330*	$20.20	350	20	−20
20	350	$20.10	*330*	50	20
70	420	$20.00	280	70	140
80	500	$19.90	210	65	290
100	600	$19.80	145	45	455
200	800	$19.70	100	80	700

MARKET CALL					
Indicative 19.90			Imbalance 213		
	BIDS		OFFERS		
X	0	0	20.50	4009	0	X
X	0	0	20.40	3744	0	X
X	0	0	20.30	3470	0	X
X	0	0	20.20	2654	0	X
X	0	0	20.10	1859	0	X
X	0	173	20.00	764	0	X
X	0	483	19.90	270	0	X
X	0	717	19.80	191	0	X
X	0	1398	19.70	0	0	X
X	0	2661	19.60	0	0	X
X	0	3515	19.50	0	0	X
X	0	4102	19.40	0	0	X
X	0	4418	19.30	0	0	X

(a)

MARKET CALL					
Indicative 19.90			Imbalance 164		
	BIDS		OFFERS		
X	0	0	20.50	5615	0	X
X	0	0	20.40	5255	0	X
X	0	0	20.30	4915	0	X
X	0	75	20.20	4044	0	X
X	0	206	20.10	3062	0	X
X	0	486	20.00	1860	0	X
X	0	988	19.90	1152	0	X
X	0	1457	19.80	900	0	X
X	0	2420	19.70	558	0	X
X	0	3869	19.60	460	0	X
X	0	4957	19.50	227	0	X
X	0	5709	19.40	124	0	X
X	0	6094	19.30	0	0	X

(b)

MARKET CALL					
Indicative 19.80			Imbalance 545		
	BIDS		OFFERS		
X	0	0	20.50	7092	0	X
X	0	73	20.40	6601	0	X
X	0	215	20.30	6228	0	X
X	0	378	20.20	5334	0	X
X	0	552	20.10	4144	0	X
X	0	939	20.00	2881	0	X
X	0	1695	19.90	2125	0	X
X	0	2391	19.80	1846	0	X
X	0	3455	19.70	1413	0	X
X	0	5085	19.60	1112	0	X
X	0	6544	19.50	855	0	X
X	0	7451	19.40	645	0	X
X	0	7937	19.30	385	0	X

(c)

FIGURE 7.1 Build-up of orders in a TraderEx call auction with significant depth. Orders to sell arriving late in the auction push the price down to $19.80 from $19.90.

			MARKET CALL							MARKET CALL		
	Indicative 19.90			Imbalance 355				Indicative 19.90			Imbalance 5	
		BIDS		OFFERS					BIDS		OFFERS	
X	0	0	20.50	1486	0	X	X	0	0	20.50	1525	0	X
X	0	0	20.40	1486	0	X	X	0	0	20.40	1525	0	X
X	0	0	20.30	1486	0	X	X	0	0	20.30	1525	0	X
X	0	0	20.20	1021	0	X	X	0	0	20.20	1021	0	X
X	0	0	20.10	626	0	X	X	0	0	20.10	626	0	X
X	0	0	20.00	322	0	X	X	0	0	20.00	322	0	X
X	0	0	19.90	50	0	X	X	0	45	19.90	50	0	X
X	0	80	19.80	0	0	X	X	0	207	19.80	0	0	X
X	0	529	19.70	0	0	X	X	0	717	19.70	0	0	X
X	0	970	19.60	0	0	X	X	0	1158	19.60	0	0	X
X	0	1047	19.50	0	0	X	X	0	1235	19.50	0	0	X
X	0	1047	19.40	0	0	X	X	0	1257	19.40	0	0	X
X	0	1047	19.30	0	0	X	X	0	1257	19.30	0	0	X
		(a)							(b)			

FIGURE 7.2 Build-up of orders in a TraderEx Call auction with less significant depth.

price. In the middle stage, the indicative price of $19.90 is shown, and 988 would trade at that price if the market was called at that moment. Figure 7.1(c) is the final stage of the call auction, and a lower price of $19.80 due to the late additional sell orders. A quantity of 1,846 will trade at that price.

Call auctions can vary in size and depth. In Figure 7.2, the first call auction stage has no overlapping buy and sell orders. The book of orders builds, and on the right is the late stage call auction, which shows that additional orders have arrived, and have resulted in a price of $19.90 as indicated with 45 as the quantity that can trade at that price.

Price Impact in a Call Auction: Your Influence on TraderEx Call Auction Prices

In a call auction, large submitted quantities to buy or to sell shares provide depth to the market. As you will see in the exercises, auctions with many orders and substantial depth will absorb large, new orders with less impact on the call price. In a call auction without substantial visible quantities to trade, large orders can have an adverse impact on the auction clearing price. In Table 7.7, we examine a Base Case, and will subsequently examine two orders. The first is an order to buy 15 at $20.20, and the other is to sell 35 at $19.80. The indicative price in the call in Table 7.7 is $19.90 and 135 is the auction quantity. Table 7.8 shows Example 1,

TABLE 7.7 Base case: $P^{Indicative} = \$19.90$, $Q^{Indicative} = 135$

Buys		Price	Sells	
At Price	Cumulative		Cumulative	At Price
0	0	$20.60	250	20
5	5	$20.50	230	0
10	15	$20.40	230	45
20	35	$20.30	185	5
15	50	$20.20	180	10
45	95	$20.10	170	20
35	130	$20.00	150	15
10	*140*	*$19.90*	*135*	50
20	160	$19.80	85	35
30	190	$19.70	50	10
10	200	$19.60	40	20
25	225	$19.50	20	20
20	245	$19.40	0	0
10	255	$19.30	0	0

TABLE 7.8 Example 1: Buy order at $20.20 increases to 25 from 15, $P^{Indicative} = \$20.00$, $Q^{Indicative} = 140$

Buys		Price	Sells	
At Price	Cumulative		Cumulative	At Price
0	0	$20.60	250	20
5	5	$20.50	230	0
10	15	$20.40	230	45
20	35	$20.30	185	5
25	60	$20.20	180	10
45	105	$20.10	170	20
35	*140*	*$20.00*	*150*	15
10	150	$19.90	135	50
20	*170*	*$19.80*	*85*	35
30	200	$19.70	50	10
10	210	$19.60	40	20
25	235	$19.50	20	20
20	255	$19.40	0	0
10	265	$19.30	0	0

TABLE 7.9 Example 2: Sell order at $19.80 increases to 95 from 35, P* = $19.80, Q* = 145

Buys		Price	Sells	
At Price	Cumulative	Price	Cumulative	At Price
0	0	$20.60	310	20
5	5	$20.50	290	0
10	15	$20.40	290	45
20	35	$20.30	245	5
15	50	$20.20	240	10
45	95	$20.10	230	20
35	130	$20.00	210	15
10	140	$19.90	195	50
20	*160*	*$19.80*	*145*	95
30	190	$19.70	50	10
10	200	$19.60	40	20
25	225	$19.50	20	20
20	245	$19.40	0	0
10	255	$19.30	0	0

in which an increase in the size of a buy order at $20.20 from 15 to 25 causes the clearing price to increase to $20.00, and the quantity to increase to 140 from 135. In Table 7.9 is Example 2 in which a large sell order for 60 added at $19.80 moves the price down to $19.80, at which 145 will trade in the call.

In TraderEx, the call auction will occur at a random point in simulation time between 2 minutes and 10 minutes after the auction opens. Depending on how fast you are running TraderEx, this could be 15 to 90 seconds of real time. After the TraderEx call auction completes, trading rolls over into the continuous order book market structure that we examined in Chapter 6.

EXERCISE 7.1: MECHANICS OF THE OPENING CALL AUCTION

Now that the rules of the call auction have been established, it is time to practice using call auctions and to examine their impact on trading outcomes. The first exercise examines how call auction outcomes influence the order book in the continuous market.

1. From the TraderEx parameter screen, check the "Call Auction" feature in the Order Driven structure as shown in Figure 7.3. Set the base rate of orders to every 5.5 minutes. Keep all of the other settings at their default levels, and keep the Scenario Number set at 1.

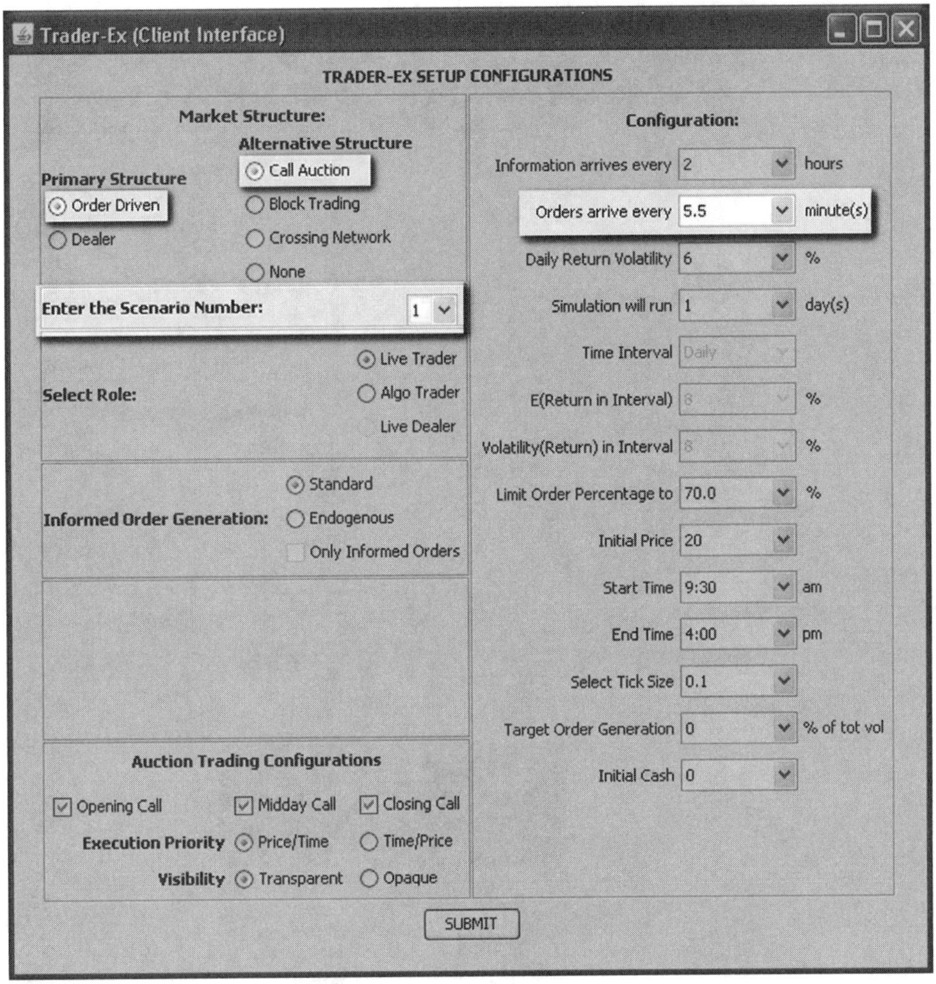

FIGURE 7.3 TraderEx setup screen—check "Order Driven" with "Call Auction" and select all three call auction occurrences.

2. Click on the "GO" button. You will see the sequence of call auction screens shown in Figure 7.4.

3. After the third screen (7.4c), the call will execute. Each scenario number will lead to a different length of time in which the auction accumulates orders and remains indicative. Without your involvement, the opening trade for 485 units at \$19.90 will appear on the ticker at the top of the screen. Continuous trading will begin after the call. In this case, the excess sell orders $(489 - 485 = 4)$ for 4 units from the call auction become the initial offer quote in the order book in Figure 7.5.

4. Click on the "RESET" button to return to the beginning of the call auction. The initial market screen will be the same as Figure 7.4. In the trading steps

(a)

MARKET CALL			
VOLUME 0	HIGH 0.00	LOW 0.00	VWAP 0.00
Indicative 0.00		Imbalance 0	

	BIDS			OFFERS		
X	0	0	21.00	893	0	X
X	0	0	20.90	860	0	X
X	0	0	20.80	653	0	X
X	0	0	20.70	653	0	X
X	0	0	20.60	592	0	X
X	0	0	20.50	493	0	X
X	0	0	20.40	352	0	X
X	0	0	20.30	153	0	X
X	0	0	20.20	121	0	X
X	0	0	20.10	80	0	X
X	0	0	20.00	0	0	X
X	0	20	19.90	0	0	X
X	0	71	19.80	0	0	X
X	0	222	19.70	0	0	X
X	0	240	19.60	0	0	X
X	0	312	19.50	0	0	X
X	0	354	19.40	0	0	X
X	0	532	19.30	0	0	X
X	0	763	19.20	0	0	X
X	0	807	19.10	0	0	X
X	0	914	19.00	0	0	X
X	0	938	18.90	0	0	X

(b)

MARKET CALL			
VOLUME 0	HIGH 0.00	LOW 0.00	VWAP 0.00
Indicative 19.90		Imbalance 46	

	BIDS			OFFERS		
X	0	0	21.00	1033	0	X
X	0	0	20.90	1000	0	X
X	0	0	20.80	793	0	X
X	0	0	20.70	793	0	X
X	0	0	20.60	732	0	X
X	0	0	20.50	633	0	X
X	0	0	20.40	492	0	X
X	0	0	20.30	293	0	X
X	0	8	20.20	261	0	X
X	0	8	20.10	142	0	X
X	0	44	20.00	62	0	X
X	0	108	19.90	62	0	X
X	0	159	19.80	62	0	X
X	0	310	19.70	62	0	X
X	0	328	19.60	0	0	X
X	0	458	19.50	0	0	X
X	0	500	19.40	0	0	X
X	0	678	19.30	0	0	X
X	0	909	19.20	0	0	X
X	0	953	19.10	0	0	X
X	0	1060	19.00	0	0	X
X	0	1084	18.90	0	0	X

(c)

MARKET CALL			
VOLUME 0	HIGH 0.00	LOW 0.00	VWAP 0.00
Indicative 19.70		Imbalance 73	

	BIDS			OFFERS		
X	0	0	21.00	1287	0	X
X	0	0	20.90	1254	0	X
X	0	0	20.80	1047	0	X
X	0	0	20.70	1047	0	X
X	0	0	20.60	986	0	X
X	0	13	20.50	887	0	X
X	0	13	20.40	746	0	X
X	0	13	20.30	547	0	X
X	0	21	20.20	515	0	X
X	0	45	20.10	396	0	X
X	0	81	20.00	316	0	X
X	0	145	19.90	316	0	X
X	0	196	19.80	274	0	X
X	0	347	19.70	274	0	X
X	0	365	19.60	141	0	X
X	0	495	19.50	141	0	X
X	0	537	19.40	141	0	X
X	0	715	19.30	52	0	X
X	0	946	19.20	0	0	X
X	0	990	19.10	0	0	X
X	0	1097	19.00	0	0	X
X	0	1121	18.90	0	0	X

FIGURE 7.4 TraderEx's initial call auction screen and two subsequent displays.

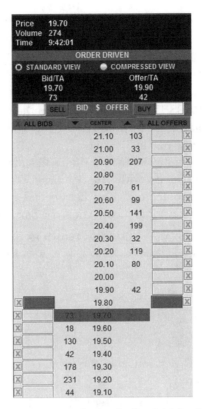

FIGURE 7.5 TraderEx's continuous order book after initial call auction executes.

detailed below, you will launch the opening call auction and participate in it in different ways. At any point during a trading day, the "RESET" button shown in Figure 7.6 will return the market to the opening call auction screen.

5. Once the auction opens, enter a buy order for 4 at $19.90 by clicking on the rectangle next to $19.90 on the left, bid side of the book.
   - What is the effect of your order on the bid–ask spread in the order book after the call auction executes?
   - After the call auction, in the continuous order book system, what price would a market order to buy 4 pay?

6. Click on the "RESET" button to return to the beginning of the call auction. The initial screen in the call auction will again be the same as Figure 7.4.

RESET

FIGURE 7.6 "RESET" will return the current TraderEx simulation to the beginning with its configuration settings retained.

At the first opportunity, enter a call auction order to buy the quantity 50 at $19.70.

- When the market was called, did your order execute? How does this affect your average purchase price compared to buying with a market order after the call?

7. Click on the "RESET" button to return to the beginning of the call auction. **At the point when the buy quantity at $19.70 is 347**, enter a call auction order to buy the quantity 50 at $19.70.

- Does your order execute? How does this affect your average purchase price compared to buying with a market order after the call?

- Compare the outcome with what occurred in #2 above. What does the call auction's time priority mean when you participate in a call auction?

8. Click on the "RESET" button to return to the beginning of the call auction. Enter 50 to sell at $19.90. What price does the auction occur at? Does your order execute?

EXERCISE 7.2: YOUR TRADEREX CALL AUCTION ORDERS

1. Click on "EXIT" and return to the opening parameter screen. Use the settings shown in Figure 7.7.

2. Buy 90 in the opening call. After watching the first five trades in the continuous market, did you benefit from participating in the call with your order for 90?

- Notice that once you have entered a buy order, you can enter a sell order only at a price that is higher than your most aggressive buy. This ensures that you will not trade against your own order in the auction.

3. Click on "RESET." In this opening call, enter a sell order for 50 at $19.70, and another sell for 50 one price level higher at $19.80.

- Which of the two orders executes? How did your participation affect the auction price and the volume traded?

EXERCISE 7.3: YOUR INFLUENCE ON TRADEREX CALL AUCTION PRICES

This exercise will examine how your orders into the auction can affect the outcome.

1. Choose the Order Book structure with Call Auctions added as an alternative structure. Set order arrival to every 9.0 minutes, set the Scenario Number to 4, and retain the default setting for the other inputs.

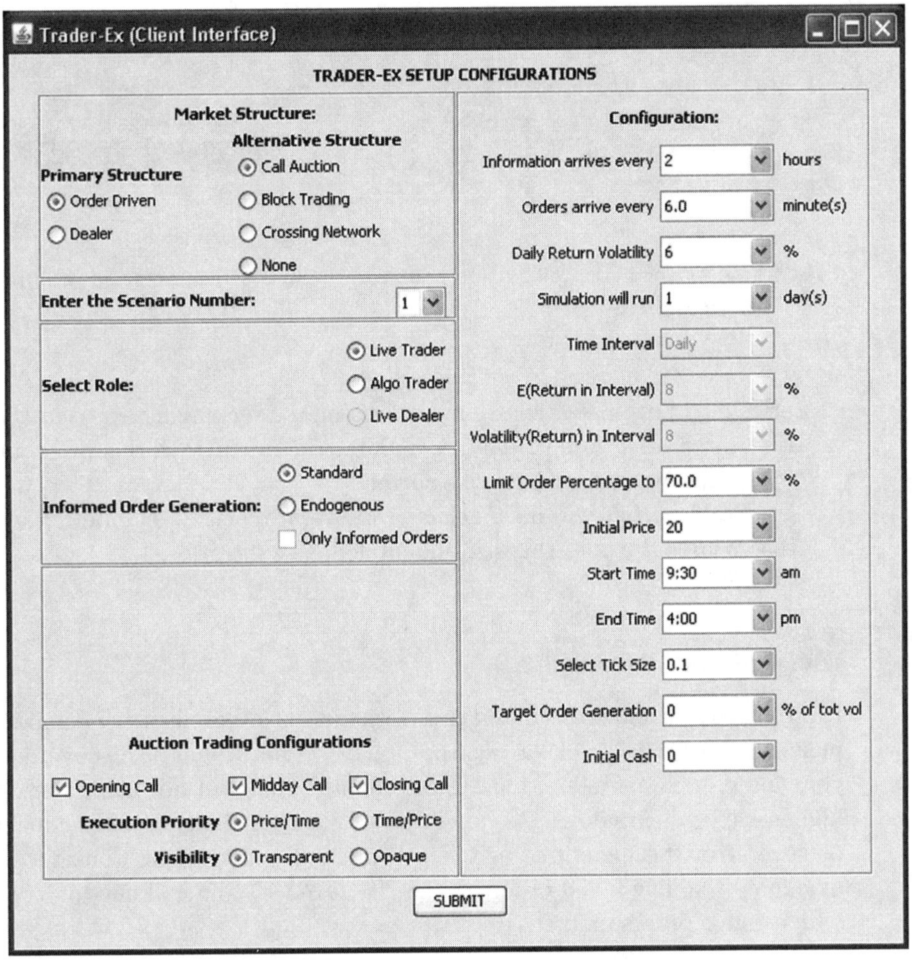

FIGURE 7.7 TraderEx configuration settings for Exercise 7.2.

2. Run through the call auction with the settings indicated to obtain the result in Figure 7.8. A call price of $19.70 and a quantity of 199 will occur.

3. Click on the "RESET" button to return to the beginning of the call auction. Once the auction opens, enter the **largest buy order** that will not move the price up. Do so by clicking on the rectangle next to $20.00 on the left or bid side of the order book. Enter the maximum quantity at this price and click "GO." Have you figured out the size correctly?

   Confirm that you have selected the right quantity by entering a quantity that is larger by one. This size should raise the price.

4. Click on the "RESET" button to return to the beginning of the call auction. Once the auction opens, enter the **largest sell order** that will not move the

(a)

X	0	0	20.20	121	0	X
X	0	0	20.10	80	0	X
X	0	0	20.00	0	0	X
X	0	20	19.90	0	0	X
X	0	71	19.80	0	0	X
X	0	222	19.70	0	0	X

(b)

X	0	45	20.10	365	0	X
X	0	81	20.00	285	0	X
X	0	145	19.90	285	0	X
X	0	196	19.80	243	0	X
X	0	347	19.70	199	0	X
X	0	365	19.60	98	0	X

FIGURE 7.8 The initial call auction book and the final screen obtained with the settings shown in Figure 7.7.

price down to $19.80. Do so by clicking on the rectangle next to $19.80 on the right-hand offer side of the book. Enter the quantity at this price, and click "GO." Have you figured the size correctly?

Confirm that you have selected the right quantity by entering a quantity that is larger by one. This size should decrease the price.

Discussion of Exercise 7.3

Did you use trial and error, or did you work out the largest an order can be before it pushes the price in the call away from the price that would be discovered without your intervention? Finding the largest quantity that will not move the call price higher when you are buying, or lower when you are selling, requires consideration of several of the quantities in the call auction order book. Consider a simple example of adding a sell order of size ΔS at $21.70 to a call auction order book with existing orders in it:

Buy Quantity			Sell Quantity	
At Price	Cumulative	Price	At Price	Cumulative
0	0	22.00	0	50
20	20	21.90	20	50
20	40	**21.80**	20	30
30	70	21.70	10	10
0	70	21.60	0	0

Question: How large can a new sell order, ΔS at $21.70, be before it moves the clearing price to a lower level, costing the sellers $0.10 a share?

Answer: It cannot be so large that the tradable quantity at $21.70 exceeds the maximum quantity (40) that can clear at $21.80. This can be written as an inequality:

$$\text{MIN}(B_{21.80}, S_{21.80} + \Delta S) > \text{MIN}(B_{21.70}, S_{21.70} + \Delta S)$$
$$\text{MIN}(40, 30 + \Delta S) > \text{MIN}(70, 10 + \Delta S)$$
$$30 > \Delta S$$

ΔS cannot equal or exceed 30. If ΔS is 30, then the same quantity of 40 will be tradable at $21.70 and $21.80, and the price with the smaller imbalance will be the auction price. The imbalance for $\Delta S = 30$ is smaller at $P = \$21.80$ () than at $21.70. Therefore, if the new sell quantity is 31, the call price will shift down to $P_{21.70}$, and 41 will trade at that price.

Buy Cumulative	Price	Sell Cumulative
0	22.00	50 + 31 = 81
20	21.90	50 + 31 = 81
40	21.80	30 + 31 = 61
70	**21.70**	10 + 31 = **41**
70	21.60	10

The general upper bound for a sell order to decrease the call price from a higher to a lower price is:

$$\Delta S \leq \text{MIN}(B_{21.80}, S_{21.80}) - \text{MIN}(B_{21.70}, S_{21.70}) + \text{MAX}(B_{21.80} - S_{21.80}, 0)$$
$$= \text{MIN}(40, 30) - \text{MIN}(70, 10) + \text{MAX}(40 - 30, 0) = 30 - 10 + 10 = \mathbf{30}$$

The situation for adding the largest buy order that will not move the price up is similar to that for sell orders. The threshold condition is met by adding the buy quantity ΔB at $21.90, such that the matchable quantities at $21.80 and $21.90 are equal:

$$\text{MIN}(B_{21.80} + \Delta B, S_{21.80}) = \text{MIN}(B_{21.90} + \Delta B_{21.90}, S_{21.90})$$

When the equation holds, the call auction algorithm picks either $21.80 or $21.90 depending on which has the smaller imbalance $|B_{21.80} + \Delta B - S_{21.80}|$ or $|B_{21.90} + \Delta B - S_{21.90}|$. If $|B_{21.80} + \Delta B - S_{21.80}|$ is smaller, then ΔB is the largest quantity that will not move the price. Otherwise, $\Delta B - 1$ is the largest quantity that will not move the price. Therefore,

$$\Delta B \leq \text{MIN}(B_{21.80}, S_{21.80}) - \text{MIN}(B_{21.90}, S_{21.90}) + \text{MAX}(S_{21.80} - B_{21.80}, 0)$$
$$= \text{MIN}(40, 30) - \text{MIN}(20, 50) + \text{MAX}(30 - 40, 0) = 30 - 20 + 0 = \mathbf{10}$$

Therefore, 10 is the largest buy order you can add at $21.90 without moving the price up from $21.80, as long as the imbalance at $21.80 is smaller than at $21.90, which means the inequality below holds:

$$|B_{21.80} + \Delta B - S_{21.80}| < |B_{21.90} + \Delta B - S_{21.90}|$$

or in this case,

$$|50 - 30| < |30 - 60|$$

With $\Delta B = 10$, the imbalance (20) is less at $21.80, so at $\Delta B = 11$, the call price will shift up to $21.90, and 31 will trade at that price.

Buy Cumulative	Price	Sell Cumulative
0	22.00	60
20 + 11 = **31**	**21.90**	60
40 + 11 = 51	21.80	30
60 + 11 = 71	21.70	10
60	21.60	0

While the call auction is a good source of liquidity and market depth, as these illustrations show, some care clearly needs to be exercised in choosing the order quantity to avoid impacting the market.

General Formula for Call Auction Order Sizing to Avoid Market Impact

We can derive the general formula for the maximum order size that will not impact the call auction price. Table 7.10 depicts a call auction that has buy and sell orders at five prices, and is about to execute at P_0 and trade $MIN(B_0, S_0)$.

The call price P_0 was selected because $MIN(B_0, S_0) > MIN(B_{-1}, S_{-1})$ and $MIN(B_0, S_0) > MIN(B_{+1}, S_{+1})$. Adding sell quantity ΔS_{-1} at P_{-1} such that

$$MIN(B_0, S_0 + \Delta S_{-1}) = MIN(B_{-1}, S_{-1} + \Delta S_{-1})$$

TABLE 7.10 A Final Call Auction Book with Buy and Sell Orders at Five Prices from Lowest P_{-2} to Highest P_{+2}

Buy Quantity		Price	Sell Quantity	
At Price	Cumulative	Price	Cumulative	At Price
b_{+2}	$B_{+2} = b_{+2}$	P_{+2}	$S_{+2} = S_{+1} + s_{+2}$	s_{+2}
b_{+1}	$B_{+1} = B_{+2} + b_{+1}$	P_{+1}	$S_{+1} = S_0 + s_{+1}$	s_{+1}
b_0	$B_0 = B_{+1} + b_0$	**P_0**	$S_0 = S_{-1} + s_0$	s_0
b_{-1}	$B_{-1} = B_0 + b_{-1}$	P_{-1}	$S_{-1} = S_{-2} + s_{-1}$	s_{-1}
b_{-2}	$B_{-2} = B_0 + b_{-2}$	P_{-2}	$S_{-2} = s_{-2}$	s_{-2}

will lead the call auction algorithm to pick either P_0 or P_{-1} as the clearing price depending on which has the smaller imbalance $|B_0 - S_0 + \Delta S_{-1}|$ or $|B_{-1} - S_{-1} + \Delta S_{-1}|$. If $|B_0 - S_0 + \Delta S_{-1}|$ is smaller, then ΔS_{-1} is the largest quantity that will not move the price. Otherwise. $\Delta S_{-1} - 1$ is the largest quantity that will not move the price.

Therefore,

$$\Delta S_{-1} = MIN(B_0, S_0) - MIN(B_{-1}, S_{-1}) + MAX(B_0 - S_0, 0)$$

is the largest sell order you can add without impacting the price as long as the imbalance is smaller at P_0:

$$|B_0 - S_0 + \Delta S_{-1}| < |B_{-1} - S_{-1} + \Delta S_{-1}|$$

Otherwise,

$$\Delta S_{-1} = MIN(B_0, S_0) - MIN(B_{-1}, S_{-1}) - 1$$

is the largest quantity that will not move the price. A sell order size 1 unit larger than these two thresholds will move the call price to the next lower level.

EXERCISE 7.4: PARTICIPATING IN THE OPENING CALL AUCTION

In this exercise you have an order to sell 400 in the first 90 minutes of trading, i.e, by 11:00 A.M. Return to the initial parameter screen and select "Order Driven" with "Call Auctions." Enter 6.0 minutes between orders and 11 as the Scenario Number as Figure 7.9 illustrates.

1. Watch the initial call auction but do not participate. Sell the full order of 400 in the continuous market, and complete the sale by 11:00 A.M. What is the average price?

2. Click on "RESET" to return to the beginning of the call auction. Participate in the auction, and try to outperform your average price result in (1). Are you able to improve your average trade price in completing the order?

3. Enter a new Scenario Number, and replay (2), but as a **buyer** of 400 this time, who uses the opening auction. Did you think there were benefits from participating in the call? Finish your order by 11 A.M. What is the average purchase price?

4. Enter the random number seed used in (3) above, and replay without buying in the opening auction, but completing your buy order for 400 by 11 A.M. What is the average purchase price? Were you better off buying with the call auction in (3), or without it in (4)?

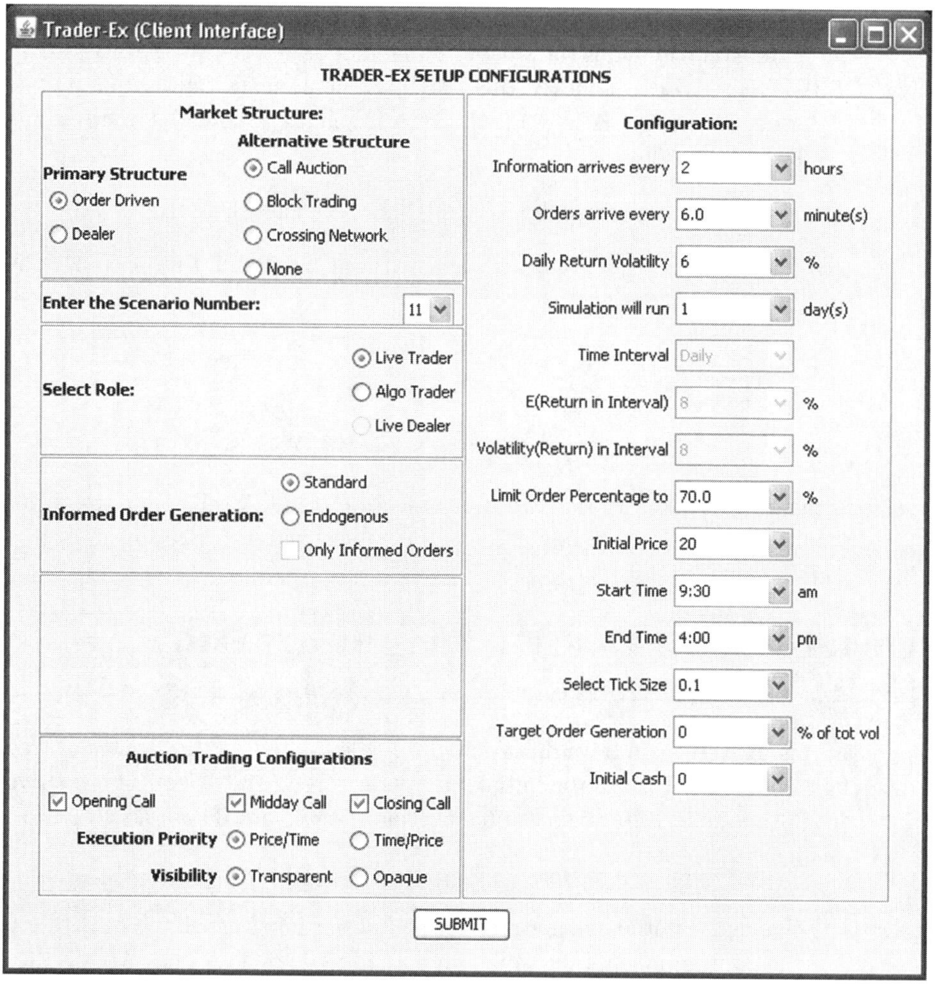

FIGURE 7.9 Parameter settings for Exercise 7.4.

EXERCISE 7.5: WORKING A LARGE ORDER WITH CALL AUCTIONS

From the TraderEx parameter screen, check off the "Call Auction" feature. In the default setting, there will be three auctions a day at the 9.30 A.M. opening, at the mid-point of the trading day (12:45 P.M.), and at the market close (4:00 P.M.).

Select the "Target Order Generation" option for TraderEx to provide trading instructions that will be 50 percent of daily trading volume in the order book as

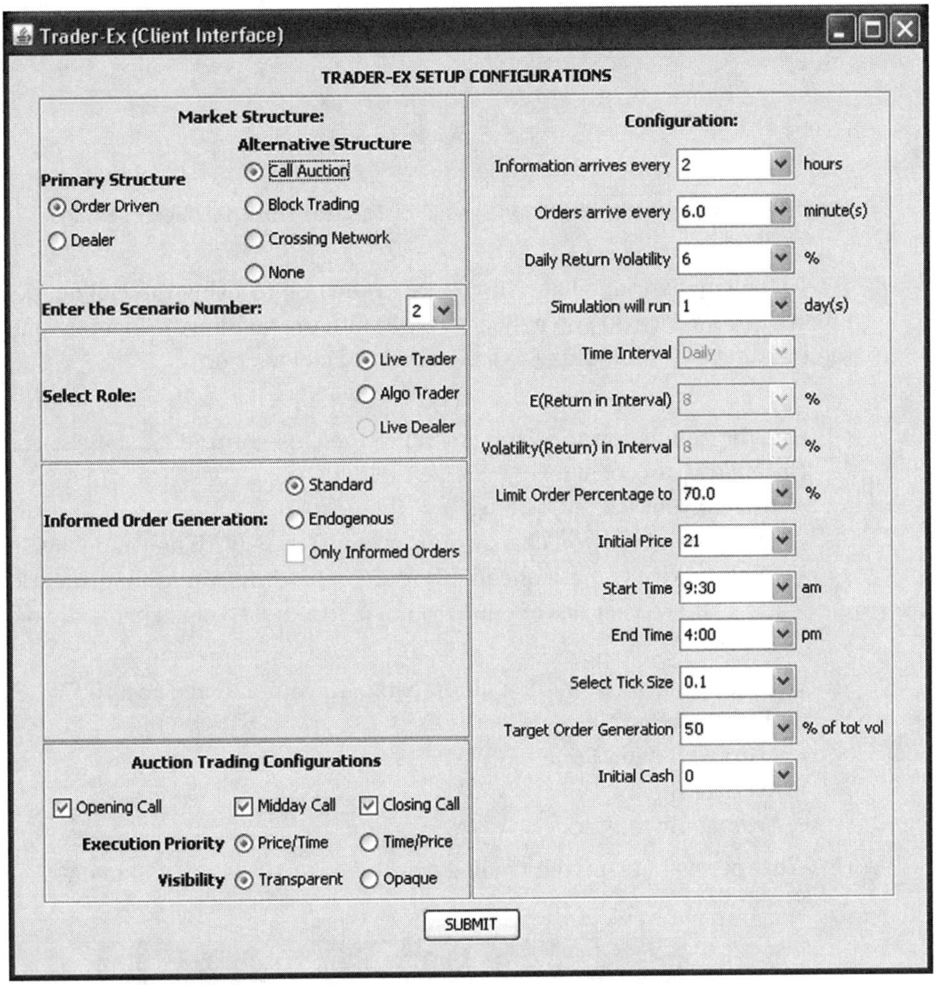

FIGURE 7.10 Parameter settings for Exercise 7.5.

shown in Figure 7.10. The addition of the call will mean that your trading will actually be 30 to 40 percent of the day's total trading. In executing this large order, you should seek to add alpha to the fund you are trading on behalf of. Try to do this by improving on the VWAP price, and by buying close to the low price of the day (or selling near the high price of the day).

Figure 7.11 shows the initial orders in the opening call auction that result from the parameter settings in Figure 7.10.

☒	0	0	20.20	121	0	☒
☒	0	0	20.10	80	0	☒
☒	0	0	20.00	0	0	☒
☒	0	20	19.90	0	0	☒
☒	0	71	19.80	0	0	☒
☒	0	222	19.70	0	0	☒

FIGURE 7.11 Initial call auction screen for Exercise 7.5's parameter settings.

In the simulation, what will your approach be to using the call auction? How much of your order do you expect to enter into the auctions? What percent of your total trading are you looking to execute in the call auction?

1. Run the simulation for a full day up to the close of trading at 4 P.M. (or 16.00). During the run consider:
   - What is your trading strategy?
   - At any point did you change your trading strategy? When and why?
   - Explain why you are ahead of, or are behind the VWAP benchmark. In Figure 7.12, the user has bought 750 but paid almost 3 cents per share more than VWAP.

2. When you reach the market close, compare your average cost to VWAP. Which of these resulted?
   - Average Buying Price < VWAP
   - Average Buying Price > VWAP
   - Average Buying Price = VWAP

3. What percentage of your trading was done in calls? _____ percent

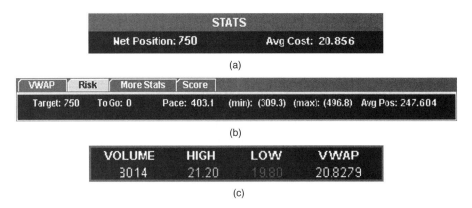

FIGURE 7.12 Illustration of performance measures for Exercise 7.5: Users reached the target position of +750 but their average buying price is about 0.03 greater than VWAP. The user's volume of 750 was about 25 percent of the market's total volume of 3,014.

4. Is the day's closing above or below your average buying price?

5. Did your trading and use of the call auctions improve the outcome you achieved for the fund manager? Why?

6. Using the "GET DATA" tool, review the TradeOrders.csv file.
   - What percentage of your trading was done in the call auction?
   - What percent was done in the continuous market by limit order?
   - What percent by market order?

7. For the continuous market:

   Limit orders _____ percent
   Market orders _____ percent

8. Do you feel that this was an optimal split between the two types of trading venues and the two types of orders in your opinion?

9. Using the "GET CHART" function or the "GET DATA" function (see Figure 7.13), graph the market's trade prices, your trades (indicate limit and market orders), and an end of day VWAP line (see example below). Identify your two best and two worst trades of the day. Were any of these in the call auction?

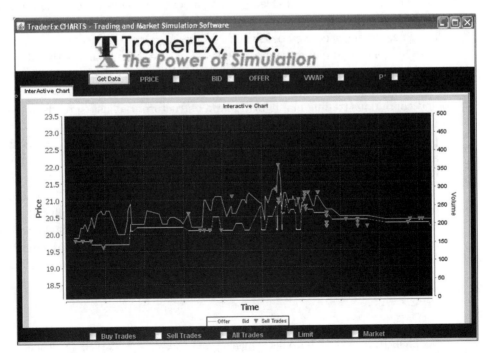

FIGURE 7.13 Graph of user trades from GET CHART function. GET "DATA" button will download data into a spreadsheet.

10. What post-trade analyses could a market participant use to improve his/her call auction use and order placement decision making in the future?

Discussion of Exercise 7.5

While call auctions have advantages for traders with large orders, making effective trading choices when a call auction is available is not simple. Here are a number of questions to reflect on.

When did you enter the call auctions? In each of the three daily auctions, you probably noticed that the more the call auction's order book built, the more confidence you could have in the price. You could also better judge how to access the liquidity on the book without impacting the price, as illustrated in Exercise 7.2. Sizing your order in a call was particularly important when you had a large order to work.

You probably were tempted to wait until the last screen was shown and then enter your order just before the price was set and the call executed. But as you saw, you needed to be careful; the TraderEx calls are held at randomly selected times, and you never know when you are looking at the last screen. Making the time of a call uncertain is a way of strengthening incentives to get your call auction order onto the book. Many actual call systems include some inducement such as this to build deeper, more active books.

One feature of call auction trading that can be a drawback is that it does not provide transactional immediacy—you have to wait for the auctions to happen. This is less of a limitation than in the past since most markets now combine call and continuous trading in a hybrid market structure. Bid–ask spreads and market impact costs mean that immediacy in trading is not a free lunch. Many institutional participants are more concerned with anonymity and keeping trading costs low, and do not wish to pay the price of immediacy. Ellul, Shin, and Tonks (2005) found that in 2000, the London Stock Exchange's call auctions handled 2.5 percent of total trading for the lowest quintile of stocks by market value, and 1.7 percent, 1.1 percent, 0.7 percent, and 0.4 percent of volume for the fourth through first quintiles of firms.[*] The authors wrote that "the call is popular on days with higher expected trading volumes, and when adverse selection costs are low." For individual stocks on particular days, the open and closing auction trades can account for 30 percent of daily volume.

---

[*]A. Ellul, H. Shin, and I. Tonks "Opening and Closing the Market: Evidence from the London Stock Exchange," *Journal of Financial and Quantitative Analysis*, December, 2005, 779–801.

Choosing the Call Over the Continuous Market

Under what conditions did you seek to fill large parts of your order in the call auctions? Under other conditions were you able to trade favorably in the continuous market? At times did you avoid trading in the continuous market and wait patiently to trade in the call? Knowing that a call was coming midday and at the close, were you less apt or more apt to enter a limit order in the continuous market knowing that, if it fails to execute, you can roll your order into the call?

A conceptual framework might help you understand your decisions. *If you only had call auctions available to trade in, how would you set your limit price?* Assume you have a reservation price for the stock, which is what you thought its true value was or your target price for it. You would use your reservation price, P^R, as the limit price. Why? If you set a different price you could have regret afterwards. Imagine your reservation price is $22 and you place your buy order into the call order at $21.80. If the call price is $21.90, you will kick yourself. On the other hand, you would not enter buy orders into the call at prices greater than $22, since that is more than it is worth, in your judgment.

Consequently, your limit price in a call auction-only environment should be your reservation price. William Vickrey, winner of the Nobel prize in Economics in 1996, demonstrated that some auction designs similarly lead participants to truth revealing strategies; i.e., to bids that are identical to the bidders' reservation prices.[*] In most stock exchange and in TraderEx, call auctions punctuate continuous order book trading. In a hybrid structure, it does not hold that your limit order price in a call auction should be your reservation price. In fact, market conditions may argue for less aggressive orders in the call auction, in favor of attaining better prices in the continuous market.

Choosing the Continuous Market Over the Call

The situation is more complex when we introduce the possibility of rolling an unexecuted order from the call into the continuous market. Assume that you have a $22 reservation price for a stock. The tactical question to ask is: "should I buy shares of BioTech at $21.90 in the call, or try for a better price in the continuous market?" Because of the possibility of price improvement in call auctions, you'll place a higher limit price on a buy order (and a lower limit price to sell) than you would in a continuous order book market. To answer the question that we just posed, let's ask a few more questions.

---

[*]William Vickrey, "Counterspeculation, Auctions, and Competitive Sealed Tenders," *Journal of Finance*, XVI, 1961, 8–37.

Question: Would you rather buy BioTech at $22.00 in the call auction, or not have your order execute at all?

Answer: Indifferent. $22.00 is your reservation price. The surplus you would receive is zero, which is what you get when you do not execute at all.

Question: Would you rather buy BioTech at $21.90 in the call, or place a limit buy at $21.90 in the continuous market when there is a 95 percent probability that your order will execute in the continuous market?

Answer: Go into the call at $21.90. Putting $21.90 on the buy order you submit to the call means that you will indeed buy if the clearing price is $21.90 or less. It would not be wise to risk the 5 percent probability of not capturing the $0.10 surplus per share available in the continuous market.

In the questions that follow, we contrast an execution in the call with an execution in the continuous market that is uncertain, but at a price that is one tick less aggressive.

Question: Would you rather buy BioTech at $21.90 in the call, or at $21.80 in the continuous market when there is an 80 percent probability that your order will execute in the continuous market?

Answer: Don't go into the call at $21.90. Accepting an execution at $21.90 in the call provides a surplus of $0.10, but the expected surplus from waiting is $(0.8) \times \$0.20 = \$0.16$.[*]

Question: Would you rather buy at $21.90 in the call, or at $21.80 in the continuous market, when there is a 20 percent probability that your order will execute in the continuous market?

Answer: Trade in the call to secure the $0.10. The expected surplus from waiting is $(0.2) \times \$0.20 = \$0.04$.

Question: Would you rather buy at $21.90 in the call, or at $21.80 in the continuous market if the probability of your order executing in the continuous market is 0.50?

Answer: Indifferent. Both options give you an expected surplus of $0.10, and you should be indifferent between them. 50 percent is a threshold probability for using the continuous market to seek a better price.

In deciding to place orders less aggressively (and therefore being less likely to execute) in the call, you should first assess the probability of getting a better price in continuous trading. In the preceding example, a greater than 50 percent chance of improving on the call auction price in continuous trading argues for waiting for

---

[*]We are assuming this is a buy-or-nothing approach, and that 20 percent of the time the other outcome is no trade. Later we will consider converting a limit order to a market order.

TABLE 7.11 Continuous Order Book after the Auction

Buy Cumulative	Price	Sell Cumulative
Call Auction		
20	P_{+2}	90
30	P_{+1}	50
80	**P_0**	**40**
130	P_{-1}	20
190	P_{-2}	10

⇓ ⇓ ⇓**Continuous Order Book** Buy Orders at Price	Price	Sell Orders at Price
Continuous Market		
	P_{+2}	40
	P_{+1}	10
40	P_0	
50	P_{-1}	
60	P_{-2}	

The call auction discussed executes at P_0 with a volume of 40. Immediately after the auction, the continuous order book provides better opportunities to improve upon the call auction price for sellers than for buyers.

trading opportunities after the call. If you believe that the actual probability of execution is greater than the threshold probability, then you should not seek an execution at that price, but rather attempt to buy one tick lower by placing a price limit one tick lower on your order in the call (and also in the continuous market if you do not execute in the call).

How would you know what is the probability of an execution one tick away from an impending call auction price? Rough estimates can come from historic data from the market, from recent experiences, and from examining the contents of the continuous order book after a call auction. A call auction that ends imbalanced toward the *buying side* will present more opportunity for a seller to obtain a price in continuous trading that is better than the call auction price as the example in Table 7.11 illustrates.

To examine this example more deeply, say you believe that the actual probability of execution of your sell order at P_{+1} is greater than a threshold probability. This leads to another question: might you do even better by putting a limit of P_{+2} on your sell order? A procedure known as *iterative dominance* can be applied to find the optimal sell order to send to the call by assessing each price, starting one tick above your reservation price.

We will use the following two terms to explain the analysis.[*]

---

[*]Schwartz, R., Francioni, R., and Weber, B., *The Equity Trader Course*, John Wiley & Sons, 2006.

Reservation Price—the maximum price a buyer is willing to pay per share for a certain number of shares, or the minimum price at which a seller is willing to sell shares. The target price an investor establishes for a security can serve as a reservation price.

Trading Surplus—the per share amount that an investor expects to gain by buying below, or selling above, their target or reservation price. In the example below, the surplus a buyer achieves increases the further below $21 he or she is able to buy shares.

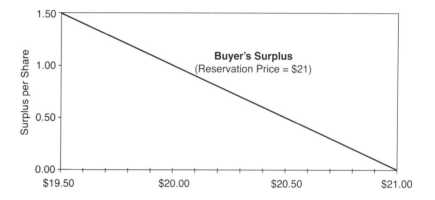

Probability of Executing in Continuous—the likelihood, in percent, of a limit order at a particular price executing in the continuous order book market after the conclusion of a call auction. Of course, traders do not have crystal balls, but experience, and prior data can enable subjective probability assessments to be made.

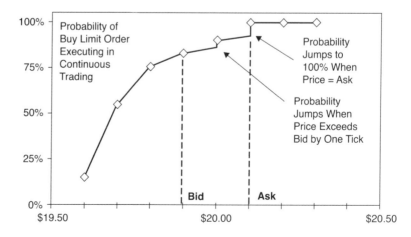

Probabilities will be increasing in price for buy orders, and decreasing in price for sell orders. In the example below, a trader examining the contents of a limit order book estimates the following probabilities of execution for a buy limit order placed at prices from $19.60 to $20.40 to execute. At the ask quote, the buy order is a market order and it executes with certainty.

Here is how the procedure works in our example. Your reservation price is $21 and you will derive surplus from selling for more. The *breakeven* or *threshold probabilities* for a sell order at prices ranging from $21.00 up to $21.40 are shown in Table 7.12.

The threshold probability in the far right column equals the surplus in the call divided by the surplus in the continuous market. The breakeven probability increases as price increases in the table above. The reason is that, as we move to higher prices, the gain in surplus achieved by increasing your price by one tick is proportionately less. If your incremental gain is proportionately less from taking the risk, the probability of the risk paying off must be higher to seek a better price.

On the other hand, the actual probability of selling at higher prices in the continuous market decreases. The reason for this is that the execution probabilities are conditioned on (take account of) the fact that your order did not execute in the call. Suppose that the clearing price at the call is $21.10 and that your limit price to sell in the continuous is $21.20. You then need a $0.10 price increase in the continuous market for your order to execute. This could happen, of course, because of a liquidity shock as we discussed in Chapter 4.

We can now solve for the optimal pair of orders to submit to the call and then the continuous market after the call auction. For a seller, identify the highest value of price in the continuous market for which you believe that the probability of executing in the continuous market is above the threshold, breakeven point. For instance, you believe that a sell limit order at $21.20 in the continuous market has a 55 percent probability of executing (higher than the threshold of 50 percent), and a sell limit order at $21.30 has a 35 percent chance of trading (below the

TABLE 7.12 Pairs of Sell Order Prices in the Call and Continuous Structures, and the Threshold Probabilities

Price Limits for Selling		Surplus in		Threshold Probability of Executing in Continuous
Call about to Execute at	Continuous	Call	Continuous	
21.00	21.10	$0.00	$0.10	NA
21.10	21.20	$0.10	$0.20	50%
21.20	21.30	$0.20	$0.30	67%
21.30	21.40	$0.30	$0.40	75%
21.40	21.50	$0.40	$0.50	80%

Threshold probabilities, when exceeded, suggest seeking a sell trade in the continuous market at a higher price than the call price.

threshold of 67 percent). Therefore, from Table 7.12, you are better off seeking a $21.20 sale price in the continuous market, and not placing the $21.10 order into the call. Note that there is no harm in entering the call with the limit price of $21.20 we have chosen for the continuous. However, you have no reason to be more aggressive in the call based on your execution probability estimates for the continuous. If your assessment is that none of the probabilities in continuous trading will exceed the threshold, then seek to sell in the call at the indicated price.

Continuous Trading Followed by a Closing Call

A closing call affects your order placement decision via its impact on the actual probability of order execution. Without a closing call auction, you may have submitted your limit order, and allowed it to sit on the book until near the end of the trading session. If it is not likely to execute as the close nears, you can cancel it and replace it with a market order to complete your instructions. The closer to the end of the day that you have placed your order, the lower is the probability that it will execute, all else the same. Clearly, the actual probability of execution is less for a day order placed at 3:30 P.M. than for one placed at 10:00 A.M. Consequently, for an otherwise identical set of conditions, at 10:00 A.M. you are more apt to enter a limit order (which could tighten the spread and supply liquidity), and at 3:45 P.M. you are more apt to enter a market order (which removes liquidity and could widen the spread).

Consider how a closing call affects your order placement decision in a continuous market leading up to the closing call. The closing call gives you another chance to realize a surplus if your limit order fails to execute in the continuous market. With the call auction as a backstop, your expected surplus per share from a buy limit order strategy at the time when you place your order in the continuous market is

$$E(\text{Surplus}) = Pr^{\text{Cont.}} \times S^{\text{Cont.}} + (1 - Pr^{\text{Cont.}}) \times E(S^{\text{Call}})$$

where $Pr^{\text{Cont.}}$ = Probability that your limit order executes in the continuous market

$S^{\text{Cont.}}$ = Surplus per share in continuous trading is the surplus that you realize if your limit order executes in the continuous market,

P^R = Reservation Price

where $E(S^{\text{Call}})$, S^{Call} = Max$(0, P^R - P^{\text{Call}})$ is the surplus that you expect to realize if your limit order in the continuous market does not execute, and you submit a limit order at your reservation price to the call.

Note: We write $E(S^{Call})$ because the specific clearing price that will be set at the call is uncertain. Notice that $S^{Call} = \text{Max}(0, P^R - P^{Call})$ because your order to buy in the call executes only if $P^{Call} \le P^R$.

The second part of the equation, $(1 - Pr^{Cont.}) \times E(S^{Call})$, is necessarily positive, so you are more apt to place a limit order than a market order in the continuous market when continuous trading is followed by a closing call, especially as the close of trading nears and the probability of realizing an execution in the continuous market ($Pr^{Cont.}$) falls.

With a closing call, across all participants in the market, more limit orders are used relative to market orders, as the end of continuous trading approaches. The introduction of a closing call therefore should result in spreads that are tighter than otherwise during the final part of the trading day.

Without a closing call the attractiveness of trading with certainty with a market order increases (all else the same) as the close of the trading day approaches. With a closing call, your optimal tactic is to enter your order into a closing call with a limit price equal to your reservation price.

Consider the following illustration for a trader with a reservation price of $22, who enters the market at 3:45 P.M. with an expected-surplus maximizing limit order to buy 1,000 shares in an order book market at $21.30:

	Probability of Execution in Continuous	Expected $S^{Cont.}$ per Share	$E(S^{Cont.})$ for 1,000 Shares
$21.50 (ask price)	100%	0.500	$500
$21.40	85%	0.510	$510
$21.30*	75%	0.525	$525
$21.20	60%	0.480	$480
$21.10	50%	0.450	$450
$21.00	40%	0.400	$400

Without a Closing Call. The trader's surplus is maximized by the limit order priced at $21.30, as indicated by the "*" at that price. At 3:50 P.M., the order remains unexecuted. In the absence of a closing call, the trader adjusts the probabilities of execution downward, leading to a recalculation of the expected surplus-maximizing order as shown in Table 7.13. At this point, there are only 10 minutes left until the closing bell, and the trader cancels the limit order and enters a market order that will trade at $21.50.

With a Closing Call. If a 4 P.M. call is introduced, how does the trader's decision making change? The trader makes probability assessments for the alternative

TABLE 7.13 Information from Table 7.12 Updated with Lower 3:50 P.M. Probabilities of Trade Execution

	Probability of Execution in Continuous	Expected $S^{Cont.}$ per Share	$E(S^{Cont.})$ for 1,000 Shares
$21.50* (ask price)	1.00	0.500	$500
$21.40	0.80	0.480	$480
$21.30	0.65	0.455	$455
$21.20	0.50	0.400	$400
$21.10	0.40	0.360	$360
$21.00	0.30	0.300	$300

clearing prices that could be set at the closing call, along with the associated surpluses that the trader would receive. See Table 7.14. The columns to the right are based on submission of a buy order priced at $21.90 into the auction.

The probabilities for the possible clearing prices (which extend from $21.80 down to $21.20) sum to 100 percent. The trader's expected surplus from a 1,000 share order with a price limit of $21.90 in the call is the value of $510, shown in the bottom right-hand cell. The value $510 is the probability-weighted sum of the surpluses for each possible clearing price individually. The expected surplus of $510 for the 1,000-share order exceeds the surplus of $500 from trading by market order.

Therefore, the addition of the closing call means the trader should not buy at the $21.50 offer but should plan to use the call. If the trader should not submit a market order at 3:50 P.M., should he or she submit a limit order? Yes. A limit order at $21.40 will generate $600 in surplus if it executes, which exceeds the expected

TABLE 7.14 Expected Closing Call Surplus from a Limit Order to Buy at $21.90

Possible Call Price	Probability of Price being Call Price	$Surplus^{Call}$ per Share	$E(Surplus^{Call})$ per Share	$E(Surplus^{Call})$ 1,000 Shares	Overall $E(Surplus^{Call})$ 1,000 Shares
$21.90	0%	$0.10	$0	$0	
21.80	5%	0.20	$0.01	$10	
21.70	5%	0.30	$0.015	$15	
21.60	20%	0.40	$0.08	$80	
21.50	30%	0.50	$0.15	$150	
21.40	30%	0.60	$0.18	$180	
21.30	5%	0.70	$0.035	$35	
21.20	5%	0.80	$0.04	$40	
21.10	0%	0.90	$0	$0	Sum = $510

surplus of $510 from the closing call. The probability of execution for a $21.40 limit order is 40 percent.

To summarize, the trader's optimal strategy at 3:50 P.M. for buying 1,000 shares is:

- Place limit buy order for 1,000 shares in the continuous market at $21.40
- If unexecuted at 4:00 P.M., go into the closing call at $21.90

Following this strategy, the trader's expected surplus, E(S) is:

$$E(\text{Surplus}) = P(\text{execution in continuous trading}) \times \text{Surplus}^{\text{ContinuousTrading}}$$
$$+ (1 - P(\text{execution in continuous trading})) \times E(\text{Surplus}^{\text{Call}})$$
$$= (0.40 \times \$600) + (0.60 \times \$510) = \$546$$

Note that this is greater than the $500 surplus you would get from executing at $21.50 by market order at 3:50 P.M. in the environment without the closing call auction. It is also greater than the $510 surplus with not placing a low-price limit order to buy in the continuous order book.

Interplay of Call and Continuous Trading Systems

We have seen that when a call is followed by continuous trading, you enter your orders at less aggressive prices in the call than you would if the call was the only game in town. When continuous trading is followed by a call, the closing call gives you an additional chance to trade. The decision making incentives keep traders' limit orders in the book and reduce end-of-day, liquidity-removing market orders. In both cases, having one facility followed by the other enables you to place your orders less aggressively in the facility that operates first. We can summarize:

- In a call-auction-only environment, you place maximally aggressive limit orders. Your limit price should equal your reservation price.
- A call auction that rolls into a continuous trading system leads to your orders being priced less aggressively in the call. The expected surplus from a subsequent execution in the continuous market leads you to price your order in an opening call, away from your reservation price.
- Ending the continuous market with a call effectively gives you another swing at the ball. You do not have to chase liquidity as aggressively at the end of the day as you otherwise would in the continuous market. If your limit order does not execute, and you need to complete the trading instruction, your limit price in the closing call should be your reservation price.

Back to the Real World

The framework we described offers a procedure for determining optimal price limits to put on your orders in continuous and call trading when the two operate together. No human trader can be expected to work these solutions out at a trading desk with a rapidly ticking time clock pressuring the trading decision. We do not expect you or anyone else to be able to do this with scientific precision. When trading decisions are being made in real time, it must be an intuitive, heuristic approach based on these principles. Your judgment about good trading and pricing decision will be strengthened by practice, especially when accompanied by an effective conceptual framework.

EXERCISE 7.6: PROPRIETARY TRADING WITH CALL AUCTION, AND NEWS RELEASES

Up to now, we have considered buy-side traders using the call auctions and continuous order book trading to fill a large buy or sell instruction. Can a prop trader receive advantages from the presence of call auctions? In this simulation, use the opening auction and the trading day to create a positive P&L, but with a zero position at the end of the day. Exercise 6.10 in the previous chapter created a similar challenge but there were no call auctions available to the prop trader. In this hybrid call-continuous market structure, though, any position you have at 4 P.M. can be submitted to the closing auction to end flat.

TraderEx will provide news stories that are associated with P* increases or decreases. When traders receive a piece of news about the company they react to it. Recall that prices do not adjust to the news (to the new value of P*) instantaneously. You have a small, critical window of opportunity to beat the market. Can the call auction improve your proprietary trading, or does it reduce profits?

To start the exercise, enter 91 as the Scenario Number, and set the arrival rate to an order every three minutes on average:

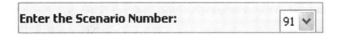

As a proprietary trader you will buy and sell based on short term price movements that you anticipate on the basis of trends, price charts, news releases, or other indicators. You will have no initial position but should respond to the news that arrives with orders and trades.

Assume that a position limit of 1,000 is imposed on you, meaning you should not exceed that many units short or long. As a proprietary trader you do not carry overnight positions, and must return to a flat or zero position by the close.

1. Run the simulation for a full day with three auctions, with the final one at the 4 P.M. close. During the run consider and make note of the following:
   - Once news was released, what was your strategy for trading in the continuous market? In the call auctions?
   - What positive or negative effects did the call auctions have on your proprietary trading?
   - How did your order handling differ as a result of receiving news stories when a call was available soon?

2. Did you return to a zero position? What was your average position? What was your largest position at any point in time?

3. What is the P&L at the end? In a proprietary trading role, do you understand what led to your P&L result?

4. Using the "GET DATA" tool, review the TradeOrders.csv file—What percentage of your prop trading was done in the call and continuous markets? Do you feel this was an optimal split between the two types of markets?

Exercise 7.6 Extension: Other Price Patterns

Replay with two other Scenario Numbers of your choice in the range 92 to 99. These will contain other news stories and different P* paths. After three runs of the simulation, examine the three P&L results you have achieved. What do you conclude about proprietary trading with call auctions?

EXERCISE 7.7: EMPHASIZING DIFFERENT DIMENSIONS OF TRADING PERFORMANCE

As described in Chapter 4, TraderEx calculates a score for a trader based on three measures of performance. VWAP is the trader's ability to transact at prices better than VWAP. P&L is the combined level of realized and unrealized profit. Risk is how far from evenly paced the trader executes the order. Figure 7.14 shows the three important measures of performance for a trader to consider.

At the TraderEx parameter screen, check off the "Call Auction" feature. In the default setting, there will be three auctions a day at the 9.30 A.M. opening, at

VWAP	Risk	More Stats	Score					
VWAP:	22.446	P & L:	54.00	RISK:	843700.75	% DONE:	75.00	TOTAL: 76.447
Weight:	100	Weight:	100	Weight:	0%	Weight:	0	

FIGURE 7.14 TraderEx performance measures and weights. Weights can be adjusted by clicking on a label and entering a weight. Score is the weighted sum of the performance measures.

the midpoint of the trading day (12:45 P.M.) and at the market close (4:00 P.M.). Select the "Target Order Generation" option for TraderEx to provide trading instructions that will be 50 percent of daily trading volume in the order book. The addition of the call will mean that your trading will be about 30 percent of the day's total trading. The parameter settings for this exercise are shown in Figure 7.15.

1. Select "Scenario Number 12." When the market opens click on "Put all of the weight (100) on Risk." What is your final risk score? Do you outperform VWAP?

2. Re-run as a pure order book market without the call structure. Keep all of the same settings, and put all of the weight on Risk again. Can you keep your pace risk lower with or without call auctions? Why?

EXERCISE 7.8: ALTERNATIVE CALL STRUCTURES: A PARTIALLY DISCLOSED CALL AUCTION AND A TIME PRIORITY CALL AUCTION

Call auctions used in some financial markets disclose far less information than the TraderEx call auction. From 8:50 A.M. until its opening call auction 10 minutes later, the Xetra system from Deutsche Boerse for example discloses only the price at which executable volume is maximized, the quantity that can be traded at this price, and the demand-supply surplus.

Price	Volume	Surplus
14.50	3,500	+500 (excess buy-side quantity)

A trader can see that by selling 500 shares, he or she will not affect the price. The first 500 shares of a submitted sell order will offset the surplus on the buying side. But beyond 500, you cannot see how much could be sold, without having to move the stock a tick up or down. In Xetra, at 9:00 A.M. a 30-second random ending period starts. In this time the call phase is stopped at random and all executable

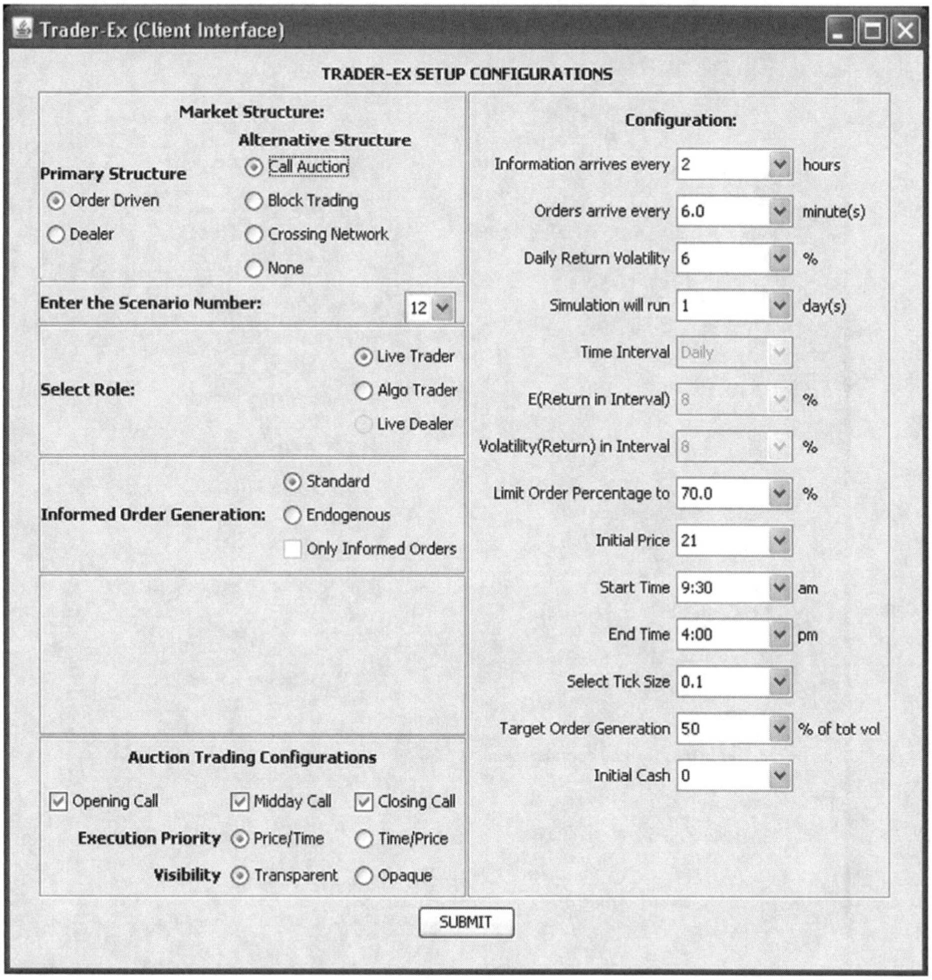

FIGURE 7.15 Parameter settings for Exercise 7.8.

orders are assigned, in the order they were received. The process is repeated at 12 noon for a two-minute call phase, and a 30-second random stopping phase, and again at 5:30 P.M. for the closing auction with a five-minute call phase and a 30-second random ending period.

TraderEx has an option that will only provide this limited view of the call auction as it forms, shown in Figure 7.16.

Exercise A:

1. Select "Scenario Number 15." In the configuration, select "Call Auction," and set Visibility to "Opaque."

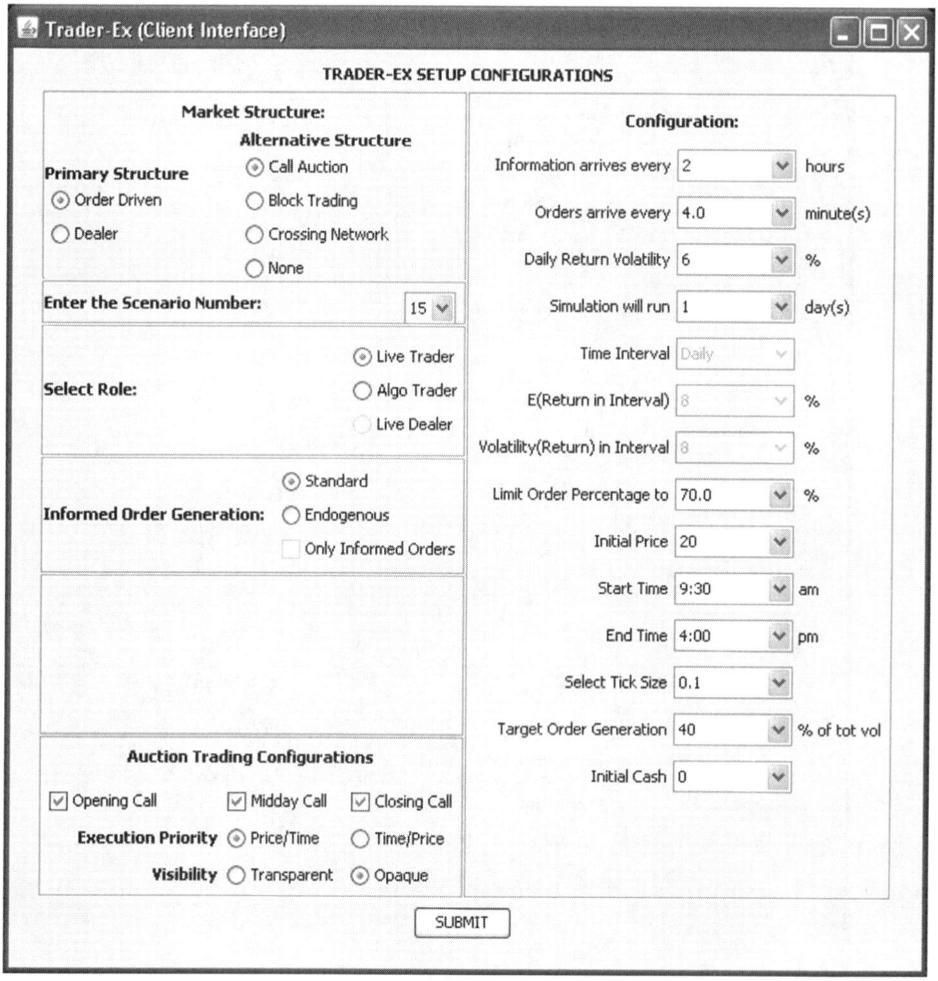

FIGURE 7.16 Parameter settings for Exercise 7.8.

2. Set the target order generation to 40 percent of the day's total trading.

3. Run the simulation, and make note of the impact the limited transparency has on your auction decisions. What percentage of your trading was done in calls?

4. Is the day's VWAP above or below your average selling price?

5. Did the reduced transparency impair your use of the call auctions? Did it impact the outcome you achieved for the fund manager? Why or why not?

Exercise B:

1. Select "Scenario Number 16." In the configuration, select "Call Auction," and set Execution Priority to "Time/Price."
2. Set the target order generation to 40 percent of the day's total trading.
3. Run the simulation, and make note of the impact the time priority has on your order timing in the call. What percentage of your trading was done in calls?
4. Is the day's VWAP above or below your average price?
5. Did time priority impair your use of the call auctions? Did it impact the outcome you achieved for the fund manager? Why or why not?

CONCLUSION

In this chapter we have given you a set of trading exercises in a hybrid call auction and order book market. You participated in the auctions and completed large trading instructions. As you experienced, the combined market structure provides new options and alternatives, and more complicated decisions to make. Market quality is also influenced by the addition of the call auctions. Hopefully, you have gained insights into auctions that will make you a more effective trader, regardless of the market structures that you encounter and the trading roles that you play in them.

CHAPTER 8

Dealer Markets: What Do the Trading Intermediaries Do?

I n Chapter 6, you played several trading roles in a continuous order book market structure. In Chapter 7, we added a call auction facility that operated three times a day. In some exercises, you were a trader handling a buy-side investor's instruction to buy or to sell a quantity of shares without paying overly high prices, or selling at prices that are too low. In other exercises, you were a proprietary trader deciding when to *supply* liquidity in an order book market by placing limit orders, and when to *demand* liquidity by using market orders to buy and to sell. As a prop trader, you sought to earn a positive profit while managing the risk of the positions you were holding. As you saw, optimizing your trading decisions requires a considerable understanding of market structure and trading conditions.

In this chapter we give you trading exercises in a quote driven, competitive dealer market. In quote driven systems, dealers post two-way quotes to buy and to sell. They supply liquidity by buying and selling from their own inventory. This entails holding a long (positive inventory) or a short (negative inventory) position. To unwind a long position, the dealer must later sell shares. To cover a short position, the dealer must later purchase shares. While holding a position, dealers face the risk of losses from adverse price swings. Dealers' survival depends on their ability to generate positive returns on their risk capital.

Dealers do not generally speculate in long-term price movements of the instruments they trade. Instead, they seek to profit from small differences between buying prices and selling prices, and they generally hold positions for short periods of time. The adage, "stock sold to a dealer is still for sale," captures this reality of a quote driven environment.

In this chapter's simulations, you will trade as a dealer and assess risk and profitability. Basic questions that a trading desk should ask are:

- How does market quality in a quote driven system compare to market quality in an order book system?
- How should you adjust your trading accordingly?
- How can you trade as a dealer in a way that limits risk, yet generates profits?

There are no simple answers to these questions.

The foreign exchange market, most options exchanges, and government bond markets including the U.S. Treasury securities market are dealer markets. MTS is a pan-European electronic trading platform for government bonds that uses a market maker model. Until the late 1990s, the NASDAQ Stock Market and the London Stock Exchange were dealer markets; today they are hybrid order book and dealer systems. Dealers post two-sided quotes (bid and ask) that are disseminated to investors and other traders. Inter-dealer brokers (IDBs) such as ICAP and eSpeed facilitate trading between dealers, and disseminate prices over market data terminals.

OPERATIONS OF QUOTE DRIVEN MARKETS

How markets are structured, the nature of the instruments that are traded (e.g., the extent to which they are liquid), and how investors bring their orders to a market largely determine whether there is a role for dealer intermediaries. Many markets would not function effectively without dealers who commit capital to meet investors' demands for liquidity. Being a dealer is very different than being an investor. Dealers have short horizons and trade from moment to moment. As one of the traders in the 1987 movie Wall Street shouted, "In ten minutes, it's history. At 4 o'clock, I'm a dinosaur!" The settings choices for the TraderEx dealer market simulations are shown in Figure 8.1.

A market maker's quotes consist of two parts: a bid to buy and an offer to sell, along with the share sizes that each of these quotes is good for. In TraderEx, the dealers' quotes are valid for 99 units. The opening screen of a dealer market simulation in Figure 8.2 shows the six competing dealers, including you (labeled Dealer ME).

The bid quotes are on the left and are adjustable to higher or lower prices with the + and – buttons. The offer quotes on the right adjust the same way. The third set of + - – buttons under "QUOTE" will move both quotes in parallel. In other words, the bid–ask pair of $19.20 and $19.80 will become $19.30 and $19.90 when the + is clicked once, and $19.40 and $20.00 when clicked twice.

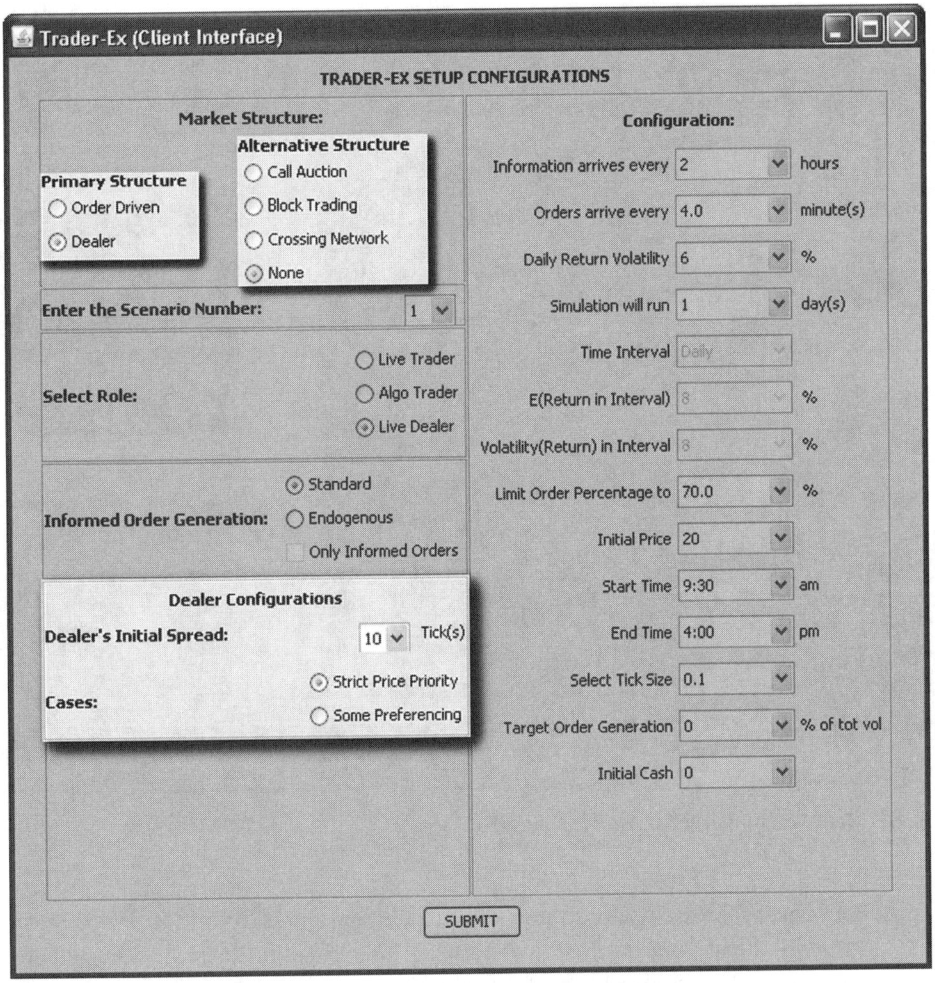

FIGURE 8.1 Configuration for dealer market structure in TraderEx.

Public investors sell at the market maker's bid, and buy at the market maker's ask. The difference between the bid and ask is the cost of dealer supplied immediacy. Dealers attempt to profit from the bid–ask spread, but concurrently must manage their risk from holding trading positions. A dealer who has a long position that exceeds his/her risk tolerance needs to revise the prices downward and hope to attract buyers. Similarly, a short position will induce a dealer to raise his/her quotes to draw in sellers and to discourage buyers. In Figure 8.3, Dealer ME (you) has accumulated a position that is long 219 units. ME is making the best bid in the market, will receive any incoming sell orders, and will buy from a seller at $20.30. Dealers Bull and Lion have posted the lowest offer, and will sell to incoming buy

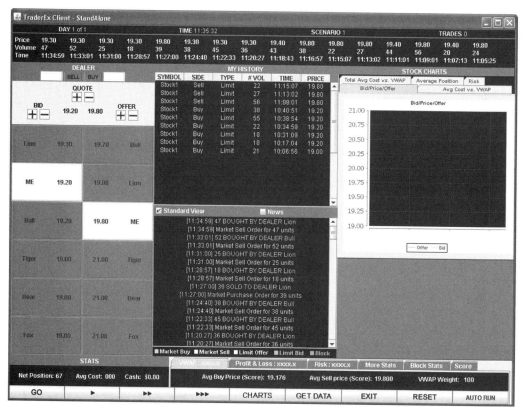

FIGURE 8.2 Initial market screen of TraderEx.

orders at $20.70. If you do not want to become long beyond 219 at this stage, you should adjust your quotes downward. ME's quotes are now $20.30–$20.80. Should they just be lowered to $20.20 and $20.70? Where do you want to position your quotes?

The dealer market simulation incorporates five computer-based market makers who will follow a set of computer programmed quote-setting rules. As Dealer ME, you will be competing with the computer driven market makers. In Figure 8.3, Dealer Bull is on the low offer quote of $20.70. Why do you think that Bull is offering at $20.70? It is likely that Bull has an uncomfortably long position, and is eager to sell. What would Bull do if you lowered your offer to $20.70 or even to $20.60? Under some conditions, Bull will respond and lower the offer price, and in other circumstances Bull will stay put at the $20.70 offer.

The TraderEx dealer quote-setting rules are based on the dealer's position size relative to a computer-imposed position limit. Dealers who are long beyond a position limit lower their bids and offers, and perhaps also sell to one of the other

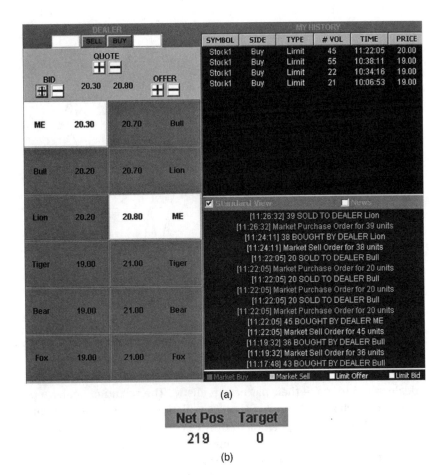

(a)

	Net Pos	Target
	219	0

(b)

FIGURE 8.3 Dealer ME has the best bid quote of $20.30 and is one tick above the lowest offer. ME's position is long 219.

market makers. Of course, you will not know the other dealers' inventory levels. As in real markets, that is carefully guarded, proprietary information. In general though, the computer-resident dealers will adjust their bids and offer quotes:

- Lower when their positions are too long
- Higher when their positions are too short

The TraderEx dealer quote changing rules were developed with input from several market makers who were active on the London Stock Exchange's SEAQ system in the 1990s. They reviewed an early version of the simulation model and its output. Examining the computer dealers' positions and trades, the real traders fine-tuned the TraderEx dealer rules by pointing out better rules and heuristics to model the

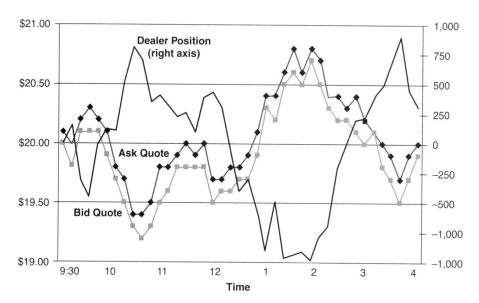

FIGURE 8.4 The average inventory of five dealers and their quote setting in a 1-day simulation run. The dealer adjusts bid and ask quotes to control their inventory positions: lowering quotes in response to a growing long position in the morning, and later raising their bid and ask as the position becomes short in the early afternoon.

dealers and to make their patterns realistic. The resulting dealer model generates behavior such as that shown for one simulation run displayed in Figure 8.4. The figure shows the average position of the five computer-based dealers and the resulting best bid and ask prices over the course of a trading day, with a high-low price range of $20.80 to $19.20, and a position range from –975 to +890.

You should not assume that any dealer quote change is motivated by a simple reaction to an imbalanced inventory. TraderEx's dealer strategies include the possibility of bluffing. A dealer who is long is interested in the share price rising. With a long position, a dealer who has just sold some shares could raise his or her offer and make the highest bid in order to draw the other dealers into raising their quotes. If the other dealers are short, they may raise their quotes to avoid further selling that would increase their risk. If so, and if you succeed in stemming the quote decreases in the stock while you are, for instance, long 219 as in Figure 8.3, ME will improve its P&L performance by selling the shares held long at a higher price.

In Figure 8.3, if Fox has a short position and is bluffing to try to lower the market quotes, he runs the risk selling even more. Eventually, a TraderEx market maker who is short beyond a position limit will need to raise his quotes as many times as necessary to entice sellers into the market and to reduce his position risk.

In TraderEx, as in most quote-driven markets, there is no secondary rule of order execution (such as time priority), and all dealers who are simultaneously making the best quote have an equally likely chance to receive the next order. For instance, if three dealers are making the highest bid, each has a one-third chance of receiving the next incoming sell order. This is consistent with a pure quote driven market where each customer selects the market maker to whom he/she wishes to direct an order. Directing an order to a specific dealer firm is know as *preferencing*, an action that will be further described in Exercise 8.4.

EXERCISE 8.1: CHANGING QUOTES TO CONTROL YOUR INVENTORY

This exercise will examine how investor order flow will impact your inventory, and the quote changes you should make to control risk and eventually return to a flat position. From the TraderEx parameter screen, check "Dealer" as the market structure. Keep all of the other settings at their default levels, and enter 12 as the Scenario Number. Then advance the simulation using the "GO" button.

1. Click on the "GO" button a few times. As you continue to click on "GO," you will see a number of trades without any quote changes having been made by you. You will then receive several customer buy orders. At about 10:30, you will have a small short position. Position your offer to be the lowest, or tied as the lowest, in the market. This will lead to more customer buy orders being routed to you. Allow your short position to build to approximately –300.

2. Note what your average selling price is from the performance dashboard at the bottom of the screen. What is the average selling price?

3. Return your position to zero by joining the bid quote as an eager buyer, and avoid being on the offer quote. What is the bid quote that you initially joined? Keep track of how many times you have to raise your bid quote to remain at the inside bid as you return your position to zero.

4. At some point buy 10 from another dealer using the "BUY" button, shown here:

Note that you will buy at the lowest offer price in the market.

5. Once you have reached a position that is flat or slightly long, examine your average buying price and your realized profit. What is the difference between your average buying price and your average selling price? Did you work out of your short position at a profit?

6. Click on the "EXIT" button, and rerun the simulation with the same settings and with 11 as the Scenario Number. Make quote changes to maintain the low offer

and build to a position of –300, then maintain the high bid quote to return to a zero or slightly long position. Did you work out of the position at a profit? What dynamics in the market made this profit different from the profit you realized in the prior simulation?

Discussion of Exercise 8.1: Price Discovery in Quote Driven Markets

Price discovery is the process of finding share values that best reflect investors' aggregate desires to own shares. In the order driven market, price discovery occurs as public participants place their limit and market orders with regard to their own assessments of share value, and according to their own beliefs about where prices might currently be heading. No single participant has individual responsibility for price discovery in a pure order driven market.

Competing market makers play a key role in discovering prices in the quote driven environment. They see substantial portions of the aggregate order flow, and they gain insight into the balance between public buy and sell pressures. They do not want to get it wrong—misjudging the order flow can be very costly for a market maker.

What is the price that dealers are trying to discover? Consider Figure 8.5. For simplicity, we assume that there is only one (monopoly) market maker, and that all orders are the same size so that we can plot *orders* rather than *shares* on the horizontal axis. The downward sloping step function describes the rate of arrival of public buy orders that can be expected per hour; i.e., $B(p(t))$ is the propensity to buy as a function of price at time t. The upward sloping step function describes the arrival rate of public sell orders. The buy and sell curves are not smooth (i.e., continuous) because price and size are both discrete variables. For the market maker environment, we cumulate orders that are *expected to arrive* at each price.[*] Specifically, the "expected arrival rate" is the number of orders that are expected to arrive in the next brief time interval (e.g., the next hour), depending on the market maker's bid and offer quotes. Nobody can be certain about future order flow, but the best a market maker can do is to post the quotes, wait, and learn. Given the uncertainties involved, the arrow pointing to the equilibrium price is labeled "stochastic equilibrium."

The intersection of the B and S curves identifies the prices that would equate the number of buy orders that are expected to arrive with the number of sell orders that are expected to arrive. We have labeled the price that balances the expected arrival rates P*. P* is the equilibrium value that the market maker's quotes should ideally bracket. If P* is $22.50, and the market maker is quoting $22.40 bid and

---

[*]The formulation is in Mark Garman, "Market Microstructure," *Journal of Financial Economics*, June 1976.

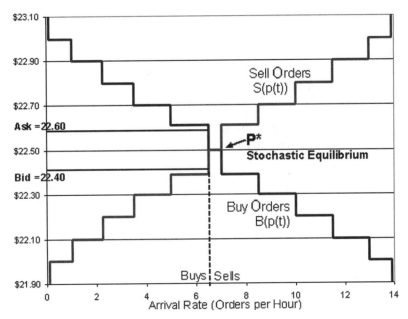

FIGURE 8.5   Price Discovery in a quote driven market. If the dealers' quotes at $22.40 and $22.60 straddle the $22.50 value of P*, then the expected arrival rate of buy and sell orders will be equal.

$22.60 offer, then the *expected* buy and sell order arrival rates are equal and the market is in stochastic equilibrium.

How does the dealer know if his quotes are properly aligned with P*? By the order flow that he receives and the inventory positions that he develops in trading. When the order flow is predominantly investor selling at the bid quote, the dealers will become long, which is a probabilistic signal that the quotes are too high. If, alternatively, the dealer gets short and continues selling, that is a sign that P* is above the offer quote, and that the prices need to adjust upward. When a dealer's quotes are at the optimal level, buy and sell order arrival rates are, on expectation, the same, and there is no systematic change or pattern to the dealer's inventory fluctuations. During the simulations you should be alert to order flow balance, and react to any imbalances that may arise.

EXERCISE 8.2: MARKET MAKER PERFORMANCE

In this exercise, you will make a market in a stock for an entire day. There will be occasional news releases on the company that could impact the P* price and the order flow. From the TraderEx parameter screen, check "Dealer" as the market structure. Keep all of the other settings at their default levels, and enter 91 as the Scenario Number. Without your intervention, the market volume would be about

7,300 units over the course of the day. As a result, you should impose on yourself a position limit of 400 units.

1. Run the simulation and monitor the news stories for their positive or negative sentiment. You should try to keep your position from becoming too long or too short beyond 400, and you are expected to end the day with no position.

2. During the trading day keep track of your largest inventory position. When did you adjust your quotes and why?

3. Record your:

    Closing position (Net Pos) (should be zero or close to zero)
    Realized Profit
    Average Position (Avg Pos)
    Market Share (%Mkt Shr)

4. With six market makers, the average market share will be about 17 percent. Did you exceed that? Why or why not?

5. Using the "GET DATA" tool, review the TradeOrders.csv file—Which positions were you able to trade out of at a profit, and which positions led to losses?

6. Using the "GET CHART" function to see a graph of the market prices, and your trades. For example:

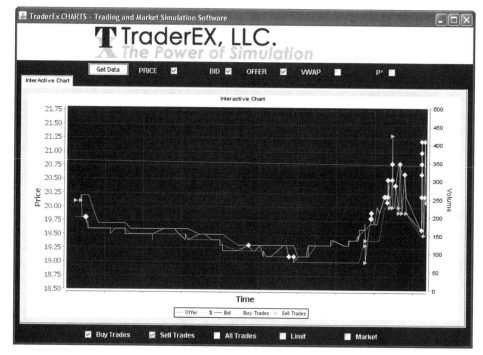

Identify your best and worst trades of the day.

7. Replay the simulation with 98 as the Scenario Number. Are you able to outperform your results from #3 above?

Discussion of Exercise 8.2: Market Maker Metrics

Compared to investors, dealers have different objectives, and use different performance metrics. A dealer's success involves a number of considerations. At the end of a trading period, dealers assess their performance based on realized profit and unrealized profit, risk, and market share. Intra-day assessments are also important to dealers. In Figure 8.3, you have a position of 219 units long and the average purchase price was $19.712. Selling at $19.70 or less will generate realized losses, while selling at $19.80 or higher will create profits. In this case, the dealer has an unrealized profit of $41.40 because the mark-to-market cost of closing his/her long position by selling at the bid price of $19.90 is:

$$\text{Unrealized P\&L} = 219 \times (19.90 - 19.712) = \$41.10$$

Although it is an important consideration, TraderEx's mark to market calculation does not factor in that the user's 219 position is much larger than the 99 unit quote size, nor that the bid is from Dealer ME, and that this bid is being used to value ME's own position. Unrealized profit is not necessarily the profit you would capture if you liquidated the position immediately.

Risk is important in assessing market makers. Dealers who carry larger positions, all else equal, are taking greater risk, and they require more risk capital to support their activity. To account for risk, TraderEx computes dealers' average position sizes. Minute-by-minute snapshots are taken, and the average position is the time-weighted average of the absolute value of the minute-by-minute Net Positions. For example, if a dealer bought at the open and had a long position of 50 for 10 minutes, and then sold 90 but was short 40 for the next 10 minutes, the average absolute position is 45. If two dealers achieve an equal level of P&L, the one who does so with a lower average position has outperformed. TraderEx accounts for position risk by using the Risk measure that was described in Chapter 4.

EXERCISE 8.3: MARKET MAKER RISK PERFORMANCE

In this exercise, you will again trade as a market maker for a full day, but the assessment score will be equally weighted between P&L results and the Risk measure that your trading generates. From the TraderEx parameter screen, check "Dealer" as the market structure. Keep all of the other settings at their default levels, and enter 16 as the Scenario Number. News stories that could impact the price will be released every hour or so.

1. After submitting the configuration settings, click on the "P&L" and "Risk score" labels, and enter equal weights for P&L and Risk.

2. Click on the "GO" button and begin.

3. At the end of your simulation run, record your:

   Closing position (Net Pos) (should be zero or close to zero)
   Realized Profit
   Average Position (Avg Pos)
   Market Share (%Mkt Shr)
   P&L / Risk / Total SCORE

4. Do you believe that you took the appropriate level of position risk in the simulation? Do you feel that the 50/50 combination of P&L and Risk in the assessment is properly balanced to control trader risk while retaining profit incentives?

5. Did your market share appreciably exceed or fall short of the 17 percent average based on six dealers?

6. Replay the simulation with 17 as the Scenario Number. Are you able to outperform your results from #3 above? Why did your performance change?

Discussion of Exercise 8.3: Position Risk and Market Maker Costs

You should have seen by now that a positive spread does not guarantee that you will achieve a profitable outcome as a competitive market maker. Market maker costs fall into two categories and can easily exceed other trading revenues, leaving a dealer with losses. Market makers face (1) the cost of carrying an unbalanced inventory, and (2) the adverse selection cost of trading with better-informed buyers and sellers. Position risk as we measure it (the time-weighted average absolute value of the position), is a proxy for the cost of an unbalanced inventory. Portfolio theory teaches us that an investor can manage risk by proper portfolio diversification, and that a properly diversified portfolio provides the investor with an expected return that is the maximum amount obtainable for a given level of risk (or an amount of risk that is minimal for a given level of returns).

A market maker, however, is not a typical investor. A market maker is buying or selling, not for his/her own investment purposes, but to sell shares to some participants or to buy shares from others. Market makers regularly acquire poorly diversified portfolios and, in so doing, accept risk that could have been diversified away. Since a market maker's desired position is zero, any position that is built up is an unwelcome risk. Position risk, however, must be incurred to realize the potential profit opportunities that are there.

According to Capital Markets theory, the additional expected return on a stock over and above the risk-free rate compensates the investor for accepting non-diversifiable risk, which is commonly measured by a security's beta. What compensates the market maker for accepting diversifiable risk? The classic answer is the bid-ask spread. Whatever makes inventory control more difficult—be it one-way order flow (i.e., short-term runs of buy orders or of sell orders), or trading large blocks, or price volatility from news releases, or thin order flow in a small cap stock, or the preferencing of orders to specific dealers—translates into more costly market making and hence wider spreads. The next exercise introduces preferencing. Adverse selection will be examined in the exercise that follows.

EXERCISE 8.4: PREFERENCING IN MARKET MAKER SYSTEMS

So far you have seen market makers compete with each other by how aggressively they (and you) set their bids and offers. If the spread is constant and the bid and offer are raised, the quotes are more aggressive on the bid side. In order to be eligible to buy in the TraderEx simulations, you had to increase your bid to match or exceed the best bid available in the market. If the bid and offer are lowered, the quotes are more aggressive on the offer side. To sell, you must lower your offer to match the new, more aggressive ask price. The only way to be more aggressive on both the bid and the offer at the same time is to narrow the spread. But all of this holds only in the absence of preferencing. So far TraderEx has imposed a rule that investor orders to sell will only go to dealers making the best bid, and that orders to buy will be routed only to dealers with the lowest offer.

In Exercise 8.4 we introduce preferencing, a well-known phenomenon in real-world dealer markets. Preferencing refers to a customer choosing to send an order to a particular market maker regardless of the prices that the dealer might be quoting at the time. This can be done because there are no time and price priority rules in a quote driven market as there are in the order book systems. The public customer (this applies primarily to institutional clients) is free to pick at will the market maker firm that he/she sends an order to, and the selection can be based on a previously established relationship. Orders, in fact, are typically preferenced to a market maker who has developed a special relationship with the customer.

In this exercise, you will make a market in a stock for an entire day. There will be occasional news releases on the company that could impact the P* price and the order flow. News stories will be released every hour or so. With preferencing, you will receive sell orders when you are not posting the best bid, and buy orders when you are not posting the best offer.

What if the market maker that the customer chooses to trade with is not posting the most aggressive quotes? If its quote is less aggressive than the best quote on the market, the market maker is not obliged to take the order, but generally will accept it to maintain a good relationship with the customer. When a market maker does accept a preferenced order, he or she will typically fill it at a price equal to the most aggressive bid or offer existing at the time the order is received. For instance, if the best bid in the market is $21.00, a sell order preferenced to a dealer quoting a $20.80 bid will be filled at $21. This practice is referred to as *quote matching*.

1. In the configuration settings, click on "Some Preferencing," and enter 95 as the Scenario Number. (The default setting that we have used up to now is "Strict Price Priority," and TraderEx has enforced this by allocating orders only to the dealer(s) making the best quote).

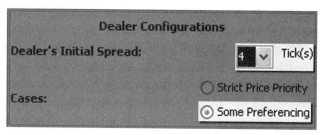

2. Click on the "GO" button and begin.

3. At the end, record your:

   Closing position (Net Pos) (should be zero or close to zero)
   Realized Profit
   Average Position (Avg Pos)
   Market Share (%Mkt Shr)
   P&L/Risk/Total SCORE

4. How did preferencing affect your trading? What impact did it have on your performance?

5. Replay the simulation with 96 as the Scenario Number. Are you able to outperform your results from #3 above? Why did your performance change?

Discussion of Exercise 8.4:
Customer-Market-Maker Preferencing

In Exercise 8.4, you may have realized that preferencing diminished your incentive as a dealer to compete via the aggressiveness of your quotes. In the price priority setting, a market maker quoting at the best bid or offer has a chance of receiving the next incoming sell order, and the probability is 100 percent if you are alone at the quote. With preferencing, however, the next order could be directed to a market maker who is not on the inside market. Complete preferencing in a market with six market makers would mean that each has a 16.7 percent chance of receiving the next incoming order.

In a market where preferencing is a common practice, what does a market maker firm accomplish by raising the best bid (or by lowering the best offer)? It will have raised the bid (or lowered the offer) that the other market makers will have to match, and may not itself receive the next order. The incentive to do this is weak. If market makers have only a weak incentive to quote aggressively, how do they compete? Answer: By developing close customer relationships. An institutional investor will use a specific dealer firm because it has received good service from that firm in the past. If a dealer either turns a customer down or executes the customer's order at an inferior price, the customer will think twice before preferencing an order to that dealer firm again. TraderEx in fact prevents "trade-throughs" from occurring at prices that would be inferior for customers.

Market makers also offer an array of ancillary services that enable them to attract order flow. For instance, they may provide customers with research reports on companies, or computer software, or data for investment analysis. They may offer direct computer links that result in faster executions than customers could achieve elsewhere.

Because of the way in which dealers compete, their spreads tend to be wider than in an order driven environment. In a pure order driven market, an incoming order executes against a contra-side order that has been selected according to two strict criteria—price and time. The most aggressively priced order executes first and, if two or more orders are tied at the most aggressive price, the order that has been placed first executes first. If there is a lengthy queue of orders at the best bid or offer, a newly arriving buy (or sell) order can quickly get priority simply by being priced one tick above the best bid (or one tick below the best offer). Aggressive pricing to get ahead of the queue results in a narrowing of the spread. Because this does not occur in a pure quote driven market, spreads tend to be wider in a quote driven than in an order driven environment.

What effect does preferencing have on market makers' profitability? More orders will be preferenced to a market maker firm that has good customer relationships. This is highly desirable for the firm. For one thing, a firm's profit is related to its trading volume. Additionally, a firm that sees a larger percentage of the order flow has an advantage with regard to price discovery and thus can set its quotes more knowledgeably.

Preferencing, however, is not an unmitigated good. It is excellent for a dealer firm to receive preferenced orders but, as we have seen, inventory control is then more difficult. With preferenced order flow, posting the most aggressive quote on the market does not ensure that a market maker will receive the next incoming order, and posting less aggressively than the best bid or offer does not ensure that the market maker will not receive the next incoming order. The greater difficulty of controlling inventory that results from this practice can negatively impact a firm's profitability.

Under what regime do market makers prefer to operate—one with preferencing or one with strict time and price priorities? Preferencing is an industry practice and dealers are comfortable with it or they would not have continued the practice. It is, nevertheless, a two-edged sword.

EXERCISE 8.5: VOLATILITY AND MARKET MAKING

The exercises up to now have had the simulation's volatility parameter set at its 6 percent default level. This means that two-thirds of the time the daily return on P* will be between –6 percent and +6 percent. For the default price setting of $20, this means that two-thirds of the time the price over a day will remain in the range $18.80 and $21.20. For an individual stock, this is a fairly high level of price uncertainty—it translates into an annual volatility of 95 percent. In the first half of 2009, the daily volatility of Microsoft, measured over the prior 30 days, ranged from 2 to 4 percent, or 30 percent to 65 percent annualized returns volatility. Reflecting the turmoil in the first half of 2009 in the financial sector, the ranges of historic daily volatilities for HSBC and Bank of America were, respectively, 2 to 7 percent, and 4 to 15 percent. This exercise will increase the daily volatility to 10 percent, which widens the price range to $18 to $22. In one-third of the cases the price will fall below $18 or rise above $22.

1. At the configuration screen, enter "10" as the Daily Return Volatility, and use 17 as the Scenario Number:

Configuration:		
Information arrives every	2 ▾	hours
Orders arrive every	4.0 ▾	minute(s)
Daily Return Volatility	10 ▾	%
Simulation will run	1 ▾	day(s)

2. Click on the "GO" button and begin. Volatility has a larger impact on the more active traders, and in this exercise you should establish a market share of at least 35 percent.

3. At the end, record your:

   Closing position (Net Pos) (should be zero or close to zero)
   Realized Profit

Average Position (Avg Pos)
Market Share (%Mkt Shr)

4. How did the heightened volatility affect your trading? What impact did it have on market bid–ask spreads and your performance?

5. Replay the simulation with 18 as the Scenario Number. Are you able to outperform your results from #3 above? Why did your performance change?

EXERCISE 8.6: LOW LIQUIDITY AND MARKET MAKING

Thus far, the exercises have kept the simulation's average base order arrival parameter at its default level of every 4.0 minutes. In this simulation, order flow and liquidity will be reduced by lowering the average order inter-arrival parameter. At the configuration screen, enter "9.0" as the Order arrival rate. Trading volumes will be reduced by just over half. Keep all other default settings, and use 20 as the Scenario Number, as shown here:

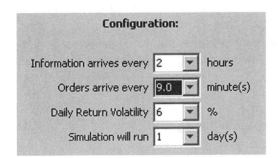

1. Click on the "GO" button and begin. Illiquidity has more effect on market makers who have positions, and in this exercise you should establish a market share of at least 35 percent.

2. At the end, record your:

   Closing position (Net Pos) (should be zero or close to zero)
   Realized Profit
   Average Position (Avg Pos)
   Market Share (%Mkt Shr)

3. How did reduced order flow and lower liquidity affect your trading? What impact did it have on market bid–ask spreads and your performance?

4. Replay the simulation with 19 as the Scenario Number. Are you able to outperform your results from #3 above? Why did your performance change?

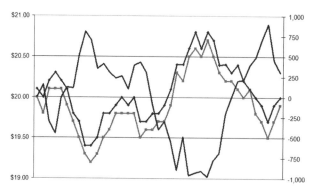

FIGURE 8.6 Price discovery in a quote driven market. In this trading day, P* drops to $19.50 but later jumps to $21. Early, the market maker quotes at $20.30 and $20.50 are too high imbalancing the market toward selling. Later, P* rises to $21, and buy orders drive the market makers into large short positions, and they raise their quotes to $21 and greater.

Discussion of Exercises 8.5 and 8.6: Volatility, Illiquidity, and Market Maker Costs

Markets with high volatility and low liquidity accentuate the two distinctive costs faced by market makers: the cost of carrying an unbalanced inventory, and the adverse selection cost of trading with a better-informed contra party.

We have already discussed the cost of unbalanced inventories that dealers face. Dealers also pay a cost of ignorance whenever they receive an order from a better-informed trader. In TraderEx, informed buyers will purchase stock from dealers whose offering prices are less than P*. Assume a market maker has posted a bid at $23.00, an offer at $23.10, and that without the market maker knowing it, the equilibrium price for a stock jumps to $23.50.

As Figure 8.7 illustrates, subsequent order flow will be predominantly from buyers. An informed trader comes in and buys at the $23.10 offer, and then another, and another until the quotes are raised enough until the offer is above the new P*. The market maker loses from these trades because informed buyers will dominate the order flow. He/she will become short, and the bid and the offer will have increased. The market maker will have sold at $23.10, and probably will not be able to buy the shares back until the bid quote reaches $23.60 or higher. Per share, the dealer will lose at least $0.50.

Having seen prices rise and settle at $23.50, the market maker will regret having traded with the better-informed counter party. The principle is general: whenever trades are triggered by better informed orders hitting market maker's quotes, the market maker will have suffered from adverse selection and, as a consequence, he/she will have "ex-post regret."

Although asymmetric information leads to dealer losses, information trading has a role in price discovery. The inventory imbalances induce the dealers to shift

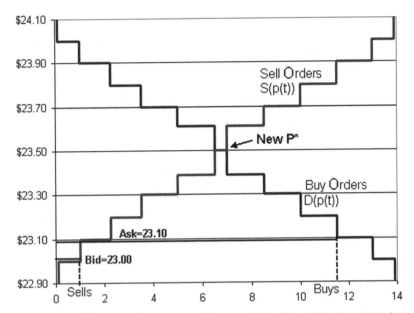

FIGURE 8.7 Price discovery in a quote driven market. P* is $23.50 and market maker quotes at $23.00 and $23.10 are too low. The expected order arrival rate for buy orders will be greater than that for sell orders until the quotes reach $23.50.

their quotes toward P*. Until the quotes regain P*, price discovery is inaccurate, and this is costly to a market maker.

Figure 8.8 illustrates the effect of a fall in P* from $23.00 to $22.50.

Let's return for a moment to the monopoly dealer model and Figure 8.5. We have used P* to identify the price that best balances the expected rate of buy and sell orders, and have shown that, in equilibrium, the market maker will set the offer above P* and the bid below P*. Remember that P* is not observable in the continuous market because the buy and sell curves are based, not on actual orders, but on the number of orders that are *expected to arrive* in a relatively brief, future interval of time (e.g., the next hour). If the quotes straddle P* (as they do in Figure 8.5), the arrival of buys is expected to balance the arrival of sells, and the dealer's inventory should, on expectation, stay in reasonable balance. However, ex post, the actual arrivals of buys and sells will likely not balance exactly because actual rates generally differ from expected rates by some random amount—even when P* has not changed.

More importantly, a serious inventory imbalance can develop if the market maker misjudges the location of P* or if, unbeknownst to the dealer, a news event causes P* to jump (either up or down). Consider Figures 8.7 and 8.8 again. Figure 8.7 depicts a situation where the demand for the stock is *greater* than the market maker has anticipated, either because of mistaken judgment or the occurrence of a bullish news event that the dealer has not yet learned about. We see in Figure 8.7

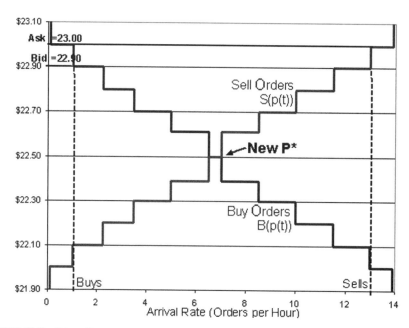

FIGURE 8.8 Price discovery in a quote driven market. P* has dropped to $22.50, and the market maker quotes at $23.00 and $23.10 are too high. The expected order arrival rate for sell orders will be greater than that for buy orders until the quotes fall to $22.50.

that P* is $23.50 and that the dealer's quotes are $23.00 bid, $23.10 offered. As informed buyers jump on the $23.10 offer, the rate of sales to the public rises and the rate of purchases from the public falls. With the order flow to the market maker out of balance, the dealer quickly acquires a short inventory position. As a control mechanism, the dealer raises the quotes, hoping once again to straddle P* and to return to a flat inventory position. In the process of adjusting the quotes, however, the market maker will be taking losses by buying shares at a price that is higher than the price at which he or she had previously sold.

Figure 8.8 depicts the opposite situation: the demand for the stock is lower than the market maker has anticipated, either because of mistaken judgment or the sudden occurrence of bearish news that the dealer does not yet know about. We see that P* is $22.50 and that the dealer's quotes are $22.90 bid, $23.00 offered. As informed sellers hit the $22.90 bid, sales to the dealer increase and purchases from the dealer fall. Now, the market maker quickly acquires a long position. In response, the dealer will lower the quotes, trying to entice buyers, and once again straddle P* with his/her quotes, and return to a flat inventory position. In the process of adjusting the quotes, however, the market maker could be selling shares at prices that are lower than the prices at which he or she had previously bought.

Achieving accurate price discovery is not easy, and inaccurate price discovery is costly for the dealer. What compensates the market maker for the cost of ignorance? The answer is the revenue that the dealer receives from transacting with liquidity traders (who are sometimes referred to as "uninformed traders"). These revenues must be large enough for the costs of dealing with better-informed traders to be offset. Could dealers exist without liquidity traders? They could not. No dealer can stay in business by trading only with better-informed participants. Without liquidity traders, the market makers would close down their operations and the quote driven market would collapse.

EXERCISE 8.7: ALTERNATIVE TRADING SYSTEMS AND MARKET MAKING

Until now the exercises have placed you in the market maker role in a pure quote driven market system. Dealer markets coexist with alternative trading systems (ATSs) in hybrid structures. How does the addition of an ATS affect the operations of a market maker? This exercise will put you in the role of a dealer who has access to a 3-times a day call auction: at the open, midday, and at the close.

1. At the configuration screen, check off "Dealer" and "Call Auction" as the structures that will be combined. In TraderEx, once the call auction begins, you will be able to click the "GO" button from 3 to 10 times and observe an indicative price in the auction. As these orders arrive at the call auction, the dealer quote screen is not shown and it is not accessible. As a dealer, you can participate in the call auctions, and your trades in it will, of course, be included in your position and your average price statistics. Retain all other default settings, and use 25 as the Scenario Number.

Market Structure:

Alternative Structure
⊙ Call Auction

Primary Structure
○ Order Driven   ○ Block Trading

⊙ Dealer   ○ Crossing Network

                    ○ None

Enter the Scenario Number: 25 ▾

Select Role: ○ Live Trader
                      ⊙ Live Dealer

---

2. Click on the "GO" button and begin. The market will open with a call, and you are to participate in it in with an order to sell 550 units. You will acquire a short

position as a dealer. Without any user participation, the final screen before the auction will appear as:

X	0	567	19.90	787	0	X
X	0	618	19.80	745	0	X
X	0	769	19.70	657	0	X
X	0	787	19.60	443	0	X
X	0	917	19.50	443	0	X

3. Once continuous quote driven trading begins, work the short position off by bidding actively and buying the shorted stock back. There will be call auctions at 12:45 and at the 4 PM close that you can use to trade and to manage your dealer position.

4. At the end, record your:

Closing position (Net Pos)(should be zero or close to zero)
Realized Profit
Average Position (Avg Pos)
Market Share (%Mkt Shr)

5. How did the call auction ATS affect your trading as a dealer? What impact did it have on market bid–ask spreads and on your performance?

6. Replay the simulation with 26 as the Scenario Number, buy 650 in the opening auction, and then totally unwind this position in the continuous dealer market that follows. Are you able to outperform your results from #3 above? Why did your performance change?

7. Replay with Crossing Network as the alternative market structure and 26 as the Scenario Number. Which of the two alternatives is most beneficial for a dealer, the call auction or a crossing network?

CONCLUSION

In this chapter we have given you a set of trading exercises in a competitive dealer market. You posted two-way quotes to buy and to sell, and made decisions under conditions that market makers in quote driven systems commonly face. As you no doubt experienced, the dealer role is not an easy one. Making decisions as a dealer, you have gained insights into market making that will make you a more effective trader regardless of the market structures that you encounter and the trading roles that you play in them.

CHAPTER 9

Dark Pools: How Undisclosed Liquidity Works

In this chapter, we examine how a dark liquidity pool can influence the choices and outcomes for traders. To this end, you will be given trading exercises based on a hybrid market structure that includes a dark pool facility and an order book system.

Dark pools offer traders with large buy or sell instructions the opportunity to trade with counterparties without having to display or to disclose their trading intentions or the sizes of their orders. The attraction of a dark pool is that, because you have not revealed your trading interest, your order will not be front run and thereby impact the market. Slippage (the difference between the price in the market at the time when you receive a large instruction and the time when you complete the order) will be reduced, and the savings obtained will enhance your investment returns.

Up to now, we have only considered visible, displayed markets in which prices and quote sizes are shown. This chapter introduces a dark pool, and you will handle block orders to trade. You will be assessed based on the criteria of achieving an attractive average price, completing the full trading instruction, and limiting the risk of trading at an uneven pace during the day. Questions that a trading professional should ask about markets that have dark pool facilities include:

- How does the quality of the market in the dark pool system compare to that of an order-book-only system?
- How should you adjust your trading strategy when a dark pool is available?
- How can you handle block orders using a dark pool in a way that limits risk yet generates profits?

Dark pools create new possibilities for price and quantity discovery in trading. The origins of electronic dark liquidity pools can be traced to the launch of the Instinet and Posit crossing networks in 1986 and 1987. These crossing systems matched buyers and sellers at the mid-point between the bid and ask. TraderEx incorporates a cross facility, and in Chapter 6, Exercise 6.13, you had the opportunity to use it. These crossing facilities performed no price discovery; they simply match offsetting volumes periodically. So too, with other dark pools.

A number of dark liquidity pools, such as ITG-Posit and Instinet Crossing, are based on mid-point reference pricing from another market. Others, including NYFIX Millenium, Pipeline, Liquidnet, and the one incorporated into TraderEx, match orders at multiple prices between the best visible bid and offer quotes, and therefore provide some limited price discovery. Several exchanges have added non-displayed order books including the NYSE's MatchPoint and Baikal from the London Stock Exchange. Average trade sizes are larger in the dark liquidity pools than in exchange and ATS markets that have more visible order books.

The TraderEx dark pool holds large orders that are not displayed on the TraderEx order book, and it allows orders to be matched at any price level from the bid to the offer quote in the order book. Trade throughs of the visible order book's market quotes, on the other hand, are not allowed in the TraderEx dark pool. (We change this setting in the software and relax the trade-through rule in Exercise 9.6.) If the market quotes are $20.20 bid and $20.40 offer, dark pool matches can happen at $20.20, $20.30, or at $20.40, but no matches can take place above $20.40 or below $20.20.

Our TraderEx dark pool is patterned on Pipeline's block trading facility. Figures 9.1 and 9.2 show Pipeline's board of ticker symbols of U.S. and European stocks. When Pipeline users see a ticker symbol that is shaded orange, it indicates that Pipeline has an order in its system for that stock. A ticker symbol that is

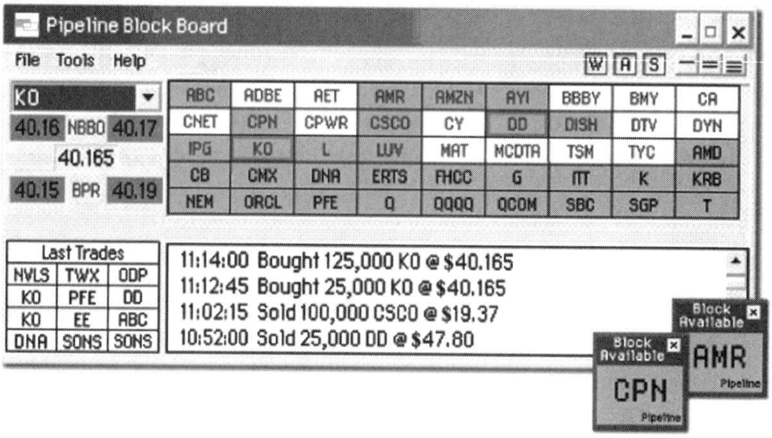

FIGURE 9.1 Pipeline display for Coca-Cola (KO).

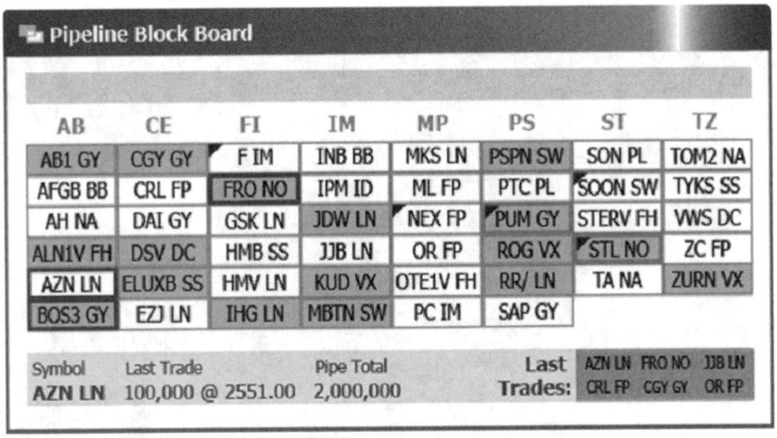

FIGURE 9.2 Pipeline display for European stocks.

outlined in light grey (red in Pipeline's actual system), or darker grey (blue in Pipeline) means that the user has an order in the system to sell (light grey) or buy (darker grey). The bottom of Figure 9.2 shows a 100,000 share Pipeline trade in AstraZeneca plc (AZN LN) at £25.51.

Dark pools are for institutional size orders, which in TraderEx are 250 units or more. Block board orders are separate from the order book, and do not interact with it. However, the price of a block board trade is determined by quotes taken from the visible order book.

In the exercises, you will be given a large order to buy or to sell, or will be operating as a proprietary trader. You will have to decide how best to time, size, and price the orders that you submit. As a simulation run progresses, you will choose between the block board and the continuous order book as you feel is best.

The Price Setting Mechanism in the TraderEx Dark Pool

Two important operational details of any dark pool are the pricing mechanism used, and how block board information is shared among dark pool participants. Crossing networks and dark pools are also referred to as "black boxes" because orders are submitted and, without any disclosure, they are either matched or returned unexecuted. Orders may match partially or completely, but there is no other feedback to traders who are not participating in the dark pool at the time. The incentive to use a dark pool comes from a trader's ability to match larger orders without pre-trade disclosure, and to save the bid-ask spread and market impact costs.

The TraderEx dark pool appears on the right side of the screen as shown in Figure 9.3. Dark pools allow participants to place orders with or without price conditions. An order without price conditions is active. In addition, an order with a limit price at the mid-quote price or better (i.e., a higher bid or lower offer), is also *active*. In our dark pool, and in Pipeline, an order with a limit price that is less

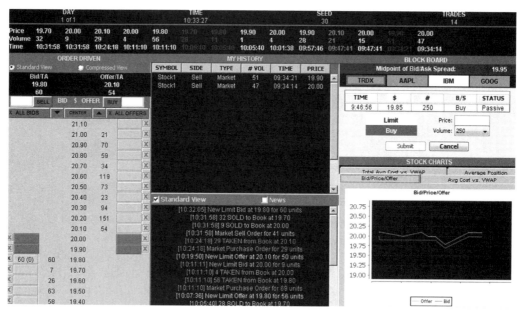

FIGURE 9.3 Pipeline display on right with order book providing reference prices that midpoint. User orders to buy are $19.80 in the order book and $19.85 to buy in the dark pool. The dark pool order is passive because it is willing to pay less, and therefore less aggressive, than the mid-quote.

aggressive than the current mid-quote is a *passive* order. The current midpoint shown in Figure 9.3 is $19.95 (the average of 19.80 and 20.10). The user's block board order in the upper right of Figure 9.3 is a passive order to buy 250 units at a price no greater than $19.85. While $19.85 is higher than the current $19.80 bid quote from the user's limit order, it is less than the $19.95 midpoint price from the order book, which explains why it is a passive order.

The TraderEx block board has a minimum order size of 250, so trades in the dark pool will be in multiples of 250 (e.g., 250, 500, 750, ...). The symbol TRDX will turn orange to signal that an order is in the system. For the order placer, the orange rectangle will be outlined in green to signify that the order is a buy order from that trader, or red for a seller.

Designers of dark pool systems face an interesting challenge. The system must keep participants' submitted orders hidden, but some small amounts of disclosure can help. Information can go to others with orders in the system, can attract outside orders, and help create trades when the contra parties are nearly matchable. The TraderEx block board (like that of Pipeline for instance), informs all traders that it holds an order. When the block board holds passive orders, it will inform any contra-side orders that a block trade is possible with some price concession. In Figure 9.4, for example, the seller has placed no price limits on his order—it

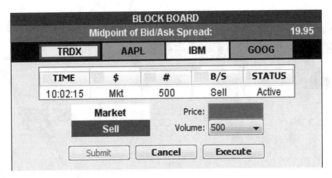

FIGURE 9.4 Block board display for a seller that has entered an active order for 500. It will sell automatically to any arriving buy order that is active. This seller currently has the option, due to a passive buy order, to use the "Execute" button to sell in the Dark Pool, but at a price less than the $19.95 midpoint.

is active—and is willing to trade at the $19.95 midpoint. The arrival of a buyer with a price limit below $19.95, however, has led the block board to give the block seller the option (as indicated by a yellow background for TRDX) to click on the "Execute" button. By doing so, she can sell at some price less than the mid-spread but not less than the bid quote.

If the seller wants this trade, he/she can click the "Execute" button shown in Figure 9.4, and the block trade will occur at some price less than $19.95, but not worse than the 19.80 bid. Unless you change the default setting that prohibits trade-throughs, TraderEx block board trades are not allowed to trade through order book quotes, which means that the bid and ask prices for the order book form the lower and upper bounds for our dark pool trades. These conditions are covered in further detail in Chapter 3.

To further illustrate, Figure 9.5 shows a current order book, and two users' block board displays on the upper right (a buyer) and the lower right (a seller). As seen in the block board of the buyer, the user has placed an active market order to buy 250 units. The order book quotes are $19.80 bid and $20.00 offer for a midpoint of $19.90. Given the current configuration of the book, if a sell order is entered into the dark pool at $19.90 or lower, there will be a trade. To be "Active," a buy order in the block board must be willing to pay $19.90 or more.

The color of the TRDX rectangles will be yellow with a green border for the active buyer with the option to Execute, and orange with a red border for the passive seller hoping for a price above the $19.90 midpoint. If the midpoint moves up to $19.95, the seller's order becomes active, and it will automatically execute against the buy order. To review the block board colors and features:

- Orange with no border color: There is a block board order for that stock.
- Orange with Red border: You have placed a sell order.

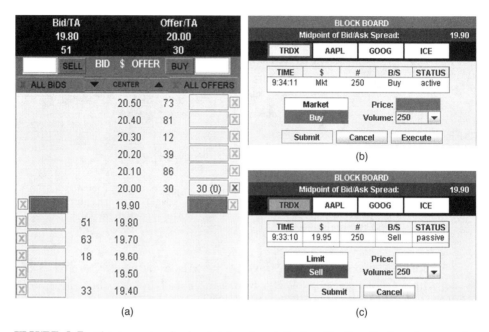

FIGURE 9.5 The current order book (above) and the two Pipeline displays for an active buyer and a passive seller showing the block board interaction between an active buy order and a passive limit sell order. The Mid-quote is $19.90, and the seller has placed a $19.95 limit price. The buyer in the block board on the left sees a yellow TRDX symbol and has the option to execute against the offer to sell above the mid-quote.

- Orange with Green border: You have placed a buy order.
- Yellow with Green border: You have placed an active buy order and there is a passive sell order for that stock.
- Yellow with Red border: You have placed an active sell order and there is a passive buy order for that stock.

From these descriptions of the TraderEx dark pool mechanism, you should see the opportunities a block board opens up for trading large quantities and not moving the price against yourself.

EXERCISE 9.1: MECHANICS OF THE DARK POOL

Our first exercise examines how the dark pool creates matches. From the TraderEx parameter screen (Figure 9.6), check the "Block Trading" feature in the Order Driven structure. In the Block Trading Configurations section at the bottom, enter

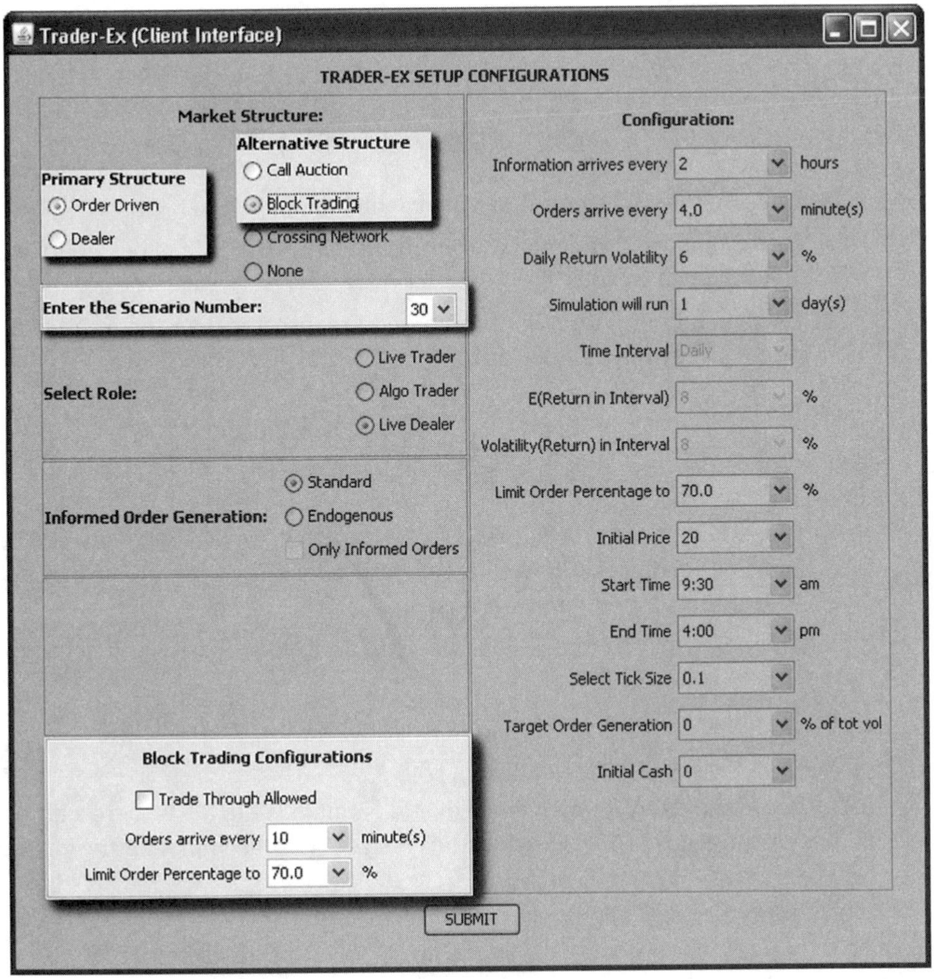

FIGURE 9.6 TraderEx Setup Screen—Check "Order Driven" with "Block Trading" and reduce the time between block order arrivals to "every 10 minutes" from "every 35 minutes." This will make the block board more active than it would be with the default settings.

"every 10 minutes". Keep all of the other settings at their default levels, and set the Scenario Number to 30. Complete this exercise using the "GO" button to advance the simulation.

1. Click on "SUBMIT," and then click on the "GO" button to launch a trading day. Looking at the order book, what prices would you expect to pay to purchase 1,000 from only the order book if you needed to complete the order by 11 A.M.?

2. Enter a block board order to buy 1,000.

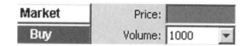

3. Click on the "GO" button to advance time in the market.

4. Once you have completed the purchase of 1,000, use the block board to sell the 1,000 back at a profit.

5. Use a sell limit with a limit price one tick greater than the average purchase price for buying the 1,000 shares:

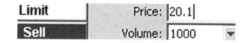

6. If you have not returned to a flat (0) position by 12 noon, convert the block board sell limit order into a block board sell market order. This order will execute at the midpoint price against an active buy order.

7. How many executions did it take for you to buy and then to sell in the dark pool?

8. Once you have returned to a flat position, what was your P&L?

9. What were your average buying and selling prices?

10. Rerun the Exercise with the Scenario Number set to 33. Is there a difference in the outcomes from using the block board? What accounts for the change in the result?

EXERCISE 9.2: SEEKING ADVANTAGES FROM DARK POOL PRICING

Click on "EXIT" and return to the opening parameter screen shown in Figure 9.7. At the TraderEx Setup Screen, check "Order Driven" with "Block Trading" and reduce the time between block order arrivals to "every 20 minutes" from every "35 minutes." This will make the Block Board somewhat more active than it would be at the default setting. Enter 31 as the Scenario Number. (See Figure 9.7.)

1. Click on "SUBMIT," and then on the "GO" button to launch a trading day. Looking at the order book, what average price would you expect to receive by selling 1,500 into the order book if you need to complete the order by 11 A.M.?

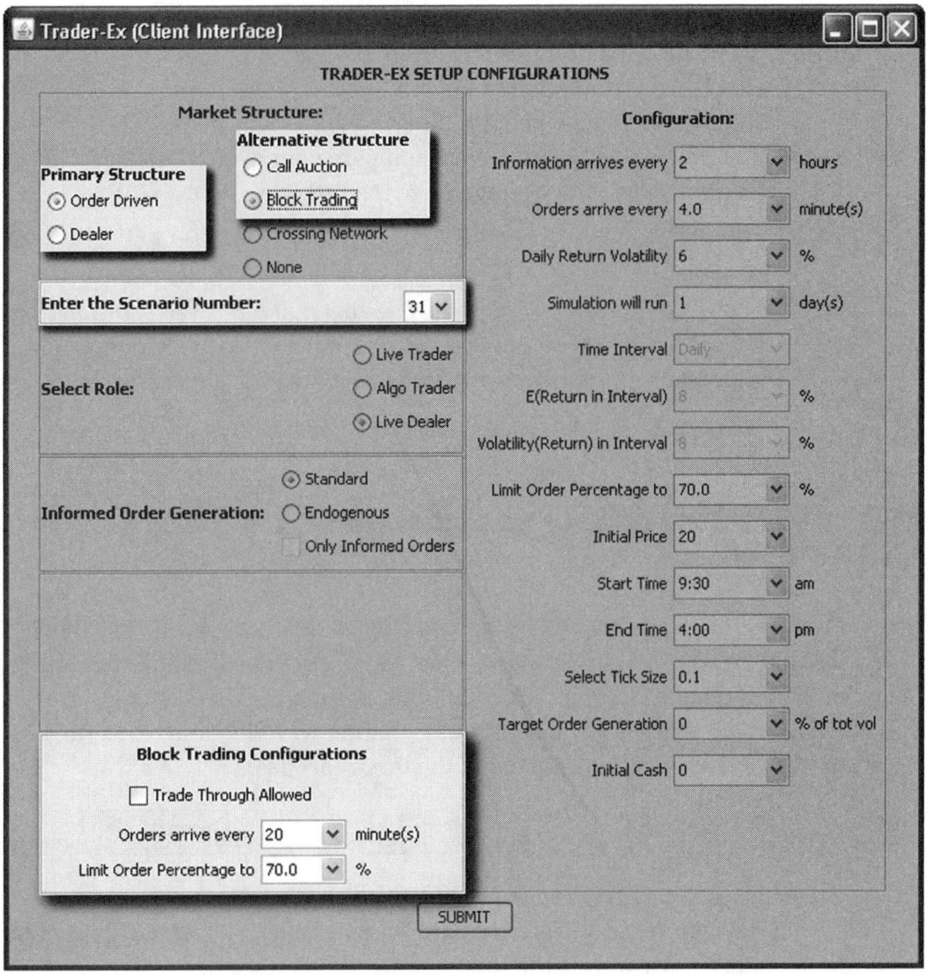

FIGURE 9.7 TraderEx setup for Exercise 9.2.

2. Enter 1,500 as a Block Board market sell order at the open. Click on the "GO" button to advance time in the market.

3. How many executions were triggered by your Block Board order?
   - What is the Completion time?
   - What is the Average Selling Price?
   - After your order is completed, compare your average selling price to VWAP—Have you sold at an average price that is higher than VWAP?

4. Click on the "RESET" button, and enter a succession of sell orders, 250 units at a time. Once one submission executes in the Block Board, enter the

next one. Stop when you have been matched six times and have established a
−1,500 (short) position from those six transactions.
  • What is the Completion time?
  • What is the Average Selling Price?
  • After your order is completed, compare your average selling price to VWAP.
    Have you sold at an average price that is higher than VWAP?

5. Was it advantageous to submit a single large instruction to the block board, or
   to break up the instruction? Why?

6. Click on "EXIT," and return to the parameter screen. Rerun the entire Exercise
   from Step 1 above with the Scenario Number set to 34. Is there a difference in
   the outcomes in 3 and 4 above? What accounts for the change in the result?

EXERCISE 9.3: WORKING A LARGE ORDER WITH A DARK POOL

From the TraderEx parameter screen (Figure 9.8), check off the "Block Trading"
feature. Enter 35 as the Scenario Number, and set the Target Order at "70 percent
of Total Volume." Retain all of the other settings at their default levels. For this
exercise, we suggest advancing the simulation with the time clock running instead
of the "GO button." Select a one of the three speeds.

1. In this simulation, you can use both the limit order book and the block board to
   fill the instructions. Watch the Target indicator to learn the instruction, which
   could increase during the run.

  • What will your approach be to using the block board?
  • What percent of your total trading are you expecting to execute in the dark
    pool?

2. Run the simulation for a full day up to the close of trading at 4 P.M. During the
   run, consider:
  • What is your trading strategy? How are you attempting to outperform VWAP
    using the block board?
  • Did you change your trading strategy or use of the block board? When and
    why?

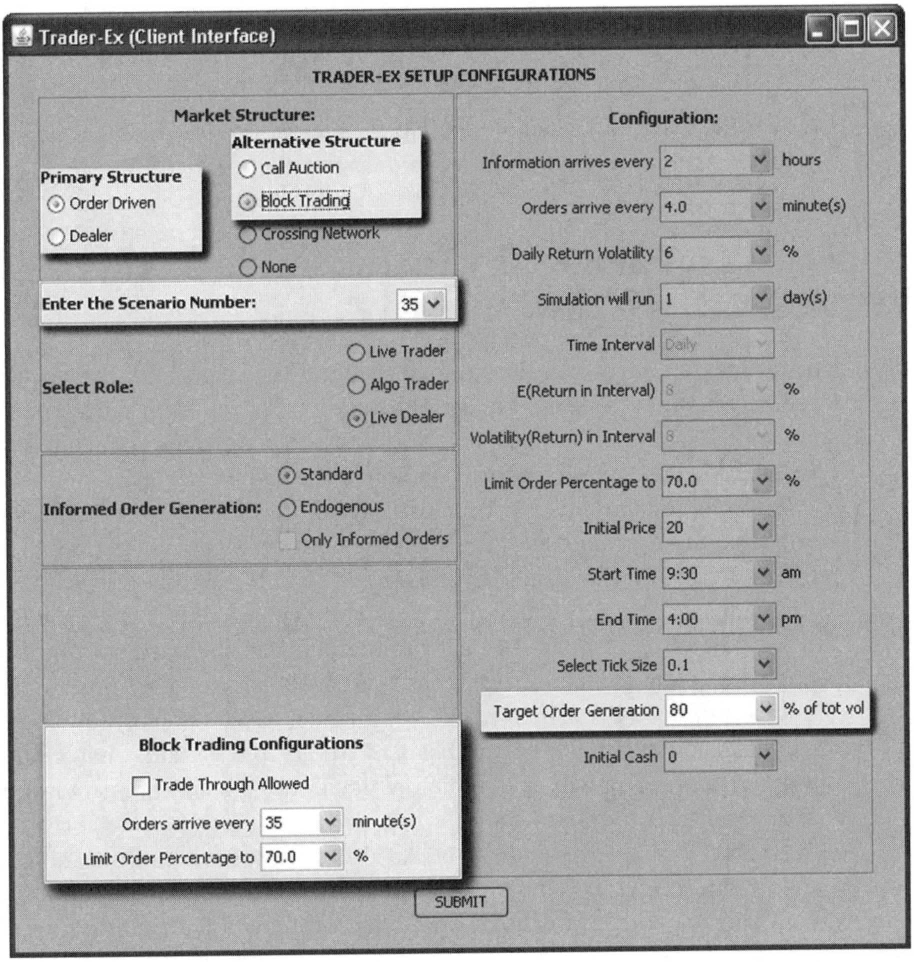

FIGURE 9.8 TraderEx setup for Exercise 9.3.

3. Record your closing position. Does it match the Target from the instruction that you were given? What percentage of the total market volume were you responsible for?

4. Record:

   Your closing P&L
   Your average transaction price to buy and/or to sell
   VWAP for the run
   Explain why you did or did not beat VWAP

5. Explain any effect that the dark pool, vis-à-vis the limit order book, may have had on the pricing, sizing, and timing of your order placement decisions.

6. Rerun with the "Block Trading" feature on, 36 as the Scenario Number, and the Target Order set at "90 percent of Total Volume." You will receive a large buy instruction. Complete the instruction by 4 P.M. and answer #3 to #5 above.

7. Was the dark pool a useful tool in both simulations for trading a large position, and for achieving prices that were near to or better than VWAP?

EXERCISE 9.4: PROPRIETARY TRADING WITH DARK POOL, AND NEWS RELEASES

Up to now, we have considered buy-side traders using the dark pool to build a large long or short position. Can a prop trader gain from using a dark pool? In this simulation, use the order book and the dark pool over the trading day to create a positive P&L, but return to a zero position at the end of the day.

In this hybrid dark pool–continuous market structure, TraderEx provides news stories that are associated with P* increases or decreases. When traders receive a piece of news about the company, they react to it. Recall that prices do not adjust to the news (to the new value of P*) instantaneously. You have a small but critical window of opportunity to beat the market. Can the dark pool improve your proprietary trading with news? What effect does it have on your profits?

As a proprietary trader, you will buy and sell based on short-term price movements that you anticipate on the basis of trends, price charts, news releases, or other indicators. You will have no initial position but should respond to the news that arrives with orders and trades.

Assume that a position limit of 2,000 is imposed on you, meaning that you should not exceed 2,000 units, either short or long. As a proprietary trader you do not carry overnight positions, and must return to a flat (i.e., zero) position by the close.

To start the exercise, enter 97 as the Scenario Number, and set the arrival rate to an order every three minutes on average. See Figure 9.9.

1. Run the simulation for a full day up to the 4 P.M. close. During the run, consider and write down the following:
   • Once news was released, what was your strategy for trading in the continuous market? In the dark pool?

| Enter the Scenario Number: | 97 ▼ | Orders arrive every | 3.0 ▼ | minute(s) |

         (a)   (b)

FIGURE 9.9 TraderEx initial parameters for Exercise 9.4.

- What positive or negative effects did the dark pool have on your proprietary trading?
- How did your order handling differ as a result of receiving news stories when a dark pool was available?

2. Did you return to a zero position? What was your average position? What was your largest position at any point in time?
   - What was your P&L at the end of the run? In a proprietary trading role, do you understand what led to your P&L result?
   - Using the "GET DATA" tool, review the TradeOrders.csv file—What percentage of your prop trading was done in the dark pool and in the continuous market? Do you feel that this was an optimal split between the two types of markets?

Exercise 7.6 Revisited: Extending an Earlier (Chapter 7) Exercise with the New Dark Pool Structure

Replay with two other Scenario Numbers of your choice in the range 91 to 99. These will contain other news stories and different P* paths. After three runs of the simulation, examine the three P&L results that you have achieved.

Discussion of Exercise 9.4

Gaming is a concern in all trading systems in general, and in dark pool systems as well. Can a prop trader manipulate the price or outcomes in the dark pool to generate a positive P&L? Do gaming activities have an impact on other users? While dark pools have advantages for traders with large orders, does the 250 minimum trade size exclude small traders in any way that you might consider unjustified, undesirable, or unfair?

In Figure 9.10, the user has entered a dark pool buy order for 250. It would be in the buyer's interest to use the order book to reduce the midpoint to an amount less than $20.05. How might that be done, at what cost, and at what risk? What are the consequences if the buyer places a market order to sell 47 into the order book?

EXERCISE 9.5: EMPHASIZING DIFFERENT DIMENSIONS OF TRADING PERFORMANCE

As described in Chapter 4, TraderEx calculates a score for a trader based on four measures of performance. VWAP is the trader's ability to transact at prices better than VWAP. P&L is the combined level of realized and unrealized profit. Risk is how far from evenly paced the trader executes the order over the course of the trading day. The final measure is full completion of the trading instruction, and is

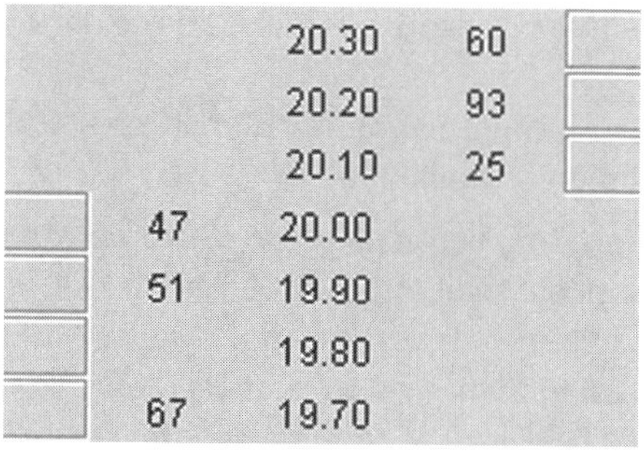

(a)

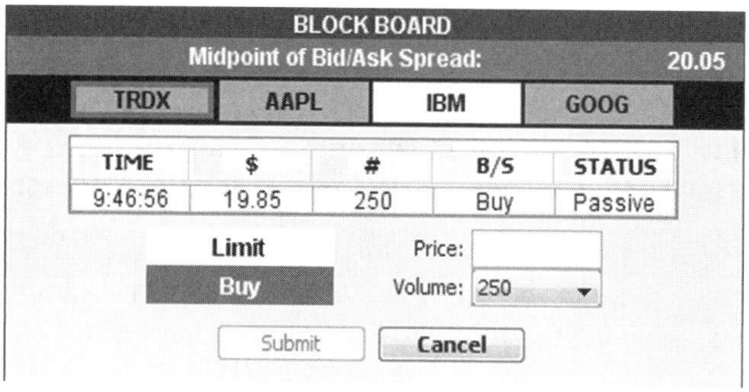

(b)

FIGURE 9.10 TraderEx order book and dark pool at the same point in time.

applied as a score reduction at the end. Completing just 70 percent of an instruction will lead to a 30 percent deduction from the final score. Figure 9.11 shows how added weight can be placed on a particular dimension of a trader's performance.

In a dark pool, large executions can make tracking VWAP more difficult. In this exercise we will look at how the pace of execution and your VWAP performance are influenced by your use of the block board.

1. At the TraderEx parameter screen, check the "Block Trading" feature to first run a trading day with the dark pool. Select the "Target Order Generation"

FIGURE 9.11 TraderEx performance measures and weights. In the illustration, weight of 100 is on the extent to which the trader has outperformed VWAP. Another 100 units of weight is placed on P&L, so that TOTAL performance is an equally weighted sum of VWAP and P&L. Adjust the weights for Exercise 9.5 to emphasize the pace at which a large buy or sell order is completed.

option so that your trading instructions will be set at 70 percent of the base level of daily trading volume in the order book. Select Scenario Number 37. After clicking "SUBMIT," click on the Risk label under "SCORE" and put a weight of 100 on Risk, and 0 on VWAP and P&L. What is your final Risk score? Did you outperform VWAP?

2. Rerun the simulation using all of the same settings as in #1, but do not add the "Block Trading" dark pool feature. Again, put a weight of 100 on Risk, and 0 on VWAP and P&L. What is your final Risk score? Did you outperform VWAP? How do these results compare with what you had in #1. Can you keep your pace risk lower using only the order book and without the block trading feature? If so, why? If not, why not?

3. Re-run #1 and #2 above with the Scenario Number set to 38. Place all of the performance weight (100) on VWAP. Run the simulation, with and without, the dark pool. Is your VWAP performance improved with the dark pool?

EXERCISE 9.6: DARK POOLS AND TRADE-THROUGH RULES

As described in Chapter 3, TraderEx, by default, imposes a trade-through rule on trades in the block board mechanism. In other words, the dark pool can only match large buy and sell orders within the price range from the market's *displayed* bid and ask quote inclusively. (Exercise 5.8 relaxed this rule.) Whether regulators should impose such a restriction on the trader is highly controversial. Some argue that it is important to protect investors from trades at poor prices, and that it helps maintain integration of pricing across markets. Others feel it disadvantages new trading systems, and that two block traders who have arrived at a price for a 100,000-share trade in a dark pool should not be restricted by the prices of limit orders in the displayed book that may be for only 100 shares.

1. At the TraderEx parameter screen, check the "Block Trading" feature and check the "Trade Through Allowed" feature. Then set the "Target Order Generation" option so that your trading instructions will be set at 70 percent of the base level of daily trading volume in the order book. Select Scenario Number 38 to receive a large buy instruction.

2. Run the simulation and enter dark pool orders that are active and passive, and ensure that some of the passive orders are outside of the quoted bid and ask prices. Orders outside of the spread mean that a trade-through is possible in the dark pool.

3. How does the chance to trade through the order book's quotes alter the dark pool's operations and the quality of the market? Were you better off with a trade-through prohibition or without? Is a trade-through prohibition a sensible regulation?

4. Rerun the simulation with a Dealer market and Block Board hybrid structure. Check the "Trade Through Allowed" feature. Select Scenario Number 39. In your role as a market maker, does the dark pool influence your trading performance? Do trade throughs taking place in a dark pool influence your dealer activities?

CONCLUSION

We conclude the chapter and the book with the following thoughts. Clearly, trading is not a simple task, and trading decisions are complex. It takes time, patience, and much practice to become a skilled participant in the equities markets. And it takes a good deal of experience to appreciate fully just how your actions in the marketplace should be determined in the context of four considerations:

- The architectural design and trading rules of the marketplace that you are interacting with (e.g., call or continuous, order driven or quote driven, transparent liquidity or dark pool liquidity).
- Your reason for trading (e.g., information, liquidity considerations, technical).
- What you are trying to accomplish (e.g., trade quickly or get a better price).
- How your performance is being assessed (e.g., P&L, risk, a VWAP measure, success in getting the job done).

A solid grasp of these four points should put you a good deal further down the road to being a successful, seasoned trader. This book's objective is to raise the quality of your trading decisions, and if we have succeeded, you will benefit from your deeper understanding, and the enhanced returns that you are now capable of generating.

About the Authors

Robert A. Schwartz is the Marvin M. Speiser Professor of Finance, and University Distinguished Professor in the Zicklin School of Business, Baruch College, CUNY. Before joining the Baruch faculty in 1997, he was Professor of Finance and Economics and Yamaichi Faculty Fellow at New York University's Leonard N. Stern School of Business, where he had been a member of the faculty since 1965. In 1966, Professor Schwartz received his PhD in Economics from Columbia University. His research is in the area of financial economics, with a primary focus on the structure of securities markets. He has published over 60 refereed journal articles, twelve edited books, and seven authored books, including *Micro Markets: A Market Structure Approach to Microeconomic Analysis*, Wiley & Sons, 2010, forthcoming; *The Equity Trader Course* (co-authored with Reto Francioni and Bruce Weber), John Wiley & Sons, 2006; and *Equity Markets in Action: The Fundamentals of Liquidity, Market Structure and Trading* (co-authored with Reto Francioni), John Wiley & Sons, 2004. He has served as a consultant to various market centers including the New York Stock Exchange, the American Stock Exchange, NASDAQ, the London Stock Exchange, Instinet, the Arizona Stock Exchange, Deutsche Börse, and the Bolsa Mexicana. From April 1983 to April 1988, he was an associate editor of the *Journal of Finance*, and he is currently an associate editor of the *Review of Quantitative Finance and Accounting* and the *Review of Pacific Basin Financial Markets and Policies*, and is a member of the advisory boards of *International Finance* and the *Journal of Trading*. In December 1995, Professor Schwartz was named the first chairman of NASDAQ's Economic Advisory Board, and he served on the EAB until Spring 1999. He is the developer, with Bruce Weber and Gregory Sipress, of the trading and market structure simulation, TraderEx (www.etraderex.net). In 2009, Schwartz was named the first recipient of the World Federation of Exchanges' annual Award for Excellence.

Gregory M. Sipress is head of Software Development at TraderEx LLC (www.etraderex.net). Prior to joining TraderEx LLC in 2006, Gregory worked as a consultant, building trading systems and financial models. He has presented executive training programs on trading and microstructure, participated in seminars for industry professionals, and organized seminars for finance faculty. He was an adjunct lecturer in Computer Information Systems at Baruch College from 2000 through 2006. He has a BS in Mathematics from State University at Albany, an MS in Business Computer Information Systems from the Zicklin School of Business, Baruch College, CUNY, an MA in Computer Science from Boston University, and an M.S. in Financial Engineering from Baruch College/Weissman School of Arts and Sciences. Gregory currently resides in Brooklyn with his wife, Lisa, and son, Hayden.

Bruce W. Weber is Professor of Information Management at the London Business School. He teaches IT and financial services topics in MBA and executive programs. He has an AB from Harvard University, and a PhD in Decision Sciences from the Wharton School of the University of Pennsylvania. His dissertation demonstrated uses of simulation modeling and behavioral experiments to compare alternative trading mechanisms. His research on IT strategy, financial systems and compliance, and the computerization of financial markets has been published in a number of academic journals, and has been cited in the popular and trade press. He is on several editorial boards including the *Journal of Management Information Systems, MIS Quarterly*, and the *Journal of Trading*. Prior to joining the London Business School in 2003, he was on the faculty of the Stern School of Business, New York University, from 1992 to 1999, and Baruch College of the City University of New York, where he was founding director of the Wasserman Trading Floor, a 60-workstation markets education center. He has co-authored "The Equity Trader Course" (with R. Schwartz and R. Francioni), John Wiley & Sons, in 2006. He is co-developer of the market trading simulation TraderEx (www.etraderex.net), a Web-based software package for teaching market structure and trading, in use at several leading business schools in the United States, Europe, and Canada. He has consulted on IT and market design issues for several major financial services firms, and the NASDAQ Stock Market and London Stock Exchange, and has presented executive training programs on IT leadership and markets technology to U.S. and European firms.

Index